HITLER'S MUSLIM ALLIES

GERMAN ARMY AND WAFFEN-SS ISLAMIC VOLUNTEERS 1941-1945

HITLER'S MUSLIM ALLIES

GERMAN ARMY AND WAFFEN-SS ISLAMIC VOLUNTEERS 1941-1945

DR ANTONIO J. MUÑOZ

FRONTLINE
BOOKS

HITLER'S MUSLIM ALLIES
German Army and Waffen-SS Islamic Volunteers1941-1945

First published in Great Britain in 2025
by Frontline Books
An imprint of
Pen & Sword Books Ltd
Yorkshire - Philadelphia

ISBN 978 1 03612 922 4

A CIP catalogue record for this book is available from the British Library

Typeset by Lapiz Digital
Printed and bound in the UK by CPI Group (UK) Ltd,
Croydon, CR0 4YY.

Printed on paper from a sustainable source by
CPI Group (UK) Ltd, Croydon, CR0 4YY

The Publisher's authorised representative in the EU for product safety is
Authorised Rep Compliance Ltd., Ground Floor, 71 Lower Baggot Street,
Dublin D02 P593, Ireland.
www.arccompliance.com

For a complete list of Pen & Sword titles please contact
PEN & SWORD BOOKS LTD
47 Church Street, Barnsley, South Yorkshire, S70 2AS, England
E-mail: enquiries@pen-and-sword.co.uk
Website: www.pen-and-sword.co.uk
or
PEN & SWORD BOOKS
1950 Lawrence Rd, Havertown, PA 19083, USA
E-mail: uspen-and-sword@casematepublishers.com

Dedication

In the hope that the Palestinian and Israeli people may one day have a lasting peace.

TABLE OF CONTENTS

TABLE OF CONTENTS

AUTHOR'S NOTE

As an academician, I have been trained to write works that are fully footnoted, so as to provide the reader with only fact-based references that justify any conclusions drawn from those facts. I decided, in this case, to do away with the hundreds (and sometimes thousands) of reference annotations that would normally appear in any academic study. I did this for the sake of writing a free-flowing study, unencumbered with the minutiae of reference detail that often distracts a reader's eyes from the story. In order to avoid this page clutter, footnotes have been kept to a bare minimum. Those readers out there who are more scholastically inclined, and who wish to study the topic further, can refer to the select bibliography of primary and secondary sources that I have prepared at the end of this work. There they will find the references that were used to write this study.

History, without its academic requirements, tends to be more compelling and entertaining, as opposed to clogging the storyline with hundreds of annotations. The key to writing history successfully is to keep the reader's attention focused on the narrative. Further still, if an author has the ability to place the reader in the middle of that story, as if they are witnessing the events as they happened, the writer would have succeeded in achieving something that is very rare and often does not occur in history books: capturing the reader's imagination and interest.

The Muslim connection to Nazi Germany

Up until almost the end of the twentieth century, the story of Muslim involvement with the Third Reich had never been discussed nor written about. It was only at the beginning of the 1990s that scholars began to delve into the connection between the Muslim world and Nazi Germany. However, the earliest work to discuss Muslim collusion with the Third Reich in any great detail was a monograph written by a former German general who actually commanded

Arab volunteers during the war.[1] Luftwaffe general Hellmuth W. Felmy was the author of this concise, but detailed, study that is still required reading for anyone interested in the topic. This pamphlet was published back in 1946 and was only intended for American military consumption. The Cold War was only just starting in 1946, and Western intelligence agencies were desperate to stay a step ahead of the Soviet Union (USSR). When the war ended, the country that eventually replaced the Nazi state as the patron of the Arab world in the Middle East was the Soviet Union. This situation became more complicated from 1948, when the State of Israel was announced. The Arab-Israeli War of 1948 pitted about half a million Jews against the millions of Muslims who lived in the region of the Middle East. To everyone's surprise, the newly created Israeli state defeated the approximately 2,000,000 Palestinians and the neighbouring Muslim kingdoms.

As stated, the USSR was actually the first nation to recognise the state of Israel on 17 May 1948, followed by Nicaragua, Czechoslovakia, Yugoslavia, and Poland. The United States recognised Israel six months later, on 31 January 1949. Although the Soviet Union had been the first state to recognise Israel as a nation, it eventually turned its attention to courting the numerous Arab kingdoms in the Middle East. This about-turn was made for a simple reason: the number of Muslim nations in North Africa and the Middle East were far more numerous than one small, Jewish state. If the USSR had assumed the role of benefactor to Israel, it would have lost political capital with those Muslim nations. As the USSR aligned itself with the Muslim Middle East, the United States took on the role of benefactor and protector of the Israeli state. The politics of the Cold War, where the conflict between communism and democracy would be done by proxy, called for America to step in and defend Israel. Israel was also a democracy surrounded by what eventually became a sea of Arab dictatorships. As a result, the United States felt duty-bound to support it.[2] Several Muslim kingdoms began to fall to revolution in the 1950s. These Arab nations now came to be ruled by military juntas or dictators. Most of these new authoritarian states, like Egypt, Syria and Iraq, began to experiment with socialism, further solidifying the political lines between East and West. By the late 1950s, Israel was a democracy surrounded by numerous (Arab) socialist states allied to the Soviet Union. So, the Cold War played itself out in the Middle East and North Africa, as it played out all over the world: as proxy wars between the East and the West.

How did the State of Israel arise?

The creation of the state of Israel is tied not only to the Balfour Declaration, but to the economic difficulties that the United Kingdom experienced at the end of the Second World War. By 1945, the United Kingdom was exhausted physically and economically. The cost of the war, in economic and human terms, had devastated this once-mighty empire. The new prime minister in the summer of 1945, Clement Attlee, was a member of the Labour Party. Attlee wanted to nationalise the heavy industries in the country and create a social welfare system that could provide healthcare and employment for the working class.[3] The overseas colonies of the United Kingdom were becoming more costly to maintain and Attlee saw this as a drain on money that was needed at home.

For example, the United Kingdom mandate in Palestine was costing about £10 million per year.[4] In addition, the British government had made further payments totalling approximately £25 million to the Palestinian government during the twenty-six years of the mandate. These payments comprised £24,751,499 in aid grants and another £170,000 from the Colonial Development Fund. Another £15 million would be incurred in the winding-up costs after the United Nations assumed the mandate. The labour government of Clement Attlee still wished to hold onto its mandate in Palestine but was loath to continue to pay the cost of maintaining it. It was believed by Clement Attlee's advisors that if his government claimed it no longer wished to carry the mandate, the United Nations would offer to carry the financial cost of maintaining it but would request the United Kingdom keep running the region. The Attlee government believed that the growing conflict between Arabs and Jews in Palestine would deter the United Nations from assuming direct control. This belief came from the mistaken assumption that the United Nations did not want to handle such a volatile issue as the Israeli-Palestinian dispute.

It was in this way that the British declared their unwillingness to continue running Palestine. To everyone's surprise, the United Nations agreed to assume the mandate in Palestine with a plan for a two-state solution that, it was hoped, would placate both sides. Once they had decreed that they no longer wished to control Palestine, the United Kingdom could not do an about-face and so reluctantly, the British withdrew their forces on 15 May 1948. The various Arab kingdoms surrounding Palestine advised the Palestinian people to reject this division of their state, assuring them that the Arab nations of Egypt, Transjordan, Syria and Iraq would crush the approximately 500,000 Jews living in Palestine. Many people today blame the current

Palestinian condition on the apparent intransigence and 'greed' of the Palestinians for wanting to keep all their land, instead of dividing it with the Israelis. However, if one looks at the situation from their perspective and the situation that presented itself in 1948, you will see that the Palestinians chose this 'all or nothing' path based on sound judgment.

First, the Muslims in the Middle East numbered approximately 80 million people in 1948. The number of Jews in Palestine was a mere half million. On this basis alone, a betting man would side with the Arabs when deciding who would come out on top of this conflict. Second, even though the Israelis had various fighting organisations (the Haganah, Irgun, and the Lehi), the number of Arabs trained in combat was numerous. Initially formed as a defensive group in the 1920s, the Haganah evolved into the main underground military force of the Jewish community in Palestine and had perhaps 30,000 men prior to the start of the 1948 war. It conducted various operations, including defence against Arab attacks, illegal immigration, arms smuggling, and attacks on Arab villages. The Haganah eventually became the core of the Israel Defense Forces (IDF) after the establishment of Israel.

The Irgun (Irgun Tzvai Leumi), also known as Etzel, was a more radical paramilitary organisation that split from the Haganah in the late 1930s due to differences in ideology and tactics. They performed the same actions as Haganah but also took part in assassinations and terror bombings. It had perhaps 3,000 men in 1947. It was led by Menachem Begin, who would eventually become prime minister of the Israeli state.[5] The Irgun conducted numerous attacks against British military and government targets, as well as Arab civilians, in its campaign for Jewish independence. The Lehi (Lohamei Herut Israel) was commonly known as the Stern Gang, and in 1947 its number was perhaps 400-500. Lehi was a smaller and more extreme splinter group from the Irgun but was committed to the same tactics and was led by Avraham Stern. Lehi carried out assassinations, bombings, and other acts of violence against British authorities, Arab civilians, and perceived collaborators. These organisations operated clandestinely and engaged in guerrilla warfare tactics against British forces, Arab militias, and Palestinian civilians during the period leading up to the establishment of the State of Israel in 1948. While their actions were controversial and sometimes involved acts considered terrorism by some, they played a significant role in the struggle for Jewish independence and the foundation of the modern State of Israel.

The strength of Arab forces was significant. The Egyptian Army alone was estimated to be around 45,000 troops. The Egyptian Army in 1948 consisted of a mixture of regular infantry, armoured units, artillery, and supporting elements. It was organised into divisions and brigades, with varying degrees of training, equipment, and combat readiness. Initially, Egypt deployed around four divisions into Palestine, including the 1st, 2nd, 3rd, and 4th infantry divisions, with additional units supporting them. However, these forces were not always deployed simultaneously due to rotations and reinforcements. Additionally, Egypt's military structure underwent changes during the conflict. The Arab Legion, the military force of Transjordan (now Jordan), had around 8-10,000 men at the outset of the 1948 Arab-Israeli War. This number increased during the conflict as volunteers and reinforcements joined its ranks. The Arab Legion played a significant role in the war, especially in operations around Jerusalem and in the West Bank. The Arab Legion was the most experienced and well-trained Arab military force involved in the conflict, benefitting from years of training by British officers and advisors. Led by British officers and under the command of Glubb Pasha (John Bagot Glubb), the Arab Legion was organised into several brigades, including infantry, artillery, and supporting units. It was considered a highly disciplined and effective fighting force, with a reputation for professionalism and combat prowess.

Lebanon also sent a contingent of troops to Palestine in 1948 as part of the Arab League's intervention in the Arab-Israeli War. The exact composition and size of the Lebanese forces varied, but they generally included several hundred to a few thousand soldiers. These forces were primarily stationed in areas bordering Palestine to support the Palestinian Arab militias and other Arab armies fighting against the newly declared State of Israel. Syria sent troops to Palestine in 1948, also as part of the Arab League's intervention in the Arab-Israeli War. The Syrian Army deployed several thousand soldiers to Palestine to support the Palestinian Arab militias and other Arab armies and these Syrian forces participated in various battles and operations throughout the course of the conflict. They included elements of the following Syrian Army units: 1st Brigade, 3rd Brigade, 6th Brigade, 7th Brigade, 10th Brigade, and 12th Brigade. Finally, the Iraqi Army contained around 27,000 men. The army was organised into divisions and brigades, and consisted of infantry, armoured units, artillery, and supporting elements. Like other Arab forces, it aimed to prevent the establishment of Israel and to seize territory in Palestine. The Iraqi units that took part in the fighting included units from the following brigades: 1st Brigade, 2nd Brigade, 3rd Brigade, 4th Brigade, 6th Brigade, and 7th Brigade.

Thus, at the start of the 1948 war, there were perhaps 34,000 trained men in the Israeli forces facing approximately 83,000 trained Arab soldiers. What the Palestinians did not factor in when deciding whether to keep all the land or give away half of it, was the fact that most of the 500,000 Jews living in Palestine were former concentration camp survivors who had nowhere else to go. Faced with a second extermination, almost the entire Jewish population took up arms or assisted in the war effort in one-way or another. Even women and girls armed themselves and were inducted into combat units. This radically increased the number of soldiers the nascent State of Israel could count on. Having nowhere to go also gave these people a sense that they had nothing to lose. Faced with extermination if the Arabs won the war, Israelis fought with a tenacity that surprised the Arab soldiers. The 1948 Arab-Israeli War led to Israel's victory and the beginning of the *Nakba* (catastrophe) for the Palestinian people. Just exactly who owns the territory that now comprises the State of Israel, including Gaza and the West Bank, is still subject to debate.

Currently, the land is controlled by Israel. The right-wing government of Benjamin Netanyahu has continued the slow but inexorable establishment of more and more illegal Israeli settlements on Palestinian-owned lands in the West Bank. The seizure of Palestinian land continues unabated. While Israel is a democracy, it has become self-evident that under Benjamin Netanyahu's conservative coalition, Israel looks more and more like an apartheid state rather than a liberal democracy. Under investigation for corruption by Israel's Supreme Court, Netanyahu has been spending much effort in the past few years at attempting to emasculate the Israeli Supreme Court and amassing more power under his premiership. Many who follow politics in Israel believe that he did this to avoid being sent to jail. The problem is that while his attention was concentrated on weakening the Israeli Supreme Court and placating his right-wing cabinet ministers by seizing more Palestinian land, he ignored the growing threat that Hamas posed. The end result was the 7 October 2023 attacks by Hamas, where approximately 1,200 Jews were massacred. One can argue either way as to who really owns the land. Some favour the Israeli claim, some favour the Palestinian claim, while some believe the land belongs to both Semitic people. My own personal belief is that peace between the Palestinians and Israelis will not come until a two-state solution is reached. Sadly, the intransigence of the current belligerents – Hamas on the Palestinian side and Benjamin Netanyahu's right-wing government on the Israeli side – indicates that for the foreseeable future, a lasting peace through a two-state solution will not be possible.

A region tied to the past

In 1990 a Spanish author, Dr Carlos Caballero-Jurado self-published a work in the Spanish language dealing with Muslim participation with Nazi Germany.[6] In 1994 two French authors published a work titled *The French Under the German Helmet: Europe 1941-1945.*[7] The importance of this French study is that it covered Arab volunteer forces from North Africa as well as in Syria that were raised by the Vichy French government during the war. It also explained how some of those Arab forces ended up serving in the German Army. The next significant work to be written was a pamphlet in the English language that was also privately published in 1995.[8] This small forty-page monograph dealt with the employment of several Arab battalions from North Africa and the Middle East. Since then, over a dozen works have been published covering the topic of Muslim participation with the Nazis during the Second World War. The following are the principal books that I suggest you acquire, if you are a serious student of the topic of Muslim participation with the Third Reich:

Dr Carlos Caballero-Jurado. *La Espada del Islam: Voluntarios Arabes en el Ejercito Aleman 1941-1945.* Alicante: Garcia Hispan, Editor, 1990.

Pierre Philippe Lambert and Gerard Le Marec. *Les Francais Sous Le Casque Allemand: Europe 1941-1945.* Paris: Jacques Grancher, 1994.

George Lepre. *Himmler's Bosnian Division: The Waffen-SS Handschar Division, 1943-1945.* Atglen: Schiffer Publishing, 1997.

Georges Bensoussan, editor. *Antisemitisme et Negationnisme dans le Monde Arabo-Musulman: La Derive; Revue D'Histoire de la Shoah le Monde Juif.* Paris: Somogy éditions dart, 2004.

Enver Redzic. *Bosnia and Herzegovina in the Second World War.* New York: Frank Cass, 2005.

Klaus-Michael Mallmann & Martin Cüppers. *Halbmond und Hakenkreuz. Das Dritte Reich, die Araber und Palästina.* Darmstadt: Wissenschaft-liche Buchgesellschaft, 2006.

Matthias Küntzel. *Jihad and Jew-Hatred: Islamism, Nazism and the Roots of 9/11.* Candor: Telos Press Publishing, 2007.

Jeffrey Herf. *Nazi Propaganda for the Arab World.* New Haven: Yale University Press, 2009.

Gilbert Achcahr. *Le Arabe et la Shoah.* Paradou: Actes Sud, 2009.

David G. Dalin and John F. Rothman. *Icon of Evil: Hitler's Mufti and the Rise of Radical Islam.* London: Routledge, 2009.

Jonathan Trigg. *Hitler's Jihadis: Muslim Volunteers of the Waffen-SS.* Kent: Spellmount Publishers, Ltd., 2012.

Andrew G. Bostom. *The Mufti's Islamic Jew-Hatred: What the Nazis Learned from the Muslim Pope.* Jacksonville: Create Space Independent Publishing Platform, 2013.

Barry Rubin and Wolfgang G. Schwanitz. *Nazis, Islamists, and the Making of the Modern Middle East.* New Haven: Yale University Press, 2014.

Israel Gershoni, editor. *Arab Responses to Fascism and Nazism: Attraction and Repulsion.* Austin: University of Texas Press, 2014.

Francis R. Nicosia. *Germany and the Arab World.* Cambridge: Cambridge University Press, 2015.

David Motadel. *Islam and Nazi Germanys War.* Harvard Belknap Press, 2017.

Francis R. Nicosia and Boğac A. Ergene. *Nazism, The Holocaust, and the Middle East: Arab and Turkish Responses.* New York: Berghahn Books, 2018.

Mario Werhas & Božidar Mikulčić. *13. SS Division Handschar.* Zagreb: Despot Infinitus, 2018.

In closing, I believe that further study of the connection between Islam and the Third Reich should be pursued. I can say without reservation or equivocation that there exists sufficient primary source material in numerous archives around the world that will help increase our knowledge of this important topic. We only have to reach out and put in the time and leg work to obtain that information.

Antonio J. Muñoz,
Summer, 2025

Chapter One

THE ORIGINS OF MODERN ARAB NATIONALISM

Who owns the Holy Land?

In order to understand the roots of Arab nationalism, one must learn about the roots of Arab-Israeli relations. This has to do principally with the land that was shared by both Palestinians and Jews. In addition, the colonial period in North Africa and the Near East is also a major factor in helping to understand the roots of Arab nationalist aspirations.[9] When I worked as a college professor teaching history, I was asked on more than one occasion where I stood on the issue of who owns the Holy Land: the Palestinians or the Israelis? Because the topic of just exactly who owns the land is such a volatile subject matter, my answer was always the same: I would reply that the land belongs to the Canaanites.[10] It was my way of creating humour and defusing a potentially heated argument. However, if one thinks about this for a while, it really makes sense, given that the Holy Land has always been fought over throughout history and has always exchanged hands on numerous occasions. The Canaanites, however, were the original owners of the area we call today the Holy Land. Before describing the arrival of the Philistines and Israelites to the territory that came to be known as Palestine, Israel or the Holy Land, the region encompassed the Kingdom of the Canaanites. Some Jews settled in the land of Canaan beginning around 1250 BCE while the majority kept moving west, towards Egypt. Most historians believe that this migration to Egypt was done for economic reasons. That is, the richness of the Nile River is what likely drew many people, Jews included, to settle there. Originally, the Israelites were a Semitic people living in what is today southern Iraq and the nation of Kuwait. Back then the region was known as Mesopotamia. Sometime around 2000 BCE they left southern Mesopotamia and began to wander west. No one knows for sure why the Israelites left during that time, but we know it was connected to the political strife occurring in the Sumer city-state of Ur.

The political conflict that followed the downfall of the Third Dynasty of Ur around 2004 BCE is most likely what prompted the exodus, as various Semitic tribes in the city and surrounding countryside vied with one another to position themselves for control of this southern Sumerian city-state. This occurred after the collapse of the Third Dynasty ruler, Ibbi Sin (ruled 2028-2004 BCE). If that is the case, then the Israelites proved to be on the losing end of this power struggle, apparently having to flee the region. Another more pejorative explanation has them forcibly evicted by other Sumerian tribes who found them too quarrelsome and haughty to deal with. In any event, they left Mesopotamia and wandered westward until they reached the land of the Canaanites. Many Israelis settled in several Canaanite cities, while the majority continued their trek into Egypt. It is believed that the bounty of the Nile River basin is what attracted many to settle there. At a time in history when the Tigris and Euphrates rivers in Mesopotamia would sometimes overflow their banks early and destroy a year's worth of crops, the Nile River offered no such travails; every year there was a bounty of food.

In the case of the Philistines, they were a sea people who lived on numerous islands in the eastern Mediterranean. They came to settle in the land of the Canaanites from the numerous island chains of the eastern Aegean Sea. The Philistines arrived sometime around 1175 BCE, or about seventy-five years after the arrival of the Israelites. The Philistines initially settled along the southern coastline of Canaan, on that part of land that would become the Gaza Strip. This made perfect sense, as the Gaza Strip lies along the eastern Mediterranean coast and the Philistines were a seafaring people. On the other hand, the Israelites who arrived in the land of the Canaanites from Mesopotamia, settled in the many towns and cities in the region. By all accounts, the Canaanites seemed to welcome them, for there was a long period of time between the arrival of the Israelites and actual conflict with the Canaanites. There is now also proof from (Israeli-run) archaeological excavations that, initially at least, most Jews who travelled to Egypt were not slaves, but served in many occupations, including as soldiers for the Pharoah. The entire duration of time in which the Israelites lived in Egypt was some 210 years. The time period where most Jews were in some form of bondage, either as slaves, serfs or as indentured servants, was some 80-164 years, depending on which Christian or Hebrew text you quote from. What we do know is that the Jewish people were said to have left Egypt, led by Moses, around 1134 BCE. Thereupon, according to the Old Testament of the Christian and Jewish Bible, the Israelites wandered for another forty years before arriving in the Kingdom of Canaan.

Roughly around 1094 BCE, the Israelites allied themselves with the Philistines in order to defeat the present owners of the land, the Canaanites. Once they had defeated the Canaanites, both the Philistines and Israelites turned against one another and fought for control of the region. Eventually, the Israelites were able to defeat the Philistines. The twelve tribes of Israel thereupon established the Jewish Kingdom around 1050 BCE. However, about 120 years later, in 930 BCE. squabbling and differences amongst the twelve tribes caused the Kingdom of Israel to split into two realms: the Kingdom of Israel and the Kingdom of Judah. The Kingdom of Israel contained ten tribes, while the Kingdom of Judah contained the remaining two.[11] Splitting their kingdom in two proved a long-term strategic mistake, as various external empires, the Assyrians, Babylonians, Persians, etc., came and conquered these two Israeli kingdoms, as well as the surrounding lands, in consecutive order. In the case of Persia, Cyrus the Great allowed many of the Jews who had been taken captive by the Assyrians and Babylonians and brought back to Mesopotamia to return from bondage to the land of Canaan where, in 1050 BCE, they had established their first kingdom.

Because of this kindness, Cyrus the Great is fondly mentioned and remembered in Jewish writing. He is well referred to in the prophecies of Deutero-Isaiah, in the Book of Daniel, as well as in the Book of Ezra. This is also because Cyrus the Great permitted the Jews to rebuild the Temple of Jerusalem (Solomon's Temple). By 332 BCE it was the turn of Alexander the Great to control the Holy Land and other regions of the Middle East, including Egypt. During this time, we know that at least a contingent of Jewish soldiers was tasked with helping to garrison Egypt for the Macedonian king, it being common practice for Alexander the Great to recruit soldiers from the local populations he conquered. The Jews had been under Persian rule for a long time, but long gone were the days of Cyrus the Great. The love the Israelites had for him had not filtered down to the present Persian emperor, Darius III (d. 330 BCE). Following the collapse of Alexander's kingdom, his generals divided his empire into four separate realms. General Ptolemy received Egypt and the territories that today comprise Israel, the region of the West Bank and Lebanon. However, competition amongst the various Hellenic kingdoms, specifically between the Seleucid Kingdom and Ptolemaic Kingdom, led to the former conquering most of Lebanon and Israel (Caanan) by 200 BCE.

The next people to rule the Israelites were the Romans. In 63 BCE General Pompey conquered Jerusalem and all of Israel. Although the Romans wisely allowed the Jews to practise their faith, and never pushed their pagan gods on them, sufficient strife between Jews and Romans eventually caused two major uprisings. At the heart of this conflict was the religious enmity felt between the indigenous population and the Romans who had settled in the region. The Jews practised a monotheistic religion, while the Romans worshipped many deities.

The initial rebellion was referred to as the First Jewish-Roman War, lasting from 66-74 CE. The second war, named the Kitos War, occurred between 115 and 117 CE and happened in areas of the Roman Empire that contained a sizeable Jewish population. By that time, Jews had either immigrated to other parts of the Roman Empire in search of economic well-being or had been forced to settle in numerous Roman cities along the Mediterranean coastline as a way of limiting the possibility of a Jewish revolt in Judeah. The third uprising was called the Bar Kokhba Revolt and lasted from 132-136 CE. It was during the First Jewish-Roman War that the famous siege of Masada took place. Jewish rebels were holed up on a hilltop and were resisting a Roman attempt to capture the fortress. The siege lasted from 70-71 CE and ended with the mass suicide of 967 Israeli men, women and children. The Israelites killed themselves because they did not want to die at the hands of the Romans or to become their slaves. The former punishment was earmarked for the men, who were to be crucified, while the latter fate was reserved for most of the women and children.

The third Jewish rebellion to Roman rule, begun in 132 CE, occurred in Judeah and came during the reign of the Roman emperor, Hadrian. The uprising was probably begun because of Hadrian's attempt to build a Roman city, to be named Aelia Capitolina, on the site of the Jewish city of Jerusalem, which had been nearly razed to the ground in 70 CE. That rebellion, too, was crushed by the Romans, but with great difficulty and only after the Romans suffered heavy losses. During this last rebellion, most Roman colonists in the region were killed by the Israelites. According to two Roman accounts of the rebellion, the Israelites massacred everyone, including women and children.[12] It took the Romans six full legions, and parts of six other legions, to finally crush this last uprising. Thereupon, Emperor Hadrian ordered that a study be made to ascertain the cause(s) for the insurgency. His advisors concluded that the rebellion had been inspired by two points of contention: (1) nationalism and (2) religious fanaticism.

Based on this report, Hadrian made the fateful decision in 136 CE to continue to refer to the site of Jerusalem as Aelia Capitolina, and to rename the region as *Palestina*. The Roman province did eventually become known by that new name, *Palestina,* but the city of Jerusalem was re-established by the Jews, and the idea of creating a (pagan) Roman city on that location had to be dropped. The Romans realised that the Israelites would have rebelled again had they pursued its establishment. Another thing Emperor Hadrian did was to further increase the expulsion of Jews from the region, and to distribute them, as before, throughout the Roman Empire. His belief was that if he reduced the Jewish population in what is today the Holy Land, revolts would cease or, at the very least, any further rebellions by the Israelites would be more manageable. His theory was proven correct, given that no further uprisings by the Israelites occurred after that. However, this decision further increased the Jewish Diaspora. Although Jerusalem's name did not change, the region did come to be known as *Palestina*. It seemed that the land of Canaan had once again exchanged hands and was now firmly under Roman rule.

Zionism

Let us now discuss Zionism, for it was a driving force that propelled many Jews to return to the Holy Land at the beginning of the twentieth century. The term Zionism refers to a return of Jews to the land they had taken from the Canaanites and renamed Judea. The ancient city of Jerusalem, built by the Israelites, served as the capital of the new Jewish state. In ancient times, the Jewish nation suffered two devastating defeats at the hands of invading conquerors. The first occurred in 586 BCE, when the Babylonians subjugated the Israeli (ten tribes) and Judean (two tribes) kingdoms and destroyed the Jewish temple in Jerusalem. The second occurred later, when the Romans conquered the area in the year 63 BCE. This conquest marked the end of Hasmonean rule in Judea and the beginning of Roman rule over the region. The Roman general Pompey the Great captured Jerusalem and incorporated Judea into the Roman Republic as a client kingdom. Later, under the rule of Herod the Great, Judea was transformed into a Roman province in 6 CE, immediately after the death of Herod. This period of Roman rule eventually led to the Jewish-Roman wars and the eventual destruction of the Second Temple of Jerusalem in 70 CE. In between these two defeats, the Jewish Kingdom had been restored by the Persian emperor, Cyrus, who had defeated the Babylonians in 537 BCE.

From a financial and cost-effective way of ruling, returning the Diaspora Jews living in Mesopotamia, and allowing all people to worship whichever God(s) they wished, was a sound strategy for the leader of a vast ethnic and religiously diverse empire. What made Cyrus the Great so 'great' was the fact that he did not care what deity you prayed to. He only asked two things of the people living under his rule: (1) that they pay their taxes, and (2) that they serve in his army. Aside from that, the various peoples living in the regions that comprised the large Persian Empire were free to run things as they saw fit. In fact, Cyrus the Great made it a practice of appointing native administrators to regions where those administrators lived. For example, an Egyptian governor would govern Egypt, a Phoenician governor would govern Phoenicia, a Jewish governor would govern the Jewish lands, etc. Throughout the history of the Jewish people and of Judaism, the return of Jews to the homeland they had conquered in ancient times has been a principal theme in their being and their identity. In effect, Zionism became a centralising programme that redefined the Jewish religious community and turned it into a nationalist movement in the late nineteenth century.[13]

How Zionism became a driving force

The Jewish lawyer, author and journalist, Theodor Herzl, is considered by most people to be the father of modern Zionism. Although proto-Zionists predated Herzl and were quite numerous, they had not been able to define precisely and concisely the dilemma of the Jewish Diaspora as succinctly as Herzl was able to do. His late nineteenth-century writings on the need for the creation of a Jewish state were the propellant that fuelled the bonfire in the hearts of Jews everywhere who yearned for a Jewish state to escape the persecution and anti-Semitism found in the world. Herzl grew up uninterested in his Jewish heritage until his adult life, when he came up against persistent anti-Semitism. Herzl believed that Jews who refused to assimilate (like the orthodox) were responsible for the hatred by gentiles of the Jews. The injustice of the Alfred Dreyfus affair in France and, more precisely, the humiliation received by Captain Dreyfus when he was ceremoniously demoted, stripped of his rank, and expelled from the French Army, with its transparent anti-Semitic overtones, was the final straw that awakened in Herzl a desire to fight for the creation of a Jewish state.[14] Only if the Jewish people had their own nation, Herzl reasoned, could Jews live in peace, free from oppression and racism. Surprisingly, Herzl was not a particularly religious person. In fact, he was sectarian and sought a non-religious state, but one where Jews from everywhere could come and live free from persecution.

Why did the United Kingdom issue the Balfour Declaration?

The Balfour Declaration, which Britain's Foreign Minister, Arthur James Balfour declared in November 1917, affirmed that the United Kingdom favoured the establishment of a Jewish homeland in Palestine.[15] Given that words in politics are extremely important, the word 'homeland' was used purposely. The British had no desire to use the word 'state' or 'nation', which would imply that the United Kingdom desired a Jewish state. The word homeland could simply imply a traditional place for a people, but not necessarily a kingdom or a nation, and so in this way, the United Kingdom could claim that it had not really condoned a Jewish state. This declaration had not been made out of pity for the Jewish plight by the British but had been done out of political expediency. It had to do with how badly the war was going for the Entente Powers. Most people who are unaware of the conflict believe that by 1917, the Central Powers (Germany, Austria-Hungary and the Ottoman Empire) were losing badly. This could not be further from the truth. The year 1917 had certainly not been a good one for the French, British, Russians and the other Entente powers. In France, numerous French regiments had mutinied and refused to return to the trenches, with Marshal Foch even having to execute French soldiers in order to restore order. In northeast Italy, where the Italians were fighting a combined German and Austro-Hungarian army, the Italians had been dealt a severe blow during the Battle of Caporetto.

Between 24 October and 19 November 1917, a combined German and Austrian army had killed 13,000 men, wounded around 30,000 Italian soldiers, and taken prisoner an astounding 270,000 men. German and Austrian losses were about 70,000. It was such a shameful loss that Marshal Luigi Cardona was forced to resign his command. This battle marked the first time that the Germans had lent significant military support to their Austro-Hungarian allies on the Italian front. A total of forty-one Italian divisions faced six German and twenty-nine Austro-Hungarian divisions under Otto von Bulow's *14. Armee*. Von Bulow's troops were able to overwhelm the Italians in the selected main breakthrough point, where a weaker Italian force was located. The result of the offensive was to push the Italians back significantly. To make matters worse for the Allies, Russia had gone through a Menshevik revolution in March 1917 and a Bolshevik revolution in October of the same year,[16] so it was doubtful if Russia would continue the war. Britain (wrongly) theorised that Russian Jewish influence in this Bolshevik revolution was substantial. When Tsar Nicholas II abdicated the Russian throne, Alexander Fyodorovich Kerensky, a member of the Russian Duma (parliament), established the Russian provisional government. Kerensky wanted Russia to withdraw from the First World War, but the Entente powers of France and the United Kingdom were loath to allow that. All along the Eastern Front, Russia was fighting 1.5 million Germans and close to 4.4 million Austro-Hungarians.

If Kerensky were to suddenly make peace with the Central Powers (the German, Austro-Hungarian and Ottoman empire), more than 5 million soldiers would be available to fight on the Western Front: a sufficient number to overwhelm the British and French defences. France and the United Kingdom threatened Kerensky that if Russia were to leave the war, two things would happen. First, the Entente powers would not recognise Kerensky's government as legitimate. Secondly, both France and the United Kingdom would demand immediate repayment for the financial and military aid that had so far been provided to the Tsar during the war. Desperate to be recognised as the legitimate Russian government and knowing that Russia was financially incapable of paying off the foreign debt, Kerensky acquiesced and kept Russia in the war.

The war, however, was extremely unpopular with the Russian people. The Russian officer corps was composed of nobles and men who had managed to engineer a commission based on either their status or wealth, not their military prowess. The Russian officer corps looked down upon the rank-and-file of the Russian Army, while the lower ranks in the Russian Army despised the officer corps, whose incompetency and arrogance were widely known. Imperial Germany, who saw a chance to destabilise the Kerensky government, engineered the return of Russian dissident, Vladimir Lenin, from exile in Switzerland. The German Army High Command sent Lenin to St. Petersburg in October 1917, hoping that the presence of this Russian communist leader would topple the Kerensky government. The plan worked flawlessly. The Bolsheviks, led by Lenin, easily overthrew Kerensky and immediately sued for peace. The result was the Treaty of Brest-Litovsk, signed in March 1918. Instantly, a million German soldiers became available for employment on the Western Front.

In Paris and London, the French and British governments were in panic mode. Both understood the significance of so many German and Austro-Hungarian troops being made available for service in the West and elsewhere. Desperation began to set in at No. 10 Downing Street and 57 Rue de Varenne. Desperation often makes individuals act irrationally. Desperation often clouds a person's judgment. Desperation can make a person believe that white is black and black is white. This is exactly what happened in the autumn of 1917. Sometimes human beings make important decisions, not based on grounded fact, but based on impressions or perceptions. This is especially true when a person is desperate and has representative biases with an instinctive desire to affirm those untrue beliefs in any way. One representative bias that Entente leaders had in 1917 was that it was the Jews who had somehow engineered the Russian communist revolution.[17]

Acting in a desperate manner, the British government speculated that if the United Kingdom was looked upon with favour by Jewry, then Jewish influence in Russia could keep the Bolsheviks in the war against Germany. This was a chimera, but sometimes perceptions are just as important as reality. It is not uncommon for people to make important decisions based on perceptions rather than actual facts. There were Zionists in both France and the United Kingdom who had been seeking recognition from European governments for the creation of a Jewish state. One such Zionist was Baron Lionel Walter Rothschild, a Jewish member of the British nobility. The chemist, Chaim Azriel Weizmann, was another Zionist who had experienced first-hand the Russian *pogroms* that on numerous occasions had decimated many Jewish communities in the Russian Pale of Settlement.[18] Both Baron Rothschild and Chaim Weizmann grabbed onto the British government's belief of a Jewish connection to the Russian revolution and used it to attain their Zionist goal of obtaining a nation for the Jewish people. Weizmann's brother, Shmuel Weizmann, who was a dedicated communist living in Russia, was the connection touted to David Lloyd George's government in London.

According to the story, Shmuel Weitzmann supposedly had a direct line to the Bolshevik government in St. Petersburg. Number 10 Downing Street bought the story, hook, line and sinker. Having been ignored for decades, Jewish Zionists used the perception shared by the governments in London and Paris (that Jews had engineered the Russian revolution) and turned it to their advantage. Both Baron Rothschild and Chaim Weizmann led Prime Minister David Lloyd George and his cabinet to believe that Jewry had sufficient influence with the Bolshevik government to keep Russia in the war. Based on the idea of *quid pro quo,* the British said: 'Help us keep Russia in the war and in return, the United Kingdom will recognise the right of Jews to return to the Holy Land.' The deal was struck when an open letter by British Foreign Secretary Arthur James Balfour and addressed to Baron Rothschild was published. The letter announced the support of the United Kingdom for the establishment of a national home for the Jewish people in Palestine.[19]

Thus, the political decision to write the Balfour Declaration was made from a desperation to keep Russia in the war, and the mistaken perception that Jews controlled the Russian revolution. That Baron Rothschild, Chaim Weizmann and other members of the Zionist leadership fooled David Lloyd George's government, there is no doubt. Neither is there any doubt that after decades of being ignored, these Zionists resorted to such methods to attain their ends. Despite the promises made by the Zionist leadership, in March 1918, four months after the Balfour Declaration was issued, the Bolsheviks, led by Vladimir Lenin, signed the Treaty of Brest-Litovsk with Imperial Germany and ended the war. The Zionist leadership used the very representative biases that gentiles had of the Jewish people to achieve their goal of a promise of a Jewish homeland in the Holy Land. It was natural, then, that Zionists everywhere would continue to push the United Kingdom to uphold its promise of helping to establish a Jewish homeland at the end of the First World War. Throughout the period between 1917 and 1939, Zionists around the world continued to remind the government in London of its promise to allow the establishment of a Jewish homeland in the Middle East. The drumbeat of constant reminders to the British government, about the promise made in the Balfour Declaration, was kept up by Zionists throughout this twenty-two-year period. Based on this assurance, Jews now began to emigrate to Palestine in larger numbers than had been seen before, which in turn, began to alarm the Arab community living there.

1882 - Egypt's crisis: the rise of modern imperialism in the Middle East

Some say that the roots of modern Arab nationalism go back to 1882 and the British occupation of Egypt. The United Kingdom occupied Egypt in 1882 primarily due to concerns over the inability of Egypt to repay loans made by British and French bankers, and concern over the protection of British interests, particularly the Suez Canal. At the time, Egypt was experiencing significant political and economic instability. The ruling *Khedive,* or viceroy, Isma'il Pasha, had incurred massive debts building infrastructure and modernising the country.[20] This led to a financial crisis, and in 1876, Egypt was placed under international financial control through the Dual Control system, overseen by Britain and France.[21] However, by 1882, tensions between the *Khedive's* government and nationalist movements, along with fears of disruption to British interests in the Suez Canal, prompted the British to intervene militarily and to occupy the country. The occupation was not bloodless; Egyptian losses, both military and civilian, numbered in the thousands. A modest estimate would be around 5-6,000 Egyptians killed, although a larger estimate of around 8-10,000 is also possible. British losses included about 850 killed and a little over 600 wounded.

The Suez Canal, completed in 1869, had become a vital link in Britain's imperial communication and trade routes to its colonies in India and the Far East. The British military intervention, known as the Anglo-Egyptian War of 1882, resulted in the defeat of Egyptian forces and the establishment of British control over Egypt, which became a de facto British protectorate. Although Egypt remained nominally part of the Ottoman Empire until 1914, it effectively became a British colony, with British officials overseeing its administration and protecting British interests, particularly in safeguarding the Suez Canal. The occupation of Egypt clearly indicated to the people of North Africa and the Middle East that European imperial powers were only concerned with their own self-interest. Slowly, anger and resentment grew over the unfairness of the occupation.

The First World War and the McMahon-Hussein Correspondence

When the First World War broke out in the summer of 1914, the British used it as an excuse to annex Egypt from the Ottoman Empire completely.[22] The war was not unwelcomed by the French or British, as many in government saw it as an opportunity to expand colonial rule by grabbing territories that currently belonged to the Ottoman Empire. Beginning in 1915 and continuing into 1916, the British High Commissioner for Egypt, Sir Henry McMahon, established contact with the very ambitious *Hijazi* ruler of Mecca, Sharif Husseini bin Ali.[23] Sharif Husseini's dream of an Arab state had developed long before the start of the First World War, envisaging a large Arab state that was to be composed of what at the time was termed Greater Syria, which also included Palestine.

The reason why McMahon had contacted Sharif Husseini was that he was hoping to obtain Arab support against the Ottoman Empire. Knowing Husseini's aspirations for an Arab state, the idea of creating a post-war Arab nation was dangled at the end of a fishing pole to Husseini by McMahon. Numerous letters were passed between the two men, with their main correspondence occurring in 1915 and 1916[24] These letters contained discussions and promises regarding Arab independence and British support for an Arab uprising against the Ottoman Empire, which was aligned with the Central Powers during the war. Lebanon was at one point mentioned in Sharif Husseini's correspondence, with McMahon writing back that Lebanon was not a good choice for an Arab state because it contained people with many faiths: Eastern Orthodox Christianity, Catholicism, Sunni Islam, Shia Islam, the Alawite and Ismaili faiths and finally, the Druze, a millenarian offshoot of Isma'ili Shi'ism. The most famous letter in this exchange is the McMahon letter of 24 October 1915, where McMahon, on behalf of the British government, appeared to offer support for Arab independence in exchange for Arab support in the war against the Ottoman Empire. However, there were ambiguities and disagreements regarding the exact territorial boundaries and promises made in these letters, particularly concerning the status of regions like Palestine. The interpretation of the correspondence became a contentious issue in the post-war period, as it influenced the negotiations and agreements that shaped the Middle East following the collapse of the Ottoman Empire. The McMahon-Hussein correspondence is a significant historical document in understanding the complexities of British policy in the Middle East during the First World War and its implications for the region's future.

The First World War and the Sykes-Picot Agreement

The Sykes-Picot Agreement, named after its primary negotiators, Sir Mark Sykes of Britain and François Georges-Picot of France, was a secret arrangement between Britain and France made during the First World War. The agreement was signed in May 1916 and aimed to define the spheres of influence and control that Britain and France would have in the Middle East following the expected defeat of the Ottoman Empire. Key points of the Sykes-Picot Agreement included a division of the Ottoman territories, by dividing the Arab provinces of the Ottoman Empire into areas of control for Britain and France. These territories included present-day Syria, Lebanon, Iraq, Jordan, and Palestine. With the establishment of British and French spheres of influence: Britain was allocated control over the region of present-day Jordan, southern Iraq, and parts of what is now Israel and Palestine. France was given control over parts of present-day Syria and Lebanon. Consideration was also given for Russian interests in Persia.

The agreement also took into account Russian interests in the region, particularly in territories such as Constantinople (Istanbul) and parts of present-day eastern Turkey. Russia was initially a party to the agreement but withdrew following the Bolshevik Revolution in 1917. The Sykes-Picot Agreement was intended to secure the interests of Britain and France in the Middle East and to prevent conflicts between the two allies over control of the region. However, its provisions were not fully implemented due to subsequent developments, including the Arab Revolt against Ottoman rule and conflicting promises made by Britain to the Arabs through the McMahon-Hussein Correspondence. The agreement's legacy has been significant in shaping the borders and geopolitical dynamics of the modern Middle East. It has also been a subject of controversy and criticism for its role in drawing artificial boundaries that did not always correspond to the ethnic, religious, or historical realities of the region.

The First World War and the Balfour Declaration

The Balfour Declaration of November 1917 diverged from the Sykes-Picot Agreement because Palestine was a part of Greater Syria, which had been promised to the French as per the secret agreement. The guarantee to allocate Palestine for a future Jewish homeland also gave the United Kingdom a reason for later demanding the Palestinian mandate, but it created another problem for Husseini and his vision of a greater Arab state. The British pledge to Husseini was now sacrificed to the requirements of Allied harmony and self-interest. The vague promises that McMahon had made to Sharif Husseini bin Ali were thought to be sufficient for the Arab leader to throw his support for a revolt against the Ottomans. As stated earlier, Sir Henry McMahon had contended that the coastal areas of Lebanon and Palestine could not be incorporated into an Arab state because peoples of other religious faiths lived there. Husseini then argued that the provinces of Baghdad and Basra belonged to the Arab heritage, but he had to reluctantly accept what was supposed to be a temporary British and French postwar occupation of Syria and Mesopotamia.

The Middle East between the wars

When Prince Faisal moved his Arab forces to Damascus in October 1918 with the intent of establishing an Arab state, the French invoked the secret Sykes-Picot Agreement and moved to seek British support, while at the same time evicting Faisal and his supporters from Damascus, which they did in July 1920. This expulsion occurred following the San Remo Conference in April 1920, where the League of Nations granted France a mandate over Syria and Lebanon. The French saw Faisal as a threat to their control over the region and moved to assert their authority by forcibly removing him from Damascus. Despite efforts by Faisal and his supporters to resist the French occupation, including the establishment of the Arab Kingdom of Syria, French military forces ultimately prevailed, leading to Faisal's expulsion and the end of his rule. After his expulsion, Faisal went into exile.

Sharif Husseini's other son, Prince Abdullah, was incensed at how the French had treated his brother. In the late summer of 1920, he began to move a sizeable Arab force from Saudi Arabia towards Damascus – presumably to try to support his brother Faisal's claim in Syria. Although he was not a real threat to French control of the region, the political repercussions of a French-Arab war would inevitably involve the United Kingdom and destabilise the region for the colonial powers. This would also alienate the rest of the Arab world and cause problems for the British and French. Prince Abdullah got as far as the east bank of the Jordan River (east of Palestine) before Winston Churchill, who was Foreign Minister at the time, decided to give the virtually worthless land surrounding Amman and east of the Jordan River to Prince Abdullah as a fiefdom. This is how Transjordan was created. Prince Faisal, who had been expelled from Syria by the French, was also placated. The government of the United Kingdom created the nation of Iraq, and the kingship of the country was offered to Prince Faisal in 1921. The borders of Iraq were drawn in a London office, amid cigar smoke, biscuits and afternoon tea.

The frontiers of Iraq were created with no consideration whatsoever over tribal, ethnic or religious concerns. In this way, Iraq came into being with a mixture of Shiite, Sunni, Fayli Kurds, Yazidi, Christians, Shabak, Kakai, Sabean-Mandaean, Bahai, Zoroastrian, Bidoon, Roma, Assyrians, and Jews. In fact, it benefitted the London government that Iraq contained a hodgepodge of peoples and faiths. No one group could claim dominance, which meant that infighting would be inevitable. This, of course, only benefitted the colonial power. It was a strategy that had been employed elsewhere, such as on the Indian subcontinent, and was the key to the creation of a vast empire by an island nation. Divide and conquer: not mere words, but actual strategy. The establishment of the kingdoms of Transjordan and Iraq were pronounced in the so-called Churchill White Paper, a study that was done shortly after the start of Jewish and Arab disturbances in Palestine in 1920.

In addition to throwing the Arabs a bone by allowing the establishment of the two kingdoms of Transjordan and Iraq, the Churchill White Paper also attempted to limit the areas in the Middle East that Jews could emigrate to.[25] Since the Jewish people claimed that the regions of Galilee (Golan), Judea (Judah), Samaria (Shomron), and Jordan (Yarden) were their rightful homeland, limiting Jewish immigration to west of the Jordan River was, in effect, denying them access to a part of their native soil.[26] This White Paper would be the first of three United Kingdom studies that would be prepared over the period of the pre-war British mandate in Palestine. In each case, the United Kingdom would attempt to diminish the Balfour Declaration by trying to limit Jewish expansionism in Palestine. However, prominent people such as Chaim Weizmann, Baron Rothschild, and other dedicated Zionists kept the pressure on each succeeding administration in No. 10 Downing Street, to abide by the Balfour Declaration.

The growth of Arab nationalism in the 1930s

The origins of Muslim support for Nazi Germany must be addressed within the context of the power struggle between Arabs and Jews who believed in Zionism, which began in earnest in the early part of the 1920s in Palestine. The struggle that was directly caused by the Balfour Declaration. Jews who believed in Zionism claimed that they were entitled to have a nation of their own in the land they had conquered long ago from the Canaanites. A land that had belonged to them for a time until, like the Jewish invaders had done to the Canaanites, other peoples had taken it from them. A land that had changed hands numerous times and had been owned by many people. A land that now had a vibrant and distinct Arab society: the Palestinians. A land that was no longer theirs to possess. In the 1920s, as Jewish immigration to Palestine grew and grew, creating fear in the general population, an antithetical Arab movement began to blossom as a direct consequence of this Zionist goal. This Arab movement was initially limited to Palestinian Arabs, for they were the ones being affected by this increased Jewish immigration. When Prince Faisal was expelled from Damascus, some of his Arab supporters also fled Syria. Some moved to Mesopotamia, while others went to Lebanon. A good number also fled south towards Palestine.

Angry and embittered at having been ousted from Syria, many now took on the cause of the Palestinians by opposing further Jewish immigration. It was thus that in Palestine, these Arab nationalists soon found themselves supporting the local Palestinian Arabs in their struggle over Jewish immigration. Many Arabs from other regions of the Middle East were empathetic to the Palestinian complaint. The leading proponent of Palestinian nationalism at the time was the Mufti of Jerusalem, Haj Amin Mohammad al-Huseini, more commonly known by his title, Haj Amin al-Huseini. Husseini's red beard and moustache echoed the ferocity and fierceness with which he would proceed to defend Palestinian rights. Strangely, it had been the United Kingdom Commissioner for Palestine at the time, Herbert Samuel, who also happened to be Jewish, who had appointed Haj Amin al-

Husseini to the Muslim Council. The Muslim Council was the highest governing body for Muslims in Palestine. Husseini quickly dominated this board and began to appoint individuals who supported his goals to various posts. He also made use of his position as Mufti of Jerusalem, appointing *mullahs* who ran the numerous Palestinian religious courts which governed Muslim Sharia Law. Initially, Husseini was opposed within the Muslim community by the so-called National Party, which was a coalition of Muslim and Christian Arabs. It was this early Arab infighting in Palestine that some scholars say inhibited the cohesion and growth of Arab nationalism, while Zionism was, for the most part, highly effective and one-minded in its purpose. This infighting among the Arabs is also what made Jewish leaders in the *Yishuv* believe that they had nothing to worry about from the Arab leadership. However, as time would prove, this self-assurance that Arab nationalism posed no threat to Zionism would soon disappear.

It became clear to the *Yishuv* that Arabs were waking up to the perceived threat that Jewish immigration posed.[27] The Mufti of Jerusalem believed that huge demonstrations would show the British that their policy of allowing further Jewish immigration to Palestine was wrought with problems and misguided. Thus began a series of demonstrations that often became riots. These riots were geared to derail the plan for a Jewish homeland in Palestine by creating the conditions that would allow the United Kingdom to revoke the Balfour Declaration. At the time, the majority of the Arabs in Palestine were uneducated, landless peasants (*Fellahin*), dependent on temporary work in privately owned farms. Many perceived Jewish immigration as a direct threat to their livelihood, since Jewish farmers had adopted a policy of only hiring Jewish workers. In addition, lands that were bought by the Jewish Council in the *Yishuv* were never resold back into Arab hands. The conclusions most Arabs reached was that Jewish immigration in Palestine was therefore detrimental. This was a point, the economic factor, which Haj Amin al-Husseini stressed in his speeches to the *Fellahin*. He realised that the lack of education on the part of the majority of the Arab listeners prevented him from speaking about such lofty ideals as pan-Arabism or Arab nationalism. He needed to speak to the points that his listeners could understand.

It was simpler to accuse the Jews of stealing land and jobs than to try to explain the intricacies of just exactly what Zionism was attempting to do in Palestine. It was true that Jewish immigration to the *Yishuv* had produced a higher standard of living in Palestine than in any of the surrounding regions. This higher standard of living was so significant that for a time at least, Arab migration to Palestine became many times higher than Jewish immigration into Palestine. In the beginning these Arab riots worked well enough to force the British government to restrict Jewish immigration somewhat, but over time the Arab plan proved to be counter-productive, and Husseini would overplay his hand. During the Arab-Jewish riots of 1930, another British study was prepared by Hope Simpson and presented by Lord Passfield to the London government. Because it did not favour them, the Jewish leadership accused the creators of the study of being biased and anti-Semitic. This new report accused the Jewish JNF agency of purchasing Arab lands and then evicting the landless *Fellahin*. It suggested that in order to avoid further conflict, further restrictions on Jewish immigration needed to be imposed.

Chaim Weitzmann was so incensed that he resigned as head of the Jewish Agency in Palestine. Other Zionist leaders were equally infuriated and voiced their opinion that the British decision was unfair and showed that the government in London was biased. Although the study was based on fact, a compromise and face-saving deal was eventually reached between the Zionists and the government of Prime Minister James Ramsay McDonald.[28] The Passfield White Paper was shortly thereafter abrogated. The 1930 riots, therefore, were a failure for Haj Amin al-Husseini and his Arab nationalist supporters. This should have indicated to Husseini that the strategy of engineering demonstrations to create the conditions for abrogating the Balfour Declaration was now ineffective. However, he continued using the same tactic, not realising that the British were not about to renege on the promise made in the Balfour Declaration. Another strategy was necessary, but he did not alter his approach. In the mid-1930s, Haj Amin al-Husseini upped the ante when a large Arab revolt began in Palestine against the *Yishuv* and the British mandate government. This expansion of the revolt would soon backfire.

This revolt could be termed as the first large-scale *Intifada* in Palestine. It proved to be an utter failure and all it succeeded in doing was to engender the wrath of the British government, which promptly disbanded the Muslim Council and all other sectors of Arab leadership in Palestine. This single act had the effect of disrupting any further organised resistance to the British mandate government, but more importantly, it left no coordinated Arab leadership body that could help the mass of the Arab population to coalesce against the highly organised Zionists, whose single goal was further Jewish immigration.[29] For instigating this rebellion, Husseini was arrested by the British mandate government in Palestine on 17 July 1939. Sir John Chancellor, the third British High Commissioner for Palestine

(1928-1931), personally issued a warrant for the arrest of the Mufti. Husseini was accused of fomenting the riots and of also being the principal ringleader behind an Arab national strike against growing Jewish immigration, which lasted from April to October 1936.[30] Faced with the fact that he could no longer make a difference in Palestine, the Mufti of Jerusalem managed to escape to Lebanon, where he came to the conclusion that peaceful means of resistance were a waste of time because the Palestinians were not getting anywhere with the British. Instead, he made the fateful decision of organising guerrilla forces that would strike directly at Jewish settlements in the Galilee region.

It was in the late 1930s that Husseini began to receive financial support from Nazi Germany. War was looming on the horizon and the British needed a steady flow of oil from her Arab-populated possessions in the Middle East. The growing German influence in the Arab world so concerned the United Kingdom that they temporarily abrogated the Balfour Declaration in 1939. Thus, the threat of a coming war managed to do what a decade of Arab demonstrations and strikes had failed to accomplish. The British did this to see if tensions in the Arab world, especially in Palestine, would decrease. This temporary cessation of legal Jewish immigration to Palestine was done for political and military considerations. Although legal immigration to Palestine was temporarily put on hold, illegal Jewish immigration continued and only increased as the Second World War progressed and Jews sought to escape Nazi-occupied Europe. When the war ended, the survivors of the Holocaust began to immigrate to Palestine by legal and illegal means. This post-war immigration to Palestine dramatically increased the Jewish community there.

Of course, this would change after the war, but before that time, it appeared that Jewish immigration had ceased, and the London government had finally sided with the Arab majority. Haj Amin al Husseini knew better, and it was therefore with the intent of expelling not only the Jews from Palestine, but the British as well, that he continued his relentless campaign against both camps. On 13 October 1939, a little over a month after the start of the Second World War, Husseini travelled from Beirut, Lebanon to Baghdad, in Iraq. There he formed the so-called Committee for the Collaboration Between Arabs – a political body he hoped would galvanise Arab nationalist groups from Syria, Iraq, Saudi Arabia, Lebanon, Palestine and Transjordan into a single, powerful body. Husseini correctly surmised that only through cooperation between the various Arab peoples and governments could both the British mandate of Palestine and Jewish immigration be defeated. What he failed to grasp, however, were the various aspirations and desires of these diverse Arab groups and their essentially local self-interest. The plight of the Palestinian *Fellahin* was far from the minds of many of these leaders. The unfortunate truth was that self-aggrandisement of their own territories was more akin to their goals.

This would eventually be proven true during the 1948 Arab-Israeli War. During that first war, the various Arab leaders failed to coordinate with one another and instead entered Palestine with the intent of carving up and gaining the largest territories for their own kingdoms. By far the most successful proved to be King Abdallah of Transjordan, who managed to gain a sizeable chunk of territory on the west bank of the Jordan River and as a result, his nation was eventually renamed as Jordan. Transjordan, originally known as the Emirate of Transjordan, became the independent Hashemite Kingdom of Jordan through a series of historical developments and diplomatic agreements. The first development was the British Mandate. After the First World War, the League of Nations granted Britain the mandate to administer Palestine and Transjordan. Transjordan was initially administered as part of the Mandate for Palestine. The second change was separation. In 1921, the British government, under the High Commissioner of Palestine Herbert Samuel, decided to separate Transjordan from the rest of the mandate territory due to administrative and financial considerations. Emir Abdullah, the son of Sharif Hussein of Mecca, was appointed as the Emir of Transjordan. The third development was independence, which Transjordan gained from Britain on 25 May 1946.

Following this independence, the country was officially named the Hashemite Kingdom of Transjordan. The next change came with territorial expansion. In 1948, the State of Israel was established, and Transjordan, along with other Arab states, participated in the Arab-Israeli War. As previously mentioned, Transjordan occupied and annexed the West Bank, including East Jerusalem, and parts of the former British Mandate of Palestine. This annexation effectively doubled the territory of Transjordan. The next development came with the changing of the country's name. In April 1949, following the territorial expansion and the annexation of the West Bank, Transjordan changed its name to the Hashemite Kingdom of Jordan, reflecting its enlarged territory and position as the sovereign state ruling over both banks of the Jordan River. Overall, the transformation of Transjordan into Jordan was a result of a combination of historical circumstances, British colonial policies, Arab nationalist movements, and geopolitical developments in the region during the early to mid-twentieth century. Little did the Palestinians know that the loss of this first Arab-Israeli conflict, which began on 15 May 1948, would result in the *Nakba* (catastrophe). The *Nakba* refers to the ethnic cleansing of Palestine and the near-total destruction of Palestinian society when one third of the Palestinian population fled the war of their own accord, another third was forcibly expelled by the Jews during and immediately after the war, with the remaining third of the Palestinian people becoming non-citizens in their own land.

Association with Nazi Germany

Having done as much as he could to prevent further Jewish immigration to Palestine, and now being hunted by the British, Haj Amin al-Husseini decided to seek further assistance from Nazi Germany. In this he employed the old Arab proverb: 'The enemy of my enemy is my friend.' He therefore wrote a formal letter of support, signed by the members of the Committee for the Collaboration Between Arabs on 21 June 1940, and sent it to Berlin via Turkey. The letter also stated that Arab nationalism was in step with the interests of Italy and Germany. A series of letters were then passed between Berlin and al-Husseini. By February 1941, the latter had met secretly with numerous Iraqi Army officers who opposed King Faisal, whom they saw as a puppet of the British. They were supported in this by Rashid Ali al-Gailani, the Iraqi prime minister from 1940-1941.

On 1 April 1941 the Iraqi Army, supported by the prime minister and a large segment of the Iraqi population, launched a *coup d'état* that toppled King Faisal. The most important letter to reach the Arab nationalist leaders was one dated 8 April 1941 and was most likely written as a response to the Iraqi army revolt. It had been approved by Adolf Hitler and in it he had directed the Nazi Secretary of State, Ernst von Weizäcker, to proclaim that Arab regions had never been occupied by Imperial Germany and that Nazi Germany had no territorial demands for Arab lands.[31] Before the Germans could offer assistance, the coup failed, even though 50,000 Iraqi troops faced about 14,000 Commonwealth soldiers from Transjordan and Basra. The famous one-eyed Israeli tank commander, Moshe Dayan, lost his left eye while working as a guide for Commonwealth forces entering Iraq. In fact, Jewish guides were used by the British from the very beginning of the war. By the end of 1942, an entire Jewish brigade was serving in the British Army.

Shortly thereafter, Hitler ordered his Special Directive No. 30 (dated 23 May 1941), and Service Regulations for Special Staff 'F' of 21 June 1941, in which *Luftwaffe* general Helmut Felmy was appointed as the general authority for all Arab affairs concerning the *Wehrmacht*.[32] On

28 November 1941 Adolf Hitler received Haj Amin al-Husseini, with *Reichsminister* for Foreign Affairs Ribbentrop present. However, Hitler restricted the conversation to cooperation between Arabs and Germans against the Jews. This was because Hitler knew that Marshal Pétain, who now headed Vichy France, was not yet ready to give up France's Arab possessions, let alone make any concessions of independence or semi-independence for France's Arab population. Of course, this all became a moot point once Britain invaded Vichy French territory in the Middle East (Syria) in 1941 and in North Africa (Morrocco and Algeria) in 1942, and finally Tunisia in 1943.

After the failed Iraqi uprising, Haj Amin al-Husseini, who was now being referred to by the Germans as the Grand Mufti of Jerusalem, and the exiled Iraqi prime minister, Rashid Ali al-Gailani, both went to work for Dr Joseph Goebbels' Propaganda Department. To this end both men and their adherents worked tirelessly to promote the Axis cause in whichever way was possible. It was not long after this that Germany and Italy began to establish their own military formations composed of Muslim volunteers.

Vichy France acquired several divisions from the pre-war French Army, composed primarily of Tunisian, Moroccan and Algerian men. When American and British Commonwealth forces invaded North Africa in November 1942, those divisions were either disbanded or switched sides and became part of the Free French forces. The Vichy French government thereupon created the so-called *Légion Impériale* with the support of Nazi ambassador Otto Abetz, who provided the funding for such things as the legion's cloth insignia. German military attire was also allocated for the volunteers. The *Légion Impériale* was established as a counter to Allied moves to absorb Vichy French forces into the Allied army. In April 1943 the *Légion Impériale* was renamed *La Légion des Volontaires Français de Tunisie* (the Legion of French Volunteers of Tunisia). Only one small battalion, the *Phalange Africaine*, was created in North Africa before the collapse of Axis resistance there in May 1943.[33] This unit will be discussed later in the book.

Muslims in the Soviet Union and the Balkans

When the Russian Civil War began in 1918, many regions of the Russian empire where Islam was the majority religion actually turned out in support of the Bolsheviks. The reason was a simple one: the Bolsheviks had made promises to give independence to those areas of the Russian empire where Muslims lived. Of course, this promise was nothing more than a lie, geared to garner the military support of the Muslim peoples against the pro-Tsarist Russian forces. Once the Bolsheviks (the 'Reds') won the civil war against the pro-Tsarist 'Whites', they simply ignored the promise they had made and instituted collectivisation methods, and repressed religion in these Muslim areas, just like they did in Christian Orthodox regions of what was now known as the Union of Soviet Socialist Republics (USSR). Muslims never forgot this betrayal, and resented having their faith suppressed.

When the Germans invaded the USSR, they quickly encountered many peoples of various ethnic races and religions who wished to rid themselves of Joseph Stalin and the communists. The Muslims were, for the most part, unhappy at the anti-religious stance of the Communist Party. Islam, like Christianity and Judaism, ran counter to communist beliefs. It was no surprise, therefore, that when recruitment of Soviet citizens began in earnest in 1942, a good portion of those recruits would be Muslim. Interestingly, the Germans met with some resistance to Nazi anti-Semitism, and their recruitment of the local Muslim population only met with mixed results in the Balkans. There must have been a difference in this region that harkened to a more tolerant time. The Muslim population here was already used to receiving the short end of the stick from both the Catholic and Eastern Orthodox Christian communities. That is why, when they were approached by the Germans, who wanted to recruit them, they were hesitant and suspicious. For example, when the Germans began to raise the Muslim SS 'Handschar' division from Muslim men living in Bosnia and Herzegovina, they had to resort to mandatory conscriptions, and later on even had to deal with a full-blown mutiny within the forming division. Granted, the Croatian fascist leader Ante Pavelić had done his very best to dissuade Bosnian Muslims from volunteering for German service, the hesitation to volunteer was already there. During the initial start of what would become a guerrilla war in Yugoslavia, many Muslim communities were targeted by both the Catholic Croatians and Eastern Orthodox Serbians, who killed Muslims where they could be found. Only later did the Catholic Croatians cease these killings and instead begin to recruit Muslim men into their forces. Faced with enemies on all sides, Muslims in the Balkans made the best of it and chose to side with whomever offered them the best chance to survive the conflict. The old proverb that 'the enemy of my enemy, is my friend' should be the guiding principle for those wishing to understand Arab-Nazi relations from 1935-1945.

Chapter Two

ARAB VOLUNTEERS IN THE GERMAN ARMY, 1941–1945

Introduction to Arab participation in the Wehrmacht

The origins of the Arab volunteer movement in the German Army date back to the failed Iraqi Army uprising of May 1941. Hitler had always expended too little interest on the political currents that moved the Arab world. Frankly, his mind was preoccupied with Europe's affairs. In the spring of 1941, most of his attention was focused on preparations for the invasion of the USSR. In addition, the need to come to Benito Mussolini's aid in the Balkans was also taking time from the *Führer*'s busy schedule. At Adolf Hitler's insistence, the prince regent of Yugoslavia, Paul Karađorđević, had been forced to sign the Tripartite Pact with Nazi Germany on 25 March 1941. Just a few days later, he was overthrown by Yugoslav Air Force officers, who immediately abrogated the treaty and installed the young, 17-year-old Peter II as king of Yugoslavia. Hitler was incensed. He immediately ordered the *Wehrmacht* high command to draw up plans to invade Yugoslavia. Now, in addition to having to invade Greece to help the floundering Italians, Hitler also had to conquer Yugoslavia to secure the southern flank of his upcoming invasion of the USSR. With so much going on, this explains why German intelligence was inadequately prepared in an area which presented favourable opportunities because of long standing friendly contacts and what appeared to be several similar goals on the part of Nazi Germany and the Arab world.

The Supreme Command of the German Armed Forces (OKW) was taken by surprise by the anti-British uprising in Iraq in 1941. In the diplomatic, propaganda, and military fields Germany had neglected to prepare for just such an eventuality. To a national military force, this was tantamount to military malpractice.[34] Having no outside support, the Iraqi Army uprising against the British and their Commonwealth forces soon petered out and failed. The opportunity to exploit the Iraqi unrest therefore rapidly slipped away from the Germans, much to Hitler's dismay. Nevertheless, an attempt to send aid and support to the Iraqis was begun during those hectic days in May 1941. The Germans hastily established a command staff under *Luftwaffe General der Flieger* Walter Helmuth Wolfgang Felmy. The headquarters staff he quickly created was simply called *Sonderstab F* (Special Staff F), where 'F' stood for Felmy. The best that this hastily organised staff could do was to make last-minute plans and half-boiled improvisations, which could only give token and therefore inadequate aid to the Iraqi insurgents.

After the collapse of the uprising, the decision to keep the staff active was made since the incident had proven Germany's inadequacies and lack of preparedness when it came to Arab and Middle Eastern matters. The total absence of a firm Arab policy was completely disregarded and the only progress that *Sonderstab F* could produce was the guarantee that in the future, if a similar Arab uprising were to happen, Nazi Germany could supply military aid. Politically, however, the Third Reich was drawing a blank card with regard to how to treat the Arabs and what they wanted, and what the Third Reich was prepared to give. Complicating matters even further was Germany's current but dubious Italian ally, Benito Mussolini. The Duce had different designs on the Arab world, so Nazi Germany needed to take the Italian demands regarding North Africa and the Middle East into consideration. Thus, a solid policy towards the Arab world would elude the Germans, mainly because there were too many variables that had not yet been decided upon. For the present, Adolf Hitler had envisioned occupying the Middle East as a means by which he could control this oil rich region. Aside from pledging to evict the French and British from the area, the *Führer* had no immediate intention to allow the Arab countries their independence.

Aspirations by Arab leaders in the region, coupled by false promises of independence after a Nazi victory, were the most the Germans were prepared to give the Arab world. But these promises would prove to be a chimera, since the Germans had no firm policy in place and their goals in this region were rather limited to control and exploitation of the natural resources. The special staff formed under General Felmy had no political influence or decision-making power, and consequently lacked any political importance in the Arab world. It was strictly a military headquarters geared to support Arabs wishing to fight the Allies. The staff, therefore, was eventually relegated to helping to form volunteer units made up of peoples from the Arab world who believed that a Nazi victory would aid their cause.

There were many that wished North Africa and the Middle East to be free of European rule altogether. Those who thought that evicting the French and British would lead to self-rule were perhaps also wondering about the Italians and the Germans. In times of war, however, immediacy of the situation usually outweighs long-term goals. As the saying goes: 'no need to worry about tomorrow, let's just get through today'. There were those people who, like the Nazis, wished to see the complete elimination of the Jewish people and therefore backed the Nazis fervently. There were also those who sought both these goals. Indeed, the Mufti of Jerusalem, Haj Amin al-Husseini, and the Iraqi leader, Prime Minister Rashid Ali al-Gailani, both sought to use the Arab volunteers eventually raised by *Sonderstab F* as the nucleus of a future Arab Army.[35] In 1943, al-Husseini was 46 years old, while al-Gailani was 50.[36] A rivalry eventually developed between the two men over who would control a future Arab army and, therefore, who would lead the Arabs in the post-war period. Both men bickered and attempted to undermine one another for the rest of the war. This feud would sap the morale of the volunteers to a certain extent and proved counterproductive. In the end, the only good that came from *Sonderstab F*'s contacts with Arab leaders and their followers was the number of their men that could be used in battle. The *Deutsches-Arabisches Infanterie-Bataillon 845* (German-Arab 845th Infantry Battalion) was one such unit.

Sonderstab F

The assignment of *Sonderstab F*, therefore, changed from a multi-purpose role that encompassed political, psychological and military goals. The initial political aims, however vague, deteriorated even more as the German options in the Arab world were diminished by the changing fortunes of war. Simply put, by the end of 1941 the opportunities that existed at the start of the war in the eastern Mediterranean, North Africa and in the Middle East, no longer existed. *Sonderstab F* was eventually relegated to being transformed into a regular army corps headquarters, and its specialised Arab units were squandered in regular combat. Instead of forming the spearhead of a joint German-Arab alliance against France, the United Kingdom and its Commonwealth allies, these formations were used piecemeal in battle. As if to underline its pure military role, on 9 April 1943 *Sonderstab F* was redesignated *Generalkommando z.b.V. LXVIII.* A year later it was renamed *LXVIII. Armeekorps.*

The North African Arab battalions

In early 1943, as the African campaign was becoming more tenuous for the Germans and Italians, the decision was made to try to recruit local Arabs into pro-German battalions. The plan was not to commit these battalions to frontline service, but rather to take up guard and security duties behind the front lines so that rear-area German forces would be available to be employed at the front. The ill-equipped and late blooming North African battalions formed by the *Afrika Korps* in Tunisia in early 1943 were destroyed by the Allied victory in that region, shortly after they had been raised. They briefly operated as coastal guard and rear area security battalions and were armed with a variety of second-hand clothing and weapons. The clothing was a mixture of German and Italian uniforms. Some even wore (Vichy) French Army attire. Weapons were also a combination of German, Italian and French arms.

Political divisions

The better trained *Deutsche-Arabische Lehr-Abteilung* (German-Arab Training Battalion), which had been in existence since July 1941, continued to suffer from a politically divisive power struggle between the Mufti of Jerusalem, Haji Amin al-Husseini and the Iraqi leader, ex-Prime Minister Rashid Ali al-Gailani. In this struggle there was even a third Arab faction that emerged and supported Fauzi Kaikyi, the former Syrian military commander. The conspiratorial intrigues of these three factions did much to sap whatever cohesiveness the Germans were trying to instil in this training battalion of Arabs from diverse parts of the Middle East. It was not until the Germans expunged the most fervent, and therefore the most troublesome, supporters of these three cliques that the *Deutsches-Arabisches Infanterie-Bataillon 845* began to function as a proper military unit. Again, the lack of a proper German policy had also allowed these various groups, each with their own personal goals, to subvert the very military unit which had been organised to represent the pro-Axis Arab world. The cadre of the *Deutsches-Arabisches Infanterie-Bataillon 845* was established in the town of Sunium, on the southernmost tip of the Greek region of Attica. There, permanent quarters were established using the weekend villas of wealthy Greek Athenians, although the majority of the personnel ended up living in tents. The climate was subtropical and the initial batch of Arab volunteers had no problems with this, since they had been raised and lived in a similar climate. Training of the battalion began immediately. The following statement describes the initial stages of the training:

> Special Staff F and the Arab volunteers gathered at Sunium in July 1941. Training of the Muslims began almost immediately. The Arabs had a fair knowledge of German and showed themselves willing to learn. Unfortunately, they lacked imagination and this made it difficult for them to understand the significance of the individual phases of a military operation. Quite a number of volunteers could not understand why they should have to go through a toughening up process, although this is an integral part of military training everywhere in the world. The Arab attitude was that it was unnecessary to make a serious effort.[37]

Another problem that quickly showed its ugly head was the mistake of using German instructors who had formerly lived in Arab countries. While at first glance these Germans, almost all of them quite knowledgeable in the language of the recruits, seemed the perfect candidates to train and become the German cadre of this Arab battalion, further experience showed that they had preconceived ideas about Arab recruits. These ideas were that Arabs were a race of menials and shirkers, and this attitude of the German cadre staff soon crept into the ranks and was detrimental to morale and training. The already pre-existing representative biases that most Germans had during this epoch was at the heart of the problem. The fact that one of the base pillars of National Socialist ideology was a racist hagiarchy also exacerbated the situation. Another unit, also under the command of *Sonderstab F*, was the all-German *Sonderverbänd 288*, which had begun training on 24 July 1941 in Potsdam. During the course of its history, it would contain not only Germans but Arabs as well. The regiment was specifically trained and equipped for desert warfare. Although this commando unit took on a few Arab volunteers who were living in Germany before being deployed, it was only after *Sonderverbänd 288* began to operate under Field Marshal Erwin Rommel's *Afrika Korps* that the unit started recruiting a large batch of Arab volunteers, some of whom were of African extraction.[38]

The structure of this unit was specifically geared for mobile desert warfare. Many of its German personnel had prior experience in the deserts of the Middle East and North Africa. A good number of them had also seen prior service in the French Foreign Legion, meaning they knew (1) French, (2) the local Berber languages (Tamazight), (3) Arabic, or all three. This unit was soon dispatched to North Africa as support for Rommel's *Afrika Korps*. Its mission would almost always place its members either behind the Allied lines or acting as the eyes and ears of the *Afrika Korps*, performing reconnaissance operations. The campaign in Egypt reached its zenith at El Alamein in 1942. As more and more

German and Italian troops, weapons and supplies kept being sunk to the bottom of the Mediterranean Sea by Allied submarines and bombers based in Malta, Erwin Rommel was eventually forced to employ the regiment in a conventional manner. The *Afrika Korps* was simply down to a skeleton of what it should have been because its replacement troops and military supplies were being destroyed. Beginning on 24 November 1942, *Sonderverbänd 288* arrived at Benghazi airport on Ju-52 transport planes, although it took several days for the entire unit to arrive.

That same day (24 November) an armed Italian merchant cruiser managed to make it to Benghazi by running through the Allied naval blockade, bringing in more members of *Sonderverbänd 288*. In addition, two Italian Spica-class torpedo boats were sent to Benghazi carrying several *Sturmgeschütz III* assault guns for the regiment. The engineer and anti-tank element of the regiment arrived by air in Derna about the same time. The initial wave that bought part of *Sonderverbänd 288* to Derna included five Ju-90 four-engine transport planes, which delivered three armoured cars, one command car, three *Panzerschreck* hand-held anti-tank guns, two 50-mm Pak-38 anti-tank guns, and about three platoons of men. The regiment had been sent to Benghazi and Derna to act as a blocking force for an expected Allied attack. It never returned to the control of *Sonderstab F* as it was eventually redesignated as *Panzergrenadier Regiment Afrika* and became an integral part of Rommel's army on 31 October 1942.[39]

Figure 1. A mono line drawing of the Freis Arabien arm patch worn by the Arab volunteers. *(Author's line drawing)*

The regiment was organised into roughly two battalions of four companies each. However, the manner in which the unit was employed was not on a traditional battalion-level. Rather, companies were chosen by the necessities the mission required and a *Kampfgruppe* (battlegroup) was created on a temporary basis until the conclusion of the mission. The table of organisation for the unit on 24 July 1941 looked as follows:

Sonderverbänd 288:
Stab Kompanie und Panzerspähwagen Zug
Sonderkompanie
Gebirgsjäger Kompanie
Schützen Kompanie
Maschinengewehr Kompanie
Panzerjäger Kompanie
Flak Kompanie
Pionier Kompanie
Nachrichten kompanie

Given that there was a total of eight companies, the size of *Sonderverbänd 288* was that of a regiment containing the equivalent of about two battalions. On 26 January 1942, *Hauptmann* (captain) Schober assumed command of the *Deutsche-Arabische Lehr-Abteilung*. The Arab volunteers were now issued with a specially manufactured cloth arm patch with the Muslim colours of red, green, white, and black and the words *Freis Arabien* ('Free Arabia') written in German underneath, with the Arabic translation written above. By April 1942 the Arab contingent in the battalion stood at 133 men, a number of whom had been former PoWs who had served in either the French or British armies. These volunteers came from Syria, Saudi Arabia, Egypt, Transjordan, Palestine, Lebanon, and Iraq. There was also a separate company which had been formed from former German members of the French Foreign Legion and was under the direct control of *Sonderstab F*. This company proved hard to control and was soon disbanded. Its men were then dispersed within the *Deutsche-Arabische Lehr-Abteilung*. The original thirty Arab volunteers were not grouped together with the new batch of 103 Arab recruits, but formed a separate company, which also contained some German NCOs and enlisted personnel. One of the reasons for this was the fact that most of the original thirty Arabs living in Germany were college graduates, who were different in demeanour and attitude than the other, uneducated Arabs. The Germans believed that social differences between both groups would cause friction in the battalion.

Figure 2. Sonderverbänd 288, 15 October 1941. *(Author's line drawing)*

There was another German special formation that was created. This eventually became the *III. Panzergrenadier Bataillon* of *Sonderverbänd 287*. It was formed on 4 August 1942 about a year later than the other two battalions. This unit contained Arab volunteers as well as a German cadre staff. This battalion was also referred to as the *Deutsch-Arabische Legion* (German-Arab Legion). The German-Arab Legion (DAL), officially *Deutsch-Arabischer Truppen (KODAT),* was a special unit (it reached regimental strength in October 1942) that emerged from the *Deutsche-Arabische Lehr-Abteilung* of *Major* Theodor von Hippel.[40] *Sonderverbänd 287* now contained three battalions.

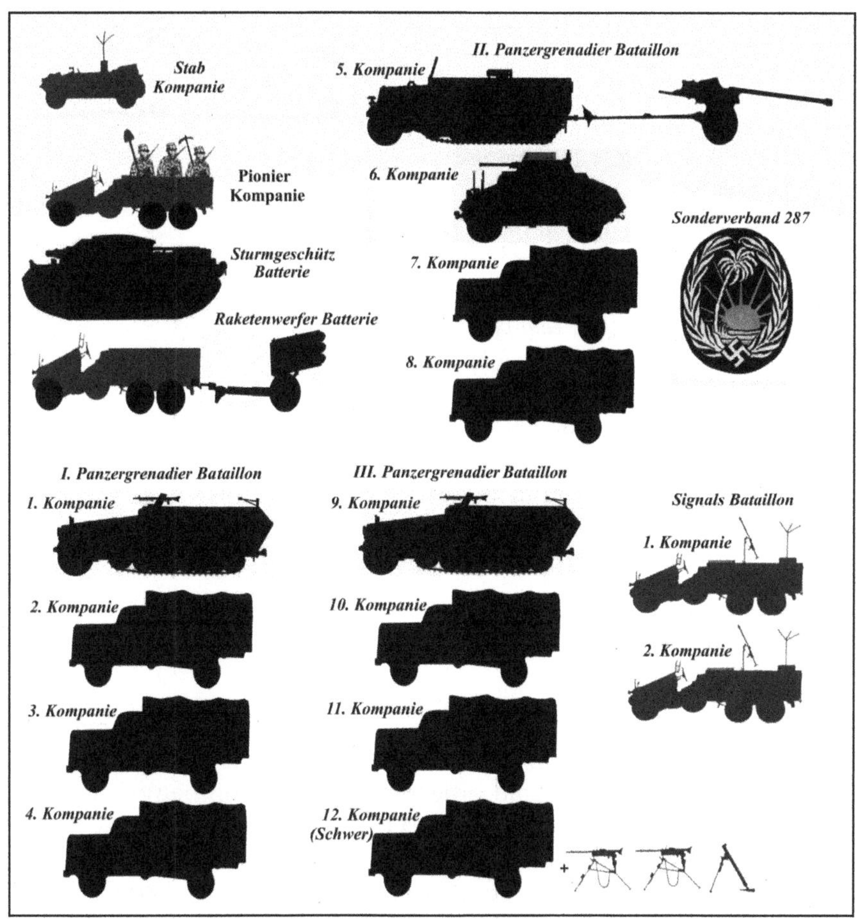

Figure 3. Sonderverbänd 287 in September 1942. *(Author's line drawing)*

The *I. Panzergrenadier Bataillon* and *II. Panzergrenadier Bataillon* were motorised and were supposed to have four companies each. The *5. Panzerjäger Kompanie* and the *6. Panzerspähwagen Kompanie* were nominally under the control of the headquarters of *II. Panzergrenadier Bataillon*. The *Deutsche-Arabische Lehr-Abteilung* at Sinium, Greece was designated as the unit's *III. Panzergrenadier Bataillon*. The organisation was as follows:

Sonderverbänd 287: [41]
- *Stab Kompanie*
- *Unabhängines Kompanien* [42]
  - *Leichte Pionierkompanie*

Sturmgeschütz Batterie
Raketenwerfer Batterie
I. Panzergrenadier Bataillon
- *1. Panzergrenadier Kompanie*
- *2. Panzergrenadier Kompanie*
- *3. Panzergrenadier Kompanie*
- *4. Panzergrenadier Kompanie*

II. Panzergrenadier Bataillon [43]
- *5. Panzerjäger Kompanie*
- *6. Panzerspähwagen Kompanie*
- *7. Panzergrenadier Kompanie*
- *8. Panzergrenadier Kompanie*

III. Panzergrenadier Bataillon [44]
- *9. Panzergrenadier Kompanie*
- *10. Panzergrenadier Kompanie*
- *11. Panzergrenadier Kompanie*
- *12. Panzergrenadier Kompanie*

Nachrichten Bataillon 287
- *1. Signals Kompanie*
- *2. Signals Kompanie*

The *Deutsche-Arabische Lehr-Abteilung* (AKA *III. Panzergrenadier Bataillon / Sonderverbänd 287)* had three companies made up of Arabs with German and a few Arab officers,[45] and one company made up purely of Germans. The *9., 10.,* and *11. Kompanie* were mainly Arab manned, while the *12. Schwer Kompanie* (heavy weapons company) was purely German. The total number of Arabs in the *III. Battalion* was only 392 volunteers. On the whole, *Sonderstab F* had a total of 5,931 officers, NCOs and enlisted men. This included the units attached to it as well as the permanent Staff personnel. When *Sonderstab F* was re-designated as the *LXVIII. Armeekorps* on 9 April 1943, the unit contained the following corps troops:[46]

Arko 168[47]
Korps-Nachrichten-Bataillon 468
Korps-Nachschubtruppen 468
Panzer-Spähkompanie 468

Table 1. Location of Sonderstab F (later redesignated as Generalkommando z.b.V.).

1943	June-Aug	*Heeresgruppe* E and *F*	Athens
	Sept	11th Italian Army	Athens
	Oct-Dec	*Heeresgruppe E and F*	Athens
1944	Jan-Oct	*Heeresgruppe* E and *F*	Athens
	Nov-Dec	2. *Panzerarmee/ Heeresgruppe F*	Serbia & Hungary
1945	Jan-April	2. *Panzerarmee/ Heeresgruppe Süd*	Hungary (Drava)
	May	2. *Panzerarmee/ Heeresgruppe Südost*	Styria (Slovenia)

Employment in Russia

On 28 June 1942 the Germans launched *Fall Blau* (Case Blue), their 1942 summer offensive in the southern regions of the Soviet Union. The goal of this offensive was no longer the capture of Moscow, but an offensive with an economic aim. The Germans needed oil to run their war machine. The capture of the Russian oil fields located in the Caucasus Mountains would supply the *Wehrmacht* with the lifeblood that could kept its men and machines moving for decades to come. Capturing the Caucasus Mountains would also open a second front in the Middle East, while also forcing neutral Turkey to consider joining the Tripartite Pact. The capture of these oil fields would also deny the same strategically important resource to the Red Army. There was another reason why in the summer of 1942 the Germans had not chosen to attack along the entire breath of the Russian Front, as they had done in 1941. Frankly, the *Ostheer* did not have the strength nor the supplies in 1942 to advance on such a wide front as they had done in 1941. By 9 August 1942 the first Soviet oil fields had been captured near Maikop. Having never been employed as a corps-sized unit, the headquarters of *Sonderstab F* suggested that it be employed in the Caucasus region with the hope that once the German Army crossed this last mountainous barrier, they would be in a position to strike at British forces in Iraq, Syria and Iran.

The Arab elements in *Sonderstab F* could then be employed in the region for which they were intended: the Middle East. The plan was sound and there were preparations at headquarters level for the eventuality of large numbers of Arabs who might volunteer to serve under *Sonderstab F* and its mixed German-Arab battalions. *General der Flieger* Helmuth Felmy certainly entertained the idea that a larger Arab force could be established, with the talk of an Arab force of brigade or division in size. However, given that the *Ostheer* was eventually pushed out of the Caucasus Mountains, this turned out to be nothing more than wishful thinking. As far as actual German-Arab formations and the battle in the Caucasus were concerned, it was *Sonderverbänd 287* which was the first unit under *Sonderstab F* that participated. The regiment was sent directly to Stalino in southern Russia, having been brought directly from the *Truppenübungsplatz Doberitz* (Troop Training Ground 'Doberitz').[48]

The unit moved to Stalino with its *I. Panzergrenadier Bataillon* and *II. Panzergrenadier Bataillon*. The *III. Panzergrenadier Bataillon* (the German-Arab Training Battalion) was not yet in Russia, as it was coming from Sinium, Greece, alongside the headquarters of *Sonderstab F*. Events in North Africa eventually required the employment of *Sonderverbänd 288* in North Africa, while *Sonderverbänd 287* was initiated into combat in the Caucasus campaign.

The headquarters of *Sonderstab F* arrived at Stalino in September 1942. It was at this time that the unit was redesignated *Generalkommando z.b.V.* (Corps Headquarters for Special Employment). Its members were allowed to wear a special corps arm patch worn on the middle of the right arm sleeve. This patch was machine woven and depicted a tilted swastika at its base, with an oval wreath of palm leaves surrounding a palm tree and a rising sun behind it.

Figure 4. Arm patch of Sonderstab F. *(Author's line drawing)*

The new designation was in line with its new assignment at Stalino, which included, among other things, a directive that outlined a training programme geared specifically for desert warfare. The directive stressed that the individual soldier had to learn to fight independently, and that training should include live fire practice with various types of weapons. This would make the individual volunteers able to employ various weapons, including captured enemy arms. The programme also included reconnaissance, observation, and orientation by use of a compass. The Arab language was to be confined to phrases for everyday use and the essentials of military terminology.

It was clear that the corps command still believed it was going to be employed in the Middle East, by way of the Caucasus Mountains. This plan was soon placed in jeopardy when *Heeresgruppe A* began to be bogged down in late September and early October 1942 as Russian resistance grew. The difficult mountainous terrain, coupled by stiffening Red Army resistance and reinforcements, finally halted the German panzers short of their objective. The line separating *Heeresgruppe A* in the Caucasus and *Heeresgruppe B* in the region of Stalingrad and the bend in the Volga River now became increasingly stretched. Soon it was necessary to send additional German forces to help cover this exposed and vital link in the Axis front line.

The only unit not committed in early October 1942 that could conceivably perform the mission of screening this exposed and weak link was *Sonderverbänd 287*, which had been kept in Stalino and remained uncommitted after its arrival in southern Russia. This motorised unit had a strength of about 2,200 men. The order to move *Sonderverbänd 287* to the southern regions of the Kalmyk ASSR (Kalmyk Autonomous Soviet Socialist Republic) arrived on 5 October 1942.[49] A day later, the two battalions moved out of Stalino and were officially attached to *1. Panzerarmee*. For a short while, *Sonderverbänd 287* was referred to as *Seekommando Xerxes* because there was a plan to employ part of the *Generalkommando z.b.V.* against Russian ports lying along the western edge of the Caspian Sea. The Germans never got that far, however, so the name was later dropped. This command contained Palestinians as well as other Arabs, and even some Germans who had lived in Palestine. There was also a sprinkling of Germans who had served in the French Foreign Legion. In autumn 1942 *Generalkommando z.b.V.* was ordered to help cover the left flank of *1. Panzerarmee*, which was coming under attack. On 28 October, *General der Flieger* Felmy wrote about this new assignment in his daily diary entry to OKW:

Considerable losses are to be expected in this endeavour. I am therefore concerned that in this mission the General Command for Special Employment with its units will soon be so exhausted that it will no longer be able to carry out a mission in the Middle East in the spring.[50]

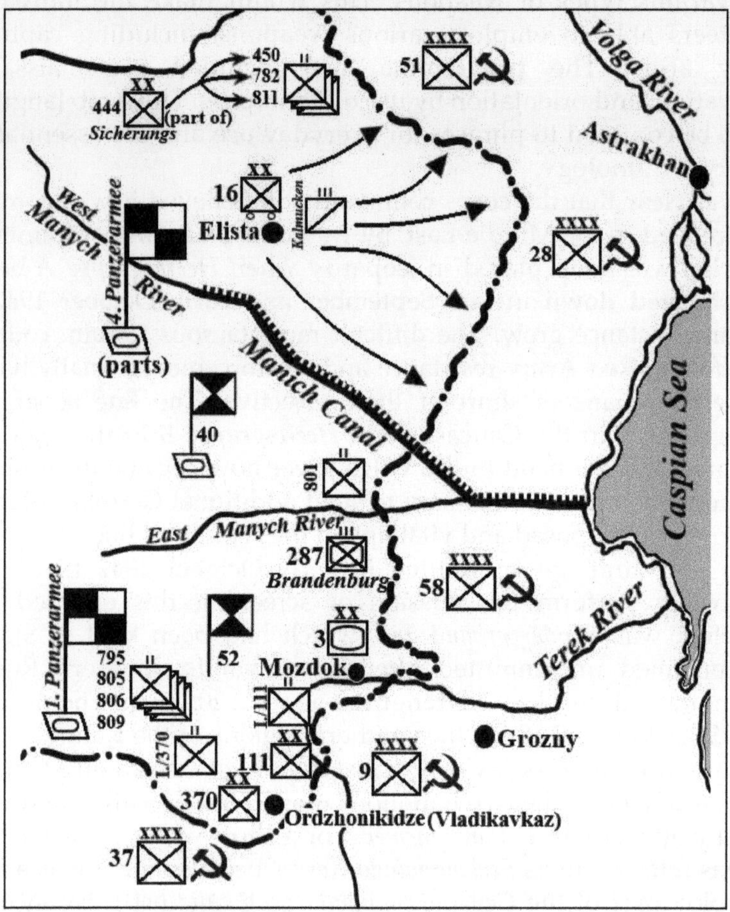

Figure 5. September 1942: the northern tip of the Russian Trans-Caucasus Front. Also shown: German units guarding the right flank of 4. Panzerarmee, and the left flank of 1. Panzerarmee. Sonderverbänd 287 was posted to an area just north of Mozdok. *(Author's line drawing)*

For operational purposes, *Generalkommando z.b.V.* was detached from the control of OKW and assigned to *Heeresgruppe A*. The plan was now to insert *Sonderverbänd 287* on the left flank of *1. Panzerarmee* in the area of Kuma between Niny-Stepnoe *(XL. Panzerkorps)* and the Manich Canal, where the southernmost mobile defence of *16. Infanterie-Division (motorisiert)* ended.[51] This German motorised division was based in the capital of the Kalmyk ASSR, Elista. From there, the division would send out deep reconnaissance forces in a wide arc. The German motorised unit was assisted in this mission by cavalry squadrons of Kalmyk volunteers who opposed the Soviet regime.

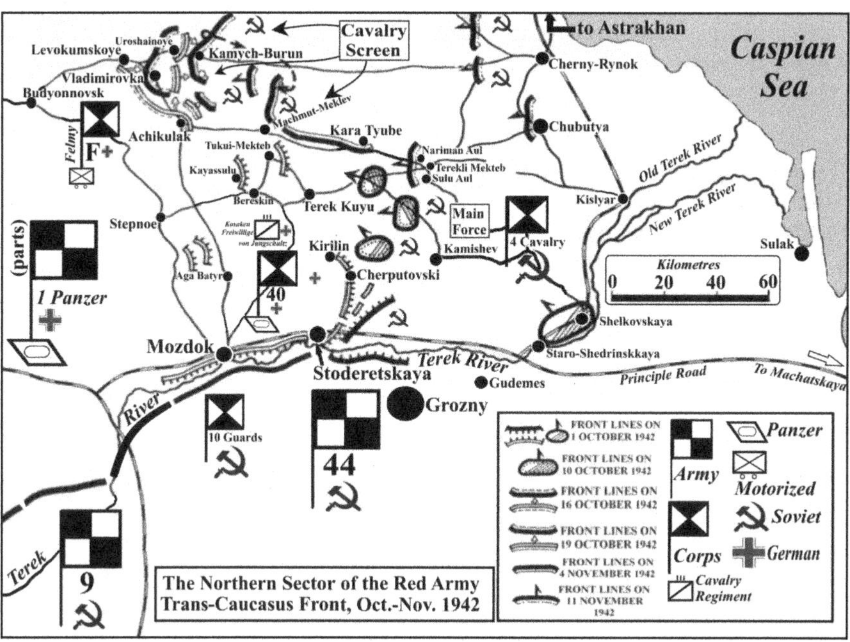

Figure 6. Location of Sonderstab F and the northern tip of the Russian Trans-Caucasus Front, 25 October 1942. *(Author's line drawing)*

The main defensive points for *Sonderverbänd 287* turned out to be Acikulak and Urozayne, on the Nogay Steppe. The regiment had arrived in its new positions with 720 Ukrainian *Hilfswilliger* (auxiliary volunteers), which had been recruited mainly in Stalino. Felmy's corps headquarters also recruited hundreds of these auxiliary volunteers before the corps withdrew from the USSR. The employment of *Sonderverbänd 287* in regular frontline fighting signalled a new chapter and changing mission for the specialised units of *Generalkommando z.b.V.* (Felmy). The requirements of the Russian Front now took precedence over the need to keep these particular and unique units uncommitted. Those who understood the initial reasons why these formations were created also comprehended that it was a crime to send them into the Russian meat grinder, which tended to chew up units and spit them out with amazing speed and volume. In order to help accomplish its new mission, *Sonderverbänd 287* was temporarily assigned the *Nordkaukasische Infanterie Bataillon 801*, which was led by a *Heer* officer, *Hauptmann* Burkhardt.

Another unit attached to the regiment at this time included *Infanterie-Bataillon Bergmann,* under the command of Dr Theodor Oberlander, an academic in peacetime who was an expert on Asia. Another unit, *Kosaken-Kavallerie-Regiment von Jungschultz* was also made a part of the *Generalkommando z.b.V.* It is interesting to note that the Teletype assigning *Generalkommando z.b.V.* to *Heeresgruppe A* specifically stated that the *Deutsche-Arabische Lehr-Abteilung* was not to be committed to combat north of the Caucasus Mountains. As *Sonderverbänd 287* was about to move to the front, a number of the Arab volunteers suddenly came down with the flu or other ailments. This was attributed by the Germans to the continued intrigues of the diverse opposing political groups within the battalion. The problem became so severe that General Felmy himself paid a visit to the unit on 5 October 1942 and addressed the Arab volunteers:

> I have received a report from your battalion commander, Captain Schober, that there is dissension and division among your ranks. This disturbs me greatly, as I have nothing but admiration for the fighting qualities of the Arabs. I remember specifically one attack which I witnessed while serving under the Turkish Army, of an Arab unit at the battle of Gaza in 1917 which greatly impressed me. Their courage was noteworthy. Unfortunately, I am at a loss for words to understand the courage which I saw then, with the defeatism and dissension which I have heard is going on among your ranks. I am not here to urge you to fight for your Arab countries if you yourselves refuse to do so. All Muslim volunteers requesting to be separated from German military service will not be impeded, but I promise you that your names will be given to the Grand Mufti. He can deal with you as he sees fit. Furthermore, your permits to reside in the Reich shall be revoked, and you will be asked to leave national territory immediately. I am going to allow you all to think over your decision until 1800 hours today, at which time every man here will be asked a simple yes or no. Your battalion commander, Captain Schober will report the results to me personally, that is all.[52]

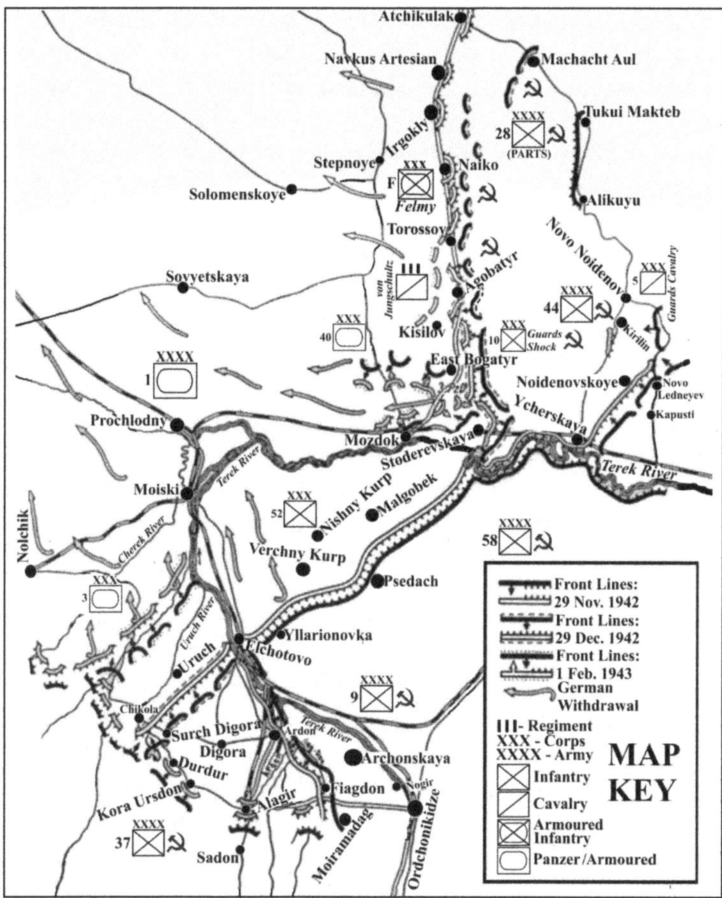

Figure 7. Location of Generalkommando z.b.V. (Felmy) from 29 November 1942 to 1 February 1943. Felmy's corps began its withdrawal on 1 January 1943 but was still in southern Russia by the beginning of February. *(Author's line drawing)*

Reports indicate that aside from those Arabs who were willing to quit at any price, most of the volunteers opted to remain in the battalion. The disgruntled and troublesome elements in the battalion were thus weeded out and sent to the German Armed Forces High Command Counterintelligence Division under guard. Thereafter the battalion returned to normal. In October, *I. Panzergrenadier Bataillon* and *II. Panzergrenadier Bataillon* had been dispatched to Budenovsk and assigned patrol duty between the left wing of *1. Panzerarmee* and the southernmost element of the *4. Panzerarmee*: *16. Infanterie-Division (motorisiert)*. The *16. Infanterie-Division (motorisiert)* had its headquarters in the city of Elista, which was the capital of the Kalmyk ASSR. As soon as *Sonderverbänd 287* arrived at Budenovsk, it helped to repel a thrust by the Soviet 4th Cavalry Corps.

The expected breakthrough by *Heeresgruppe Süd* into Iran through the Caucasus Mountains never materialised. On 19 November 1942 the Russians launched a massive winter counteroffensive that helped to destroy almost two Romanian armies and the Hungarian 2nd Army. The offensive also wiped out the German *6. Armee* at Stalingrad. This winter offensive did not end until late spring 1943. By that spring, the Nazi threat to the oil fields in the Caucasus had been averted. Events in the Mediterranean during November 1942 were also developing negatively for the Axis. On 8 November, a large American, British and Commonwealth force landed on the Atlantic coast of Morocco and Algeria and was threatening to cut off Rommel's *Afrika Korps* and the Italian Army in North Africa from its bases in Tripolitania, Libya. In the meantime, fighting in Russia continued. The decision to transfer the desert-trained *Generalkommando z.b.V.* and its specialised units to North Africa was soon reached. In late January 1943 the corps headquarters and its sub-units were ordered to withdraw from the Soviet Union, but by the beginning of February 1943 the corps and its units were still in southern Russia.

However, due to the serious nature of the military situation facing the Germans in southern Russia, only the *(Deutsch-Araber) III. Panzergrenadier Ausbildung Bataillon* immediately shifted to Palermo, Italy in anticipation of its employment in North Africa. It was not until January 1943 that this battalion from *Sonderverbänd 287* was actually sent across the Mediterranean Sea and landed in Tunisia. In order to retain some sort of control over the battalion, the *Generalkommando z.b.V. F* sent a representative to *Heeresgruppe Süd* in Italy, *Oberstleutnant* Meyer-Ricks, who assumed his post on 7 December 1942.[53] As it turned out, *Oberstleutnant* Meyer-Ricks and *Hauptmann* Schober would prove quite instrumental in helping to raise several Arab volunteer battalions for the Axis cause in Tunisia.

The withdrawal from the Caucasus region continued into February 1943 when the remnants of *444. Sicherungs-Division* withdrew alongside the *LVII. Panzerkorps, with Generalkommando z.b.V. Felmy* on its flank. During this time, *444. Sicherungs-Division* operated in various groups, one of which was named Combat Group Krause and contained the *I. Bataillon* and *II. Bataillon* of *Polizeiregiment 6*. The *III. Bataillon* of *Polizeiregiment 6* had been destroyed in January 1943 while serving with the 8th Italian Army. On 3 February 1943 both police battalions, alongside an assault gun battery, were operating around the town of Koissug.[54] On 16 February 1943, the *II. Bataillon* of *Sonderverbänd 287* was attached to *Kampfgruppe Krause* in the region of Tatsinskaya. This had occurred because on 17 February, the *I. Bataillon* of *Polizeiregiment 6*, which had been operating under *Kampfgruppe Krause,* was withdrawn from the *444. Sicherungs-Division* due to heavy losses. However, the *I. Bataillon* of *Polizeiregiment 6* was still being listed as operational as late as 30 January 1943. On 16 February, the *I. Bataillon* of *Polizeiregiment 6* was transferred to the control of *454. Sicherungs-Division*.[55]

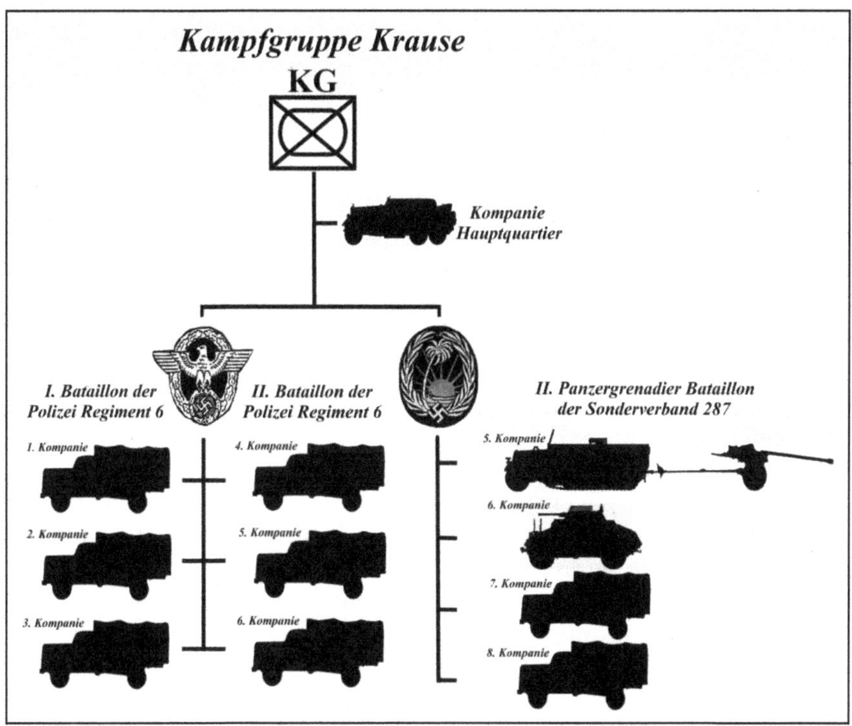

Figure 8. Combat Group Krause, February 1943. *(Author's line drawing)*

A later document states that *I. Bataillon* of *Polizeiregiment 6* was disbanded on 31 March 1943, when it listed that the *1.*, *2.*, and *3. Kompanien* were lost. However, this police battalion was still listed as part of the order of battle for the *454. Sicherungs-Division* as late as 23 March 1943. In any event, *Kampfgruppe Krause* was a temporary affair that was employed simply out of expediency. By March 1943 *II. Bataillon* of *Sonderverbänd 287* was back under *Generalkommando z.b.V Felmy*.

The German-Arab Training Battalion in the Mediterranean

A special recruiting organ was established called the *Kommando Deutsche-Arabische Truppen*, or *Kodat*. In Vichy French Tunisia, the *Deutsche-Arabische Lehr-Abteilung* began to recruit hundreds of Muslims, many of whom were unemployed, from various tribes into

Arab auxiliary battalions. While the Vichy French government of Pierre Laval recruited Arab labour battalions to build fortifications, the Germans armed and clothed their Arab auxiliaries and gave them the less hazardous duty of coastal defence, as well as rear area guard and security duties at important military installations. In this way, German forces who would otherwise be performing those duties were now free to be used at the front. The *Freies Arabien* arm patch mentioned earlier, was freely distributed to these battalions. Among the ranks of these Arab volunteers were numerous men of obvious African extraction, which no doubt reminded some of the older German officers of the East African *Askari* soldiers from the First World War,[56] when the *Askaris* had faithfully served the *Kaiser* and Imperial Germany under the leadership of General Paul von Lettow-Vorbeck in German East Africa. For four long years, General Paul von Lettow-Vorbeck was able to hold off 300,000 United Kingdom and Commonwealth forces with only 3,000 German troops and 11,000 African *Askaris*. To his credit, von Lettow-Vorbeck was never captured or defeated in battle. As a result, he became well known in Europe, while in Germany, his military successes and the fact he was never defeated made him a national hero.

The sight of Arabs in German uniform, wearing sleeve bands with the words Free Arabia embroidered on them in both German and Arabic, made a great impression on the Arab volunteers and the local population. This in turn, actually helped to garner more enlistments. Soon numerous Arab companies were being raised. The Arab volunteers were separated by region, so there were companies made up of Moroccans, while other companies were composed of Tunisians, and still others were made up of Algerian volunteers. All these companies were grouped into battalions and were manned by Arab volunteers with a cadre of German officers and NCOs. For the German officers and NCOs, service in these battalions was choice duty, given that they did not have to serve on the front lines and therefore the chances of getting killed were significantly reduced. Approximately five German ex-Foreign Legionaries were attached to each company as NCOs. There was a lack of supplies due to the stranglehold which the Allies had on Axis supply ships moving to and from North Africa.

It was thus that many of these new volunteers had to make do with Vichy French army uniforms and worn-out French rifles. One source says that as many as 6,300 Arabs were recruited this way.[57] If this is true, then theoretically the Germans could have formed almost thirteen battalions of 500 men each. The two major drawbacks of these new Arab battalions were (1) the inadequate quantities of uniforms, equipment, and arms and (2) the very limited amount of time the Germans had to train these new units.

There were two types of Arab formations raised for service under the German Army: those created for combat and guard duty, and those which were to serve under the supervision of German engineers as construction troops. The Arabs that were to serve as construction workers wore a white brassard on the right sleeve of their jacket with the inscription *In Dienste der Deutschen Wehrmacht* (In the Service of the German Armed Forces). Those who were earmarked for the combat battalions wore the *Freies Arabien* arm patch. It should be noted that the Arab battalions created in 1943 in Tunisia were exclusively used as guards behind the front lines. Only those Arab units created to serve under *Sonderstab F* saw combat on the front lines.

Jm Dienst
der
DeutschenWehrmacht

Figure 9. The white brassard worn on the right sleeve of the field blouse of the Arab volunteers serving in German-sponsored construction battalions. *(Author's line drawing)*

The Phalange Africaine

Eventually, the Vichy French government raised a combat battalion made up of Arab volunteers as well. This was actually a formation made up of Arabs and Frenchmen who had been living in North Africa, with many of the Frenchmen having been born in Algeria and Tunisia. The metropolitan French referred to those born in French-Algeria as *Pieds-Noirs* (black feet).[58] This tended to be a pejorative term, although some French-born in Algeria took it as a badge of honour. Although most *Pieds-Noirs* had never even visited metropolitan France, they supported the Vichy government. This mixed Arab and French battalion was dubbed the *Phalange Africaine* (African Phalanx). It consisted of around 400 men, two thirds of whom were Algerian-born Frenchmen and the remaining third pure Algerian Arabs. Command of this mixed formation was given to

Figure 10. Insignia of the Phalange Africaine. A cloth shield employing a black thread background, surrounded by a gold thread outer edge. The double-headed axe emblem was made of stamped bronze and attached to the cloth emblem by a pinback. It was worn on the right breast pocket of the field blouse. *(Author's line drawing)*

Figure 11. The French arm shield of the Phalange Africaine. It was made from cloth and worn on the right sleeve of the field blouse. It sported the French tricolour (blue, white, red) with a black background and the name FRANCE in white lettering above the tricolour. *(Author's line drawing)*

Captain Pierre-Simon Ange Cristofini, a Corsican, who was a former captain of the 3rd (Algerian) Tirailleurs Regiment. The *Phalange Africaine* only managed to recruit a total of 406 men, of which only 132 were local Arabs. The men in this battalion wore French colonial uniforms with German helmets. The decal on the German helmet sported a rectangle with the French tricolour (blue/white/red). The battalion was initially quartered and trained at the Bordj-Ceda camp. From this unit, a 210-man company was eventually detached from the battalion and sent to serve under the Germans, who quickly dubbed the unit *Französische Freiwilligen Legion,* and posted it to the *II. Bataillon* of *Panzer Grenadier Regiment 754,* which formed part of *334. Infanterie-Division.* On 13 February 1943 the 132 Arabs of the *Phalange Africaine* were absorbed into the *Deutsche-Arabische Lehr-Abteilung.* The Germans eventually recruited enough Arab volunteers to outfit two Tunisian, one Algerian, and one Moroccan battalion. As for the

French volunteers, on 18 March 1943 they swore allegiance to Marshal Pétain and on 25 April experienced their first action against elements of the British 8th Army. The unit lost seventy men killed. Still later in the month, the *Phalange Africaine* fought against General Charles de Gaulle's Free French forces. In this battle, fourteen men of the battalion were captured by Free French troops, who instantly had them shot for treason.[59] Thereafter, the battalion quickly disintegrated.

Employment in Tunisia

Although the four battalions were primarily composed of Tunisians, Algerians, and Moroccans, they also contained small numbers of other Arabs. These included Egyptians, Syrians, Iraqis, Senussi, Tuaregs, and other desert Arabs. Each battalion consisted of three infantry companies armed with carbines and light machine guns, plus a heavy weapons company equipped with mortars and heavy machine guns.[60] The infantry companies were all at full strength and had 150 men each, while the heavy weapons companies had around 200-220 men each. If we add up the totals for these four battalions, we come up with a count of some 2,600-2,700 men. This is a far cry from the 6,300 quoted by another source. I am inclined to believe that perhaps no more than 3,000 were recruited and that the strength of the DAL and these Arab battalions in total only numbered some 3,500 men (about seven battalions). On 24 February 1943 *Oberstleutnant* Meyer-Ricks and *Hauptmann* Schober were both killed during an Allied air raid. The loss of these two specialised officers severely crippled the training of these battalions and permanently disabled further effective recruitment of the local Arab population. Because *Generalkommando z.b.V.* was still heavily engaged in southern Russia, no suitable replacements were on hand to assume the critical posts of these two officers:

> Although as a general rule the death of a commander did not result in the dissolution of a German military unit, in a case such as this where special conditions prevailed the loss could have serious consequences. Both dead officers had performed their duties well, and both spoke Arabic fluently. It was difficult to find other men who were as expert in the field of German-Arab relations. Finally, a Colonel von Hippel, who had seen service in the former German African colonies, was entrusted with the command of Kodat by the 5th Panzer Army.[61]

This was the same *Oberst* Theodor von Hippel who had been in command of the *Deutsche-Arabische Lehr-Abteilung* when that unit had captured the British commandos at Hammamet. *Oberst* von Hippel was a member of the famous *Brandenburg* commandos; the operational arm of the German Armed Forces secret service, the *Abwehr*. Hippel had arrived in Tunisia in February 1943, just in time to surrender with the rest of the Axis forces three months later, in May. In the meantime, *Generalkommando z.b.V.* had finally been withdrawn from Russia, but had left all its sub-units under the command of *XXIV. Panzerkorps.*[62] The order for the transfer came on 24 February 1943. The decision had been made to move *Generalkommando z.b.V.* to Reggio, in southern Italy. This was in expectation of its employment in North Africa. Anticipating this, General Felmy flatly stated that he could not employ his command in North Africa because his HQ lacked its supporting units, including the communications battalion, which was vital to every higher-level headquarters command. This fact saved the men of *Generalkommando z.b.V.* from ending up as prisoners of war when *Panzerarmee Afrika* surrendered in May 1943. Meanwhile, the North African Arab volunteer battalions were being organised and trained by the men of the *Deutsche-Arabische Lehr-Abteilung*, which was also tasked with coastal defence duties from the port of Cape Bon, to the coastal town of Sousse (Susa) in the Gulf of Hammamet.

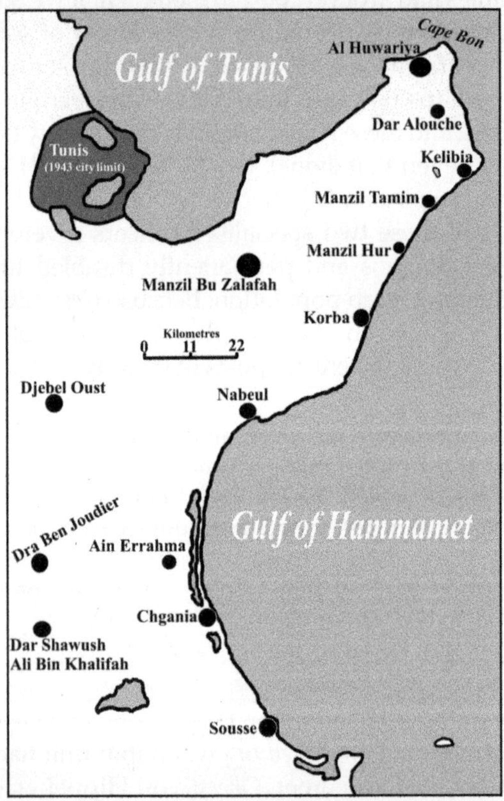

Figure 12. The Arab volunteer battalions had to cover a 205-kilometre stretch of coastline from Cape Bon to Sousse. *(Author's line drawing)*

This was a distance of 205 kilometres (almost 137 miles). That means that *III. Bataillon / Sonderverbänd 287* and the four Arab battalions that were being organised and trained there had to cover, on average, 41 kilometres (27 miles) per battalion. The mission of coastal guard watch, therefore, was quite a challenge. Nevertheless, during one night in the spring of 1943, the British managed to land an eight-man commando team by submarine at Hammamet. This squad belonged to No. 6 Commando, which at the time was led by Lieutenant Colonel Derek Mills-Roberts. The plan was to blow up the headquarters of *Hauptmann* Fritz von Koenen's *Brandenburg* commando unit.

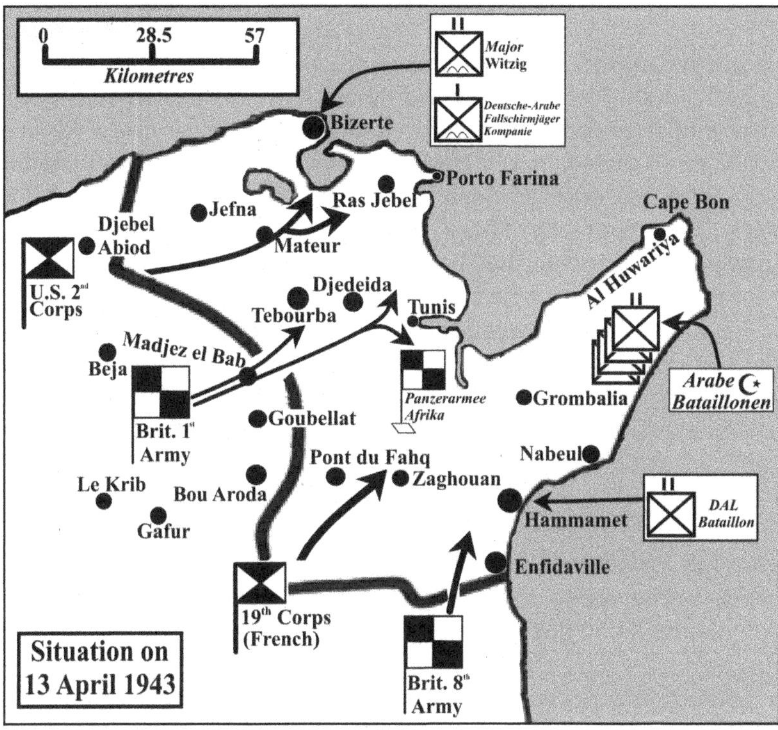

Figure 13. The last phase of the North African campaign: the defeat of the Axis forces in Tunisia, April-May 1943. *(Author's line drawing)*

Hauptmann Koenen led a reinforced 300-man commando company *(13. Kompanie)* of *Lehr-Regiment Brandenburg z.b.V. 800*. The company had been created in 1941 for service in North Africa. Von Koenen himself was the son of a former German colonist who had established a farm in Southwest Africa (Namibia), when Imperial Germany ruled there. As such, he was familiar with Africa and the people who lived on that continent, which is one of the reasons why he was chosen to lead this company in North Africa. Von Koenen's commandos had led numerous successful sorties behind the Allied lines in Tunis and Algeria, and because of this, he and his unit had become infamous at British 8th Army headquarters. The plan was to kill the staff officers of this commando company and destroy its headquarters. However, the attempt by the small commando force was unsuccessful. Within 48 hours the entire eight-man team from No. 6 Commando was caught or killed by the *Brandenburgers* acting in conjunction with the Arab volunteers of *III. Panzergrenadier Bataillon / Sonderverbänd 287*. The commander of this small British commando force, a captain, drowned while attempting to return to the submarine from whence his unit had disembarked.

Arab paratroopers

There were other instances when different German commands tried to make use of Arab volunteers. For example, *1. Fallschirmjäger Regiment* recruited about a company of Arab volunteers and gave them parachute training with the hope of later employing them behind enemy lines. Similarly, Otto Skorzeny, Hitler's leading commando, employed Arab volunteers, but this event shall be discussed later. By mid-March 1943 the British 8th Army had reached the Mareth line in southern Tunisia. Very soon, Allied pressure to break through there became so critical that the Germans reluctantly sent in one of the Tunisian battalions to the front lines. As expected, this move proved disastrous. Upon arrival at the front, the Tunisian volunteers lit fires to stay warm. Unaware that this new battalion had arrived, the Germans in the local area fired on their positions. The British forces in front of the Arabs were thus able to see the Arab positions and immediately attacked the Arab battalion. Under artillery fire and a mechanised assault that followed, the Arab battalion quickly collapsed and folded. The Arab companies were overrun by a British motorised force, with about two thirds of the Arab soldiers being taken prisoner. The remaining third were either killed or deserted, taking to the hills. Those not killed or taken prisoner were later reported MIA.[63] Not a single soldier from the battalion managed to escape. Only one German officer and two NCOs, all of them wounded, managed to make it to an aid station immediately behind the front. The command staff of *5. Panzerarmee* concluded from this brief but bloody engagement that it would be better if the Arab battalions were kept behind the lines, performing security and coastal guard duty. Nevertheless, another use of the Arabs came in April 1943:

> In mid-April 1943 some of the German personnel in the German-Arab Training Battalion, and all Muslims who had finished their training, reinforced by German ex-French Foreign Legion troops, were consolidated into a task force near Ferryville in Tunisia. This group included two infantry

> companies and one heavy company, the latter composed of one heavy infantry howitzer platoon, one 20 mm anti-aircraft platoon, one anti-tank platoon, and one heavy machine gun platoon. During the following weeks this task force was employed in the northern sector of the front, southwest of Matör and in the Sedyenane Valley. It served as the tactical reserve of an Austrian division, and later with the 999. leichte Afrika Division.[64]

Few details are known about this unit, but it is known that it was employed next to *Major* Witzig's parachute battalion. On 1 May the combined German-Arab Training Battalion *Kampfgruppe* relieved a battalion from the *Hermann Göring Panzer-Division*. That same day the unit succeeded in repelling a US attack. On 3 May the battalion performed rearguard duty for an infantry regiment and on 6 May it was placed as the reserve battalion for a *Luftwaffe* (Air Force) regiment that had recently been formed for infantry duty from ground crews and staff. The final end of this ad-hoc German-Arab battalion was as follows:

> On the afternoon of 7 May the group was to have assumed responsibility for the protection of an anti-aircraft unit established along the Bizerta-Tunis railroad. As the task force was about to move into position the antiaircraft unit was overrun by American tanks. The following day the supply trains of the task force were disbanded, its records destroyed, and the remnants of the group, less than 100 men, assembled at Porto Farina, north of Tunis. Here from 4-5,000 other Axis soldiers waited in well-disciplined ranks for ferries to evacuate them. The majority of the Arab soldiers in the task force remained with German troops and went voluntarily into captivity with them.[65]

US Army records state that about 2,000 Arab prisoners were located in US PoW camps in Opaluka, Alabama as of 10 April 1946. This gives us an indication of the size of the German recruitment of Arabs in North Africa in just a few months' time and confirms the estimate of around 2,700 total recruits, not including the *Deutsche-Arabische Lehr-Abteilung*. In some instances, Arabs were executed individually for treason, as happened in 1944 and reported in the British newspaper, the *Daily Mail*. In this particular case, the Arab sentenced to death, Kaci Djilali, had been in the *Deutsche-Arabische Lehr-Abteilung* and had also served with *Sonderverbänd 287* in southern Russia. A small one-sentence story appeared on the bottom of the front page of the 1 April 1944 issue:

> DEATH FOR NAZI ARAB: Algiers, Friday. – Sentence of death for treason was passed by a French military court today on an Arab, Kaci Djilali, who fought in Russia against the Red Army and in Tunisia against the Allies - Reuters.[66]

We do not know what offence or act Kaci Djilali did that warranted his execution. He was shot by Free French forces, who had assumed official control of Tunisia on 15 May 1943. Many Arabs had been employed by France in their pre-war army and also under Vichy French rule. After North Africa was liberated, the Free French forces simply conscripted those former Vichy French divisions containing a French cadre staff but overwhelmingly composed of Arabs. These former Vichy French divisions were made part of the Free French Army. Given Djilali's service with the German Army, however, perhaps his execution was meant to serve as an example to other Arabs still supporting the Axis cause. It is possible that his commitment for the Axis caused him to be singled out for retribution, the idea being that the Arabs would be dissuaded from assisting Germany or Italy for fear that the same fate that happened to Kaci Djilali would await any other Arab who sided with the Axis powers. Ironically, Kaci Djilali was executed in the same year and exactly six months to the day before the death of one of the founding fathers of Tunisian independence against French rule, Abdelaziz Thâalbi, who passed away on 1 October 1944.

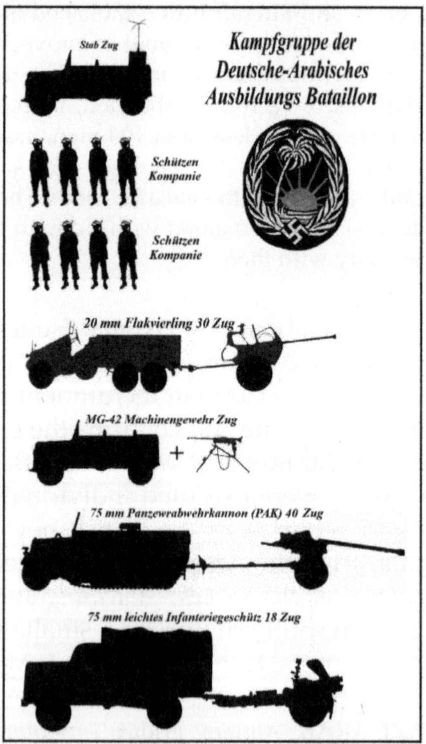

Figure 14. Kampfgruppe created from the Deutsch-Arabische Ausbildungs Bataillon. *(Author's line drawing)*

Arab Commandos

During the period in which the *Deutsche-Arabische Lehr-Abteilung* was stationed in the Gulf of Hammamet, a German paratrooper captain, *Hauptmann* Gerhard Schacht, from the *1. Fallschirmjäger Regiment,* arrived in town and began recruiting volunteers for an Arab parachute company. He had been given permission by Army Group South (Italy) to train between 80-100 Arabs from the German-Arab Command (*Kodat*), for instructions in demolition and engineering work. For this reason, they were transferred to the *Fallschirmjägerschule Wittstock* (Wittstock Parachute School) near Berlin, Germany. There were others in the German camp who took an interest in the Arab volunteers and their potential as saboteurs and commandos. Otto Skorzeny was one such German who between November 1943 and June 1944 trained 60-75 Italians, 20 Serbians, 15 Frenchmen, and 25 Arabs in the *A-Schule* (A School) established by the *Abwehr* in a country estate between The Hague and Scheveningen in the Netherlands. These Arabs had come from the now dissolved Italian-Arab (parachute) legion. In addition, a W/T course, lasting several months, was begun in December 1943. The technical direction was in the hands of a pro-German Dutch engineer and the course was conducted by a German technician from the Havel Institute. The students included two Italians, four French and Belgian volunteers, and two Arabs.[67]

One such Arab commando was a Palestinian named Fawzi al-Qutb, who had escaped Palestine in 1943 after getting into trouble with the British authorities. The then 25-year-old al-Qutb was a follower of the Mufti of Jerusalem, who managed to get him posted to *SS-Sturmbannführer* Otto Skorzeny's commando and sabotage school, located in the Netherlands.[68] After a one-year training course in the most refined techniques of sabotage and commando operations, he was ordered to lead a four-man team of German saboteurs into Palestine. He refused and was immediately handcuffed and sent to a prison camp in Silesia, where he lingered for three months until the Mufti of Jerusalem was able to get him out, offering to give him a job in Berlin preparing Arabic propaganda for the Germans. In 1945 he was caught by the Soviet attack on the German capital and only managed to escape by dressing himself as a wounded German soldier. He was caught by US troops near Salzburg, Austria and placed in a PoW camp, before later being allowed to return to Palestine.

His most notable achievement was the destruction by bombing of the Palestinian Post building on 1 February 1948, when his expertise in explosives, learned while serving under the Germans, was finally put to use. He figured slightly in the Arab-Israeli bombings and counter-bombings while the British still held a mandate over Palestine. But what of the 80-100 Arabs who went to Wittstock for parachute and demolitions training? Apparently, this small Arab parachute company was used behind the Allied lines in North Africa with good results. *Major* Witzig's exploits included the delay of US forces by blocking the Jefna tunnel pass, then advancing on to Sadjenane, further west. The Arab Parachute Company, under *Hauptmann* Schacht, was used by *Hauptmann* Rudolf Witzig's *11. Fallschirm-Pionier-Bataillon.*[69] These Arab parachutists had first to prove that (1) they had two year's prior service in the army, and (2) that they had the stamina to complete the rigorous paratrooper training. *Hauptmann* Schacht noted:

> The command (Kodat) was composed of Moroccans, Algerians, Tunisians, Senussi, Tuaregs, Syrians, Egyptians, Iraqi, and desert Arabs. Volunteers had to provide proof of two years of service in the army of their own country before they were accepted. Former French colonial troops mixed with Italian Sahara veterans, British-trained colonial fighters of the Middle East countries, and Foreign Legion soldiers. One old sergeant had even served in the Turkish Army in World War I.[70]

The *Deutsches-Arabisches Infanterie-Bataillon 845*

After the Germans lost the fortified swamp positions in Tunisia between Mareth and Gabes, there was no longer any opportunity to employ the *Generalkommando z.b.V.*, which by then had been withdrawn from Russia.[71] It was therefore decided that the corps command would become a motorised corps headquarters and on 8 April 1943, it was redesignated as the *Generalkommando z.b.V. LXVIII (motorisiert).* The corps had no units of its own, save *Sonderverbänd 287*, which was the size of a reinforced regiment. However, *Sonderverbänd 287* was itself withdrawn and sent to southern France on 15 March 1943, where it was redesignated as *Grenadier Regiment 92 (motorisiert).* It contained the *I.* and *II. Bataillon* of *Sonderverbänd 287*, plus an engineer company and artillery battery. This redesignation occurred on 2 May 1943. It was then that *Grenadier Regiment 92* was sent to act as part of the occupation force in Serbia. Without *Grenadier Regiment 92* (i.e. the old *Sonderverbänd 287*), *Generalkommando z.b.V. LXVIII* was once again left without any units of its own to control. The *Deutsche-Arabische Lehr-Abteilung* (*III. Bataillon / Sonderverbänd 287*) was in Tunisia and could not be used any time soon by the corps. Nevertheless, a *Wehrmacht* High Command order dated

29 March 1943 emphasised that *Generalkommando z.b.V. LXVIII* would continue to function as its field agency for all Arab matters:

> The pertinent order contained a paragraph to the effect that the Special Corps was to organize a staff to deal with all political issues and propaganda connected with the Muslim world. This staff was to serve with the German-Arab Battalion.[72]

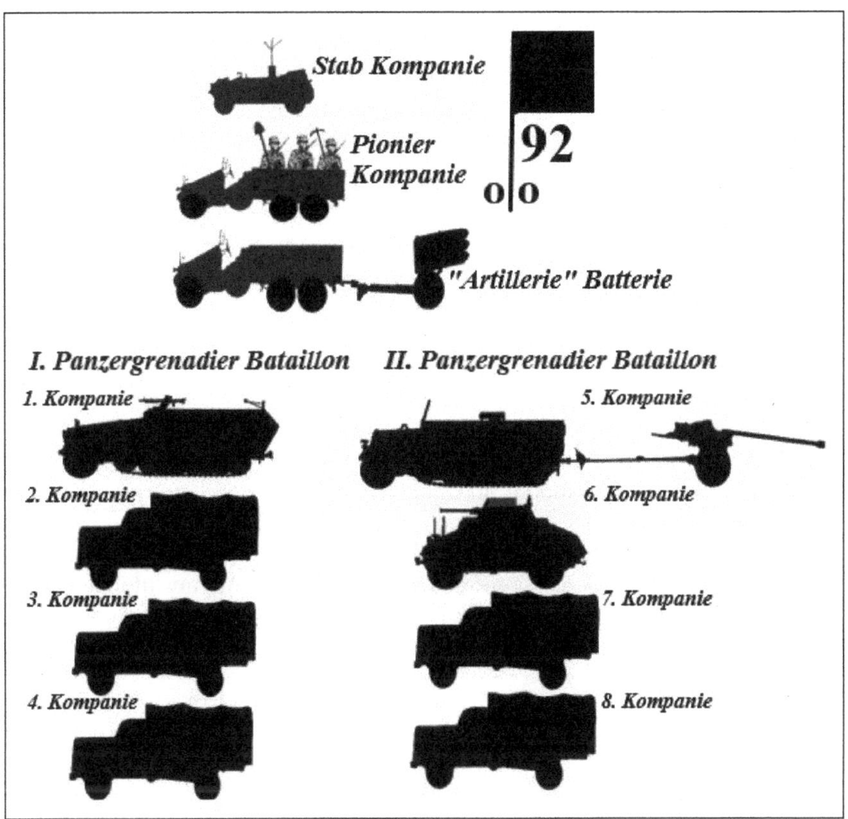

Figure 15. Grenadier Regiment 92 (motorisiert), which was created from the I. and II. battalions of Sonderverbänd 287. *(Author's line drawing)*

When the corps command finally left Russia, it was diverted to Greece where there was a need for a German corps command to control several smaller units. The corps arrived in Greece towards the end of May 1943. Meanwhile elements of the *Deutsche-Arabische Lehr-Abteilung,* which had remained at Palermo, Italy while the bulk of the

Battalion was employed in Tunisia, was incorporated into a new Arab unit: the *Deutsches-Arabisches Infanterie-Bataillon 845*, a battalion that was organised at *Truppenübungsplatz Döllersheim* (Döllersheim Military Training Area),[73] located north and northeast of Linz, in lower Austria. The main camp was about 18 kilometres (12 miles) east of Zwettl, which was itself north of Linz and was an annex to the larger camp. Initially the new Arab battalion contained four companies. It was in the summer of 1943 that *Deutsches-Arabisches Infanterie-Bataillon 845* was assigned to the *Generalkommando LXVIII. Armeekorps (mot.)*. The title of *Generalkommando z.b.V. LXVIII* was dropped and the headquarters became a regular German Army infantry corps. The title was now simply: *LXVIII. Armeekorps (motorisiert)*. The corps quickly issued a training directive for the unit on 30 June 1943:

> The Battalion is under the direct command of the Generalkommando. Initially it will organise into units all Arabs ready to serve the German cause and will train them in guerrilla tactics.
>
> For this purpose, it will give the Arabs:
>
> Basic infantry training.
>
> Training in teamwork for surprise raids to be carried out by squads and half-squad sized units.
>
> Training in demolition techniques (ranger type training).
>
> ...If possible, squads should be composed of men from the same locality. The Battalion's 5th Company will be a parachute company. Lieutenant Rolf is appointed commander of this company. Also attached to the *Generalkommando* is the Arab Recruiting Centre (Westa) in Paris. At present this agency is mainly an intelligence unit. After its transfer to the zone of O.B. Süd the Battalion will be employed for guard duties in addition to its normal training routine.[74]

What is very interesting about this document relating the training and organisational layout of *Deutsche-Arabisches Infanterie Bataillon* is that for the first time since Tunis, it mentions the *Arabisches Fallschirmjäger Kompanie* (Arab Paratrooper Company) that had attached itself to *Major* Witzig's *Fallschirmjäger Pionier Bataillon*. This Arab parachute company would go on to take part in the final battles of the war, along the Oder River, and the battle for the German capital.

Table 2. Employment of LXVIII. Armeekorps.

Date	Command	Higher Command	Location
1943			
Feb	-	*Heeresgruppe F* [75]	Greece
24 Mar	*HG E*	*HG F*	Greece
26 April	*HG E*	*HG F*	Greece
28 July	*11. Armee* (Italian)	*HG F*	Athens
9 Sept	*Armeegruppe Südgriechenland*	*HG F*	Athens
5 Oct	*HG E*		
1944			
1 Jan	*HG E*	*HG Süd*	Athens
Nov	*2. Panzerarmee*	*HG F*	Serbia, Hungary
1945			
Jan	*2. Panzerarmee*	*Süd*	Hungary
May	*2. Panzerarmee*	*OB Südost* [76]	Styria (Austria)

This Arab parachute company had been evacuated to the Italian mainland and was initially stationed in Rome, just before the collapse of Axis resistance in North Africa in April 1943. The company was temporarily attached to the *Deutsches-Arabisches Infanterie-Bataillon 845* while stationed in Greece. Another aspect which becomes clear is that the new *Deutsches-Arabisches Infanterie-Bataillon 845* would still continue to train in what were obviously unorthodox and unconventional warfare techniques. This type of training would later prove to be instrumental in allowing the Arab battalion to operate against the Greek guerrillas with greater effectiveness. Given his background, an Arab soldier from this period of history had the potential to be a formidable guerrilla fighter, one that would be adept at using all of the tricks that other guerrilla movements have employed throughout history. According to *General der Flieger* Felmy, the Arab volunteers of *Deutsches-Arabisches Infanterie-Bataillon 845* showed great courage and would surpass their Greek guerrilla opponents at every turn.[77]

Operations in Greece

When *Deutsches-Arabisches Infanterie-Bataillon 845* arrived in Greece, it was initially given the responsibility for railway security protection north of Salonika, under *XCI. Armeekorps, Heeresgruppe E.* This army corps had been created simply by redesignating *Oberfeldkommandantur 395* as *XCI. Armeekorps*. After completing its training in November 1943, *Deutsches-Arabisches Infanterie-Bataillon 845* was once again posted to *LXVIII. Armeekorps* in the Peloponnese region of Greece, where it came under the control of the German *41. Festungs-Division* (41st Fortress Division). This division controlled numerous static, fortress, and garrison battalions and brigades, many of which were formed from a total of twenty-two penal battalions of the German Army that were stationed there. There were some cases of desertion, as in the case which occurred on 19 November 1943, when three Arab members deserted with their weapons. Overall, however, the battalion did not suffer from high desertion rates.

One source says that *Deutsches-Arabisches Infanterie-Bataillon 845* did not come under the control of the *41. Festungs-Division* until the spring of 1944, when it was transferred to the Lani region, with its base headquarters in Amfiklia, a town situated at the northern foot of Mount Parnassus, in the valley of the Cephissus River, just west of the city of Thebes. Its first large-scale anti-partisan operation occurred on 7 April 1944 when the battalion, plus around 3,000-4,000 other German troops, was employed against the 2nd ELAS Division, then operating in the Helicon Mountain range, by the Gulf of Corinth. The battalion stayed in this region near the Aegean Sea until its move to the Peloponnesus in the spring of 1944. It was in the Helicon Mountain range of southern Greece that *Deutsches-Arabisches Infanterie-Bataillon 845* proved its worth. As stated earlier, guerrilla warfare was a form of combat which seemed to suit the Arab mindset of the period. A few typical examples from the experiences of *Hauptmann* von Voss, the commander of *1. Kompanie / 845. Deutsche-Arabisches Infanterie Bataillon* show the type of situation frequently encountered by German officers in their dealings with the Arab volunteers:

> One day, Ali ben Mohammed reported to the medical officer and requested to be hospitalised. The officer examined Ali and found him in excellent health. 'Why do you want to be hospitalised?' He asked. 'You're not sick.' 'Others get into the hospital, why can't I?' 'You are healthy and you're not going into a hospital!' Ali turned to the door, which had a glass panel, and pushed his head through it. Covered with blood, and with pieces of glass sticking into his scalp, he faced the doctor and asked: 'Am I sick now?' On another day, the company was drilling. Everything seemed to be going well. Suddenly, one Machmut hurled his rifle away and flung himself on the ground. 'Ich nix soldat!' (Me no soldier!), he cried. His friend Mabruk was so ashamed at Machmut's behaviour that he drew his bayonet and gave himself five or six blows over the head with it, exposing the bone under his scalp.

> On another occasion two Arabs were teasing a soldier about his homosexual inclinations. That same night the soldier in question took his rifle, placed it behind the ear of one of his two tormentors, and pulled the trigger. During an action against partisans, Colonel von Eberlein, the commander of a security division, radioed that he was caught between two rivers.[78] I told some of my Arabs, who were fond of the fierce old man with all his medals. All of them volunteered to go with me to the colonel's rescue. When we came to the river, they refused to let me wade across; they insisted on carrying me across on their shoulders. My Arabs never filched any of my personal belongings, though as a rule they stole like magpies. They liked to stuff themselves with good food, they liked to get drunk, to loot and rape; but they also knew how to die bravely, and they resisted pain remarkably well.[79]

The *Deutsches-Arabisches Infanterie-Bataillon 845* was also instrumental in capturing some Allied agents who were assisting the Greek guerrillas, among them was Captain Stephen McGregor, who was caught in Monte Parnasso. But it was the Greek communist Major General Stefanos Sarafis who paid them begrudging praise when he singled them out amongst what were 2,500-3,000 Axis troops attacking his 2nd ELAS Partisan Division in the region of Helicon in April 1944:

> Between 7-11 April a force of Germans, Battalionists, Italians, and Moroccans – about 2,500 men in all – tried to clear the Helicon district of ELAS troops.[80] They landed from small craft in the Corinthian Gulf, in the Zaltsa and Ayii Saranda Bay, and after being reinforced from Thebes, Levadia and Amfissa, advanced towards Koukoura, Kyriaki, Distomo and Chostia. There was fierce fighting for four days at Kyriaki. Enemy dead and wounded: 250 including 45 Battalionists.[81] In these operations they pillaged and burnt houses and raped girls.[82]

No doubt, some of the raping and pillaging was done by the Arab soldiers in *Hauptmann* von Voss *1. Kompanie,* and the rest of *Deutsches-Arabisches Infanterie-Bataillon 845* for that matter. On 15 August 1944 the battalion was said to have been under the control of *117. Jäger-Division.* The recruiting of more Arab volunteers had never ceased. Offices were set up all over Europe and by a careful review of Allied PoWs, many more Arabs came forward and joined the German Army. It was in this way that a second battalion of Arabs was raised at Zwettl, near the Döllersheim Training Area on 1 September 1944. The training of this second Arab battalion began that very month. The unit was designated as *II. Bataillon der 845. Deutsch-Arabische Infanterie Bataillon.* During October and November 1944, as the second battalion was undergoing training, the *Deutsches-Arabisches Infanterie-Bataillon 845* made a fighting withdrawal from Greece during the general German retreat from that country. The Greek partisans harassed the unit, given that it was part of the rear guard. Although they were employed in this manner, the morale of the battalion did not waver, in fact, if anything it got better. An example of their bravery is given by General Felmy while the battalion was operating in Bosnia-Herzegovina:

> When the German Army evacuated southern Greece in October 1944, and retreated northward through the Balkans, the 845th German-Arab Battalion usually furnished the rear guard. Remarkably enough, the Muslim troops soon became accustomed to the severe cold and even though they suffered high losses they remained effective. The German forces retreated from Greece into Yugoslavia, frequently delayed by air raids and partisans. Throughout the withdrawal the Arabs gave a good account of themselves. Towards the end of November, the 1st Company/ 845th German-Arab Infantry Battalion attacked Hill 734 at Uzice four times in succession despite the bitter cold and deep snow. A fifth attack was successful.[83]

Due to heavy losses, it was decided on 10 January 1945 to disband *II Bataillon der 845. Deutsche-Arabisches Infanterie Bataillon,* which had been training at Zwettl, in lower Austria. Instead, its men were distributed amongst the depleted line companies of the original *845. Deutsche-Arabisches Infanterie Bataillon.* However, the German cadre personnel of the now-disbanded *II Bataillon* did not follow the Arab recruits into Yugoslavia. Instead, the Germans were transferred into the *48. Infanterie-Division* that during this time was reforming in the Czech Protectorate.

Panzergrenadier Brigade 92 and Grenadier Alarm Regiment 92

Grenadier Regiment 92 (motorisiert) / Panzergrenadier Brigade 92

In October 1944 *Grenadier Regiment 92 (motorisiert)* suffered heavy losses during the battle for Belgrade. After further losses while making a fighting withdrawal from Serbia to Bosnia-Herzegovina, it was reinforced and reformed on 11 January 1945 and renamed *Panzergrenadier Brigade 92.* This time it was redesignated as a motorised infantry brigade by the expansion of the engineer company and artillery battery into battalions. In addition, an anti-tank battalion was also added.[84] In February the brigade was a reserve force for *2. Panzerarmee.* It took part in the defensive battles between the Sava and Drava rivers, as well as battles in the area around Kaposvár, just south of Lake Balaton. Part of the brigade took part in *Unternehmen*

Frühlingserwachen, also referred to as the *Plattenseeoffensive* (Lake Balaton Offensive) – the last German offensive of the war. The attack was aimed at trying to defend the Hungarian oil fields in and around Lake Balaton. Throughout the war, the oil fields near Lake Balaton supplied approximately 40 per cent of Germany's total oil supply. Beginning on 14 March 1945, the Red Army 2nd and 3rd Ukrainian Front counterattacked and began to push the Germans back. That same day, *Panzergrenadier Brigade 92* was committed as a rear guard of *6. Armee* in the northeast region of Lake Balaton, near Veszprem. The brigade then operated in the area of the 3rd Hungarian Army, southwest of Esztergom (Gran).

Grenadier Alarm Regiment 92

From late March 1945, the regimental staff and staff company of *Panzergrenadier Brigade 92* were deployed individually but with the two training and replacement battalions that supplied men for the regiment/brigade. In essence, the headquarters staff of *Panzergrenadier Brigade 92* was withdrawn and attached to the two training and replacement battalions for the brigade. They were then employed as an 'alarm' unit under *Division 608 z.b.V.* in Lausitz near Cottbus.[85] This special divisional headquarters employed the following formations:

Brigade Stab 100
Grenadier-Regiments-Stab Hellbach
Grenadier-Regiments-Stab Peter
SS-Polizei-Regiment 1
SS-Polizei-Regiment Krause
SS-Gendarmerie-Bataillon 6
Drei (3) Alarm Bataillone
Sechs (6) Volkssturm Bataillone
Grenadier-Alarm-Regiment 83
Grenadier-Alarm-Regiment 92[86]
Grenadier-Alarm-Regiment 95
Nachrichten-Kompanie 608
Versorgungs-Regiment 608

Panzergrenadier Brigade 92

When a Red Army drive succeeded in breaking through the defences of the 3rd Hungarian Army's 1st Hussar Division, *Panzergrenadier-Brigade 92* was ordered to counterattack and managed to plug the gap just east of the town of Kisbér. The brigade then moved to defensive positions in the area west of Tatabanya until 18 March 1945. Thereafter, *Panzergrenadier-*

Brigade 92 took part in further defensive battles under 3rd Hungarian Army but was attached to *96. Infanterie-Division.* From 18-26 March 1945 the fighting occurred in the area of Tatabanya and Felsőgalla, just southwest of Lábatlan. The brigade then defended the bridgehead around Lábatlan on the Danube River until the end of March. A general withdrawal was then ordered across the river. *Panzergrenadier-Brigade 92* moved west towards the area north of Komorn/Donau - Neuhäusl. The brigade then withdrew under *8. Armee.* This led *Panzergrenadier-Brigade 92* from the area of Neuhäusl to the region around Neutra (Nitra), then on to the Tatra Mountain range (referred to as the 'small Carpathians'), before then moving on to the area northeast of Pressburg (Bratislava).

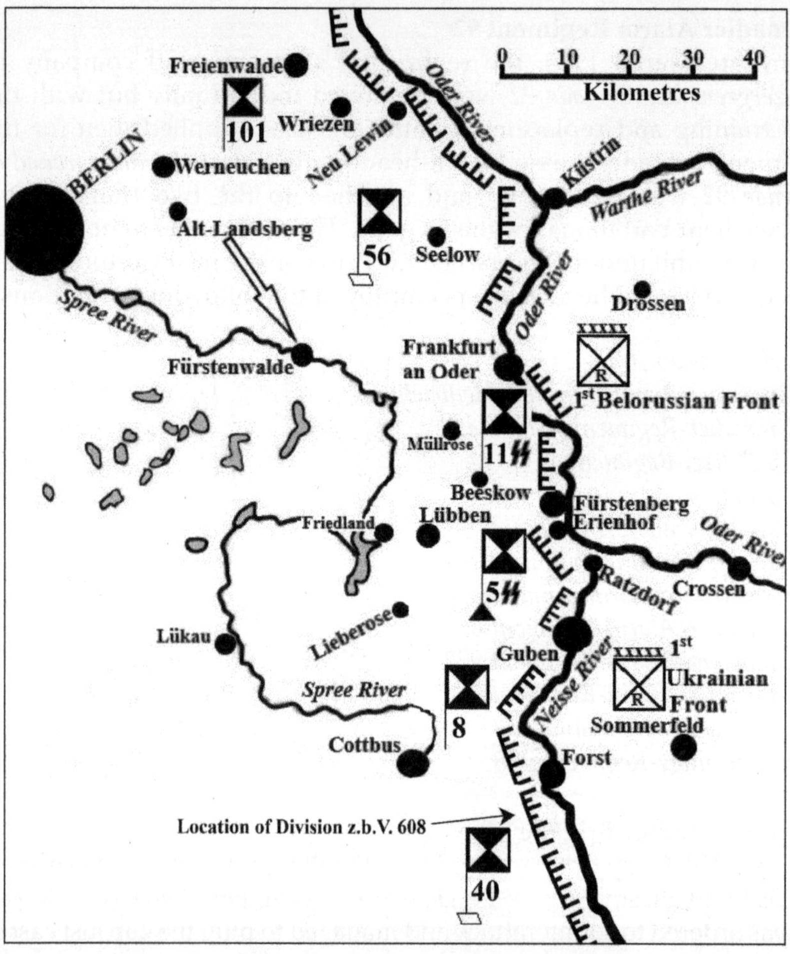

Figure 16. Grenadier Alarm Regiment 92 under Division Stab z.b.V. 608 near Cottbus, along the Oder River front, March-April 1945. *(Author's line drawing)*

From 4 April 1945 there was a general withdrawal from the northwestern part of the Tatra Mountains to the area around Marchegg and Breitensee, in the Gänserndorf district of Austria. *Panzergrenadier-Brigade 92* then took part in the defence of Pillichsdorf (Waldberg), northeast of Vienna. From 6-11 April it took part in the rear-guard battles as part of *96. Infanterie-Division,* and later that month served alongside the *37. SS-Freiwilligen-Kavallerie-Division 'Lützow'.* Along with this SS cavalry division, *Panzergrenadier-Brigade 92* fought its way back across the Hornsberg area from 14-15 April, before moving to the Hollabrunn area until 5 May, where, on the orders of the *Oberkommando der Wehrmacht* and *Heeresgruppe Süd,* the brigade was finally disbanded. Its men were told to head west, hoping to be taken by British or American forces, rather than to fall into the hands of either the Russians or Yugoslav partisans.

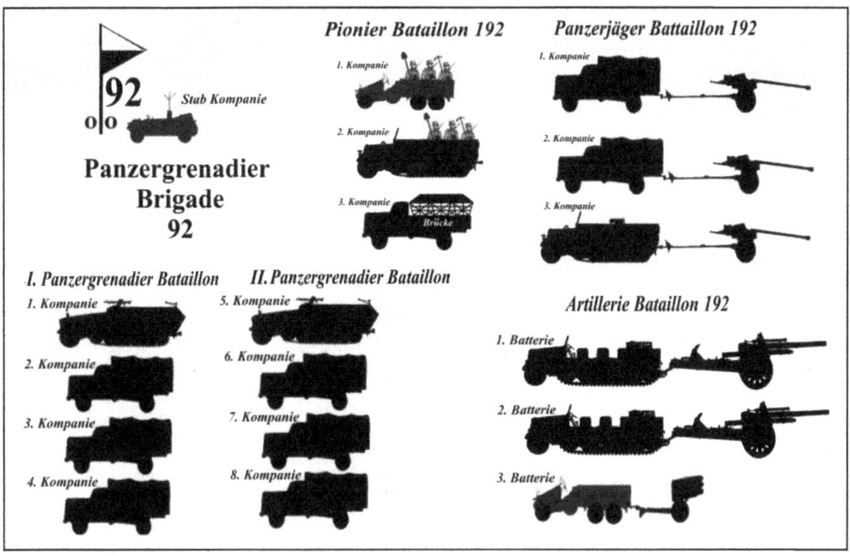

Figure 17. Panzergrenadier Brigade 92, 30 January 1945. *(Author's line drawing)*

Arab paratroopers defend Berlin

Another blow to the strength of the original *845. Deutsche-Arabisches Infanterie Bataillon* came in November 1944, when about 100 of the remaining Arabs in the *5. Kompanie,* the one that was parachute trained, deserted en masse from the unit, choosing to join their old *Fallschirmjäger* commander from their battles in North Africa: *Hauptmann* Gerhard Schacht. The Arabs who had served with Schacht learned that he was organising a special parachute regiment for action on the eastern front. Schacht, now with the rank of major, would eventually become the commander of *Fallschirmjäger-Regiment* 25 of *9. Fallschirmjäger-Division*. This division would fight in front of Berlin during the final two months of the war. *Major* Schacht discussed his Arab volunteers in a personal letter to a friend, in which he wrote the following:

> In November 1944, word got around that I had been entrusted with the activation of a parachute regiment for special employment. Before this month was over approximately 100 Arabs had deserted from their jobs with various staffs to volunteer for service in the new regiment. Under the leadership of officers who had commanded them during the Tunisian campaign, they formed an extra company for the regiment. During the fighting in March and April 1945 in Pomerania and on the Oder marshes, the Arab Company fully proved its effectiveness. In at least two instances I owed my life to the Arabs. Their losses were in proportion to their courage.[87]

When the Red Army offensive along the Oder River began on 16 April 1945, the defensive positions of *9. Fallschirmjäger-Division* were quickly broken. While *Fallschirmjäger-Regiment 26* withdrew northwards, towards Wriezen, *Fallschirmjäger-Regiment 25,* which contained the Arab parachute company, withdrew west, eventually reaching Berlin, where it fought and was destroyed. One of the ironic twists in the battle for the German capital was that the defenders included men from virtually every part of Europe and the Middle East: English, South African,[88] French, Spanish, Danes, Dutch, Norwegian, Swedish, Latvian, Estonian, Russian, Belarusian, and even Arab volunteers – all fighting alongside 13-17-year-old *Hitler Jugend,* 60-70-year-old *Volkssturm,* and what remained of the once powerful *Ostheer*.

Final employment in Yugoslavia, 1944-1945

But what of the original *Deutsches-Arabisches Infanterie-Bataillon 845*? The one that was fighting in Bosnia-Herzegovina in autumn 1944? As it turned out, it was withdrawn from Greece while attached to the *41. Festungs-Division* as it moved from Larissa, through Bitolj and Skoplje, Macedonia. It then travelled with the division to Kraljevo. In January

1945 it was completely reorganised in the Slavonski Brod area of eastern Croatia. The new organization was as follows:

Grenadier-Regiment 1230 [89]
Grenadier-Regiment 1231 [90]
Grenadier-Regiment 1232 [91]
Deutsches-Arabisches Infanterie-Bataillon 845
Füsilier-Bataillon 41 [92]
Artillerie-Regiment 141 [93]
Panzerjäger-Abteilung 141 [94]
Pionier-Bataillon 141 [95]
Divisions-Versorgungseinheiten 141

From Kraljevo, the Arab battalion moved on towards Užice, and from there headed towards the Sarajevo area in Bosnia, where it ended the year regrouping and refreshing.

In March and April 1945, *Deutsches-Arabisches Infanterie-Bataillon 845* was still fighting under *41. Festungs-Division,* just southeast of Vinkovci in Syrmia. Its higher corps command was the *XXXIV. Armeekorps*. The *41. Festungs-Division* had by then been redesignated as an infantry formation. In late April the battalion had been pushed back to Vukovar and ended up under the *104. Jäger-Division of XV. Gebirgs-Armeekorps.* Later, the unit was shifted to Zagreb:

> In April it participated in the retreat that brought General Hauser's 41st Fortress Division to positions west of Zagreb, in Croatia. Here the battalion was captured. As far as can be ascertained the Arabs were concentrated in special PoW camps and released after about one year of captivity. [96]

They were then expelled from Yugoslavia, with most returning to the Arab state or European colony they had come from.

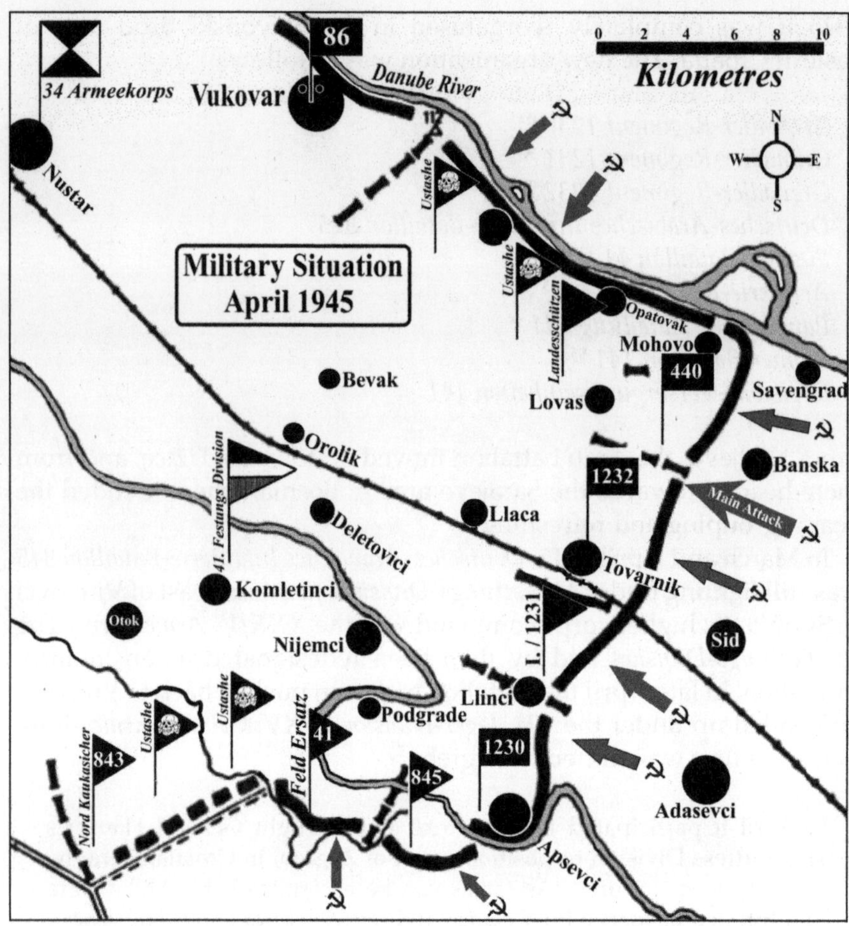

Figure 18. Positions of 41. Festungs Division and other Axis forces in April 1945. Notice the Deutsche-Arabisches Infanterie Bataillon, located west of the town of Apsevci. *(Author's line drawing)*

Vichy French-Arab units

La Brigade nord-africaine

In April 1944 a new anti-communist formation was created using a core of Muslim volunteers from North Africa who had been living in France. The idea to create this force had been the brainchild of the SS Security Services' Paris HQ and assistance was sought from the Algerian leader, Mohamed el-Maadi, in January 1944.[97] Maadi was the editor of the Arab language magazine *Er Rashid* ('The Messenger').

As such he was in a position to greatly influence his fellow Algerians and others in the local Muslim communities in France. In this way he was able to recruit 400 Arab men for the new formation, of which only 300 were chosen since the other 100 or so had such terrible criminal records that even the SD was unwilling to hire them. This all changed later, as the need for more manpower grew and soon even common criminals were being accepted into the *Brigade nord-africaine.* The effect this had was that the unit eventually received a reputation as looters and rapists within the French community. Even the hated *Milice* did not want to be associated with them, although initially it was simply out of racism. In fact, the SD had been trying to get these Muslim volunteers into the *Milice* since 1943, but to no avail. The commanders of the various companies within the *Brigade nord-africaine* were all Frenchmen who wore the SD uniform, while their Muslim volunteers wore a similar uniform to the *Milice.*

Henri Lafont

The overall commander of the brigade was a Frenchman by the name of Henri Chamberlain, who used the *nom de guerre* of Henri Lafont and had a long history before the war of criminal behaviour. He had the rank of an *SS-Hauptsturmführer* and split the unit into five companies. His father died when Lafont was 11 and on the day his father was buried, his mother abandoned him. He grew up on his own and was forced to fend for himself. In 1940, while in a French jail, he met two *Abwehr* agents who befriended him and suggested he work for the Germans. Lafont initially got a position with the French police through his connection with the *Abwehr.* However, he surrounded himself with former criminals and even some corrupt policemen, like his second in command, Pierre Bonny, and went into business for himself, extorting people and stores. The last straw for his police boss came in July 1940, when he forcibly freed twenty-seven criminals from French jails and made them a part of his growing criminal gang. He was only spared from being jailed or killed because he managed to locate and arrest the Belgian spymaster Otto Lambrecht and hand him over to the *Gestapo,* who thereupon protected Lafront. The *Abwehr* then approached Lafont and asked him to help insert two agents into French-controlled Algeria, in North Africa.

However, Lafont botched the mission. The agents were arrested and the Vichy French government sentenced him to death, although they could not reach him in occupied France, and the Germans refused to extradite him. From late 1940 through to the beginning of 1942, the *Gestapo* employed Lafont and his 100 or so associates to counteract the French resistance. Lafont and his men excelled at hideous ways to torture his fellow countrymen.[98] As a result, he and his band of criminals gained a terrible reputation with the French Resistance as being the worst of the worst of all of the *Carlingue.*[99] In 1942 Lafont's trouble with the French police ended when he became a member of the German *Devisenschutzkommando* (Foreign Exchange Protection Command) which was supposed to be in charge of overseeing the banks and fighting the Black Market. In this position, he enriched himself while also ingratiating himself with top Nazi brass, including the head of the Paris SD, *SS-Standartenführer* Helmut Knochen.

Creation of the Brigade nord-africaine

In the beginning of 1944 Lafont contacted Mohamed el-Maadi, who was a former French colonial captain, and proposed the creation of an organisation called *La Légion nord-africaine.* Mohamed el-Maadi was rabidly anti-communist and was an active member of the secret French Army organisation, *La Cagoule.* Members of this group had taken part in assassinations of important left-wing politicians and newspaper editors during the period of the Third Republic and into the Vichy French period. The more than 300 Arabs chosen for this battalion were grouped into platoons and were dressed in the uniform of the *Milice française* (French militia). The men of the battalion initially operated in the region of the Dordogne, although it is known that the *Première Compagnie* (1st Company) and *Troisième Compagnie* (3rd Company) also operated in Montbéliard.[100] Three platoons of the *Brigade nord-africaine* fought the *Maquis* in the region of Corrèze and Tulle. One company fought in the region of Dordogne, Mussidan and Sainte-Marie-de-Chignac, while another fought in the area of Brantôme and in Franche-Comté, in eastern France.

In July 1944 the *Brigade nord-africaine* was reformed and soon disbanded because of desertions by Arabs within the unit. The reason for the desertions was that it was clear the war was turning against the Germans. Some of its former members travelled to Germany with Capitaine el-Maadi, while others joined the *Freies Indien Legion* (Free India Legion). The India Legion was the *Infanterie-Regiment 950 (indisch)* of the German Army, which was now making its way towards the relative safety of southern Germany. The Arab companies were now basically reduced to the size of platoons of perhaps twenty-five to thirty Arab volunteers each. Each platoon was named as a section. Therefore, the 1st Platoon was referred to as the 1st Section, the 2nd Platoon was the 2nd Section, etc. These sections were commanded by the same SD company commanders as follows:

1 Section – SS-Untersturmführer Charles Cazauba
2 Section – SS-Untersturmführer Paul Clavič
3 Section – SS-Untersturmführer Paul Millebuaux
4 Section – SS-Untersturmführer Alex Villaplana
5 Section – SS-Untersturmführer Lucien Prĕvost

Desertions continued throughout the withdrawal and by the time the remnants of *Brigade nord-africaine* reached Grenoble, on their way north to the German border, barely thirty Arabs remained within the unit. All except one of the French SS second lieutenants who had served in the battalion ended up joining the *33. Waffen-Grenadier-Division der-SS 'Charlemagne'.*

Conclusions

An estimated 500 Syrians, 150-200 Palestinians, 450 Iraqis, 150-200 Lebanese, and perhaps 5-6,000 Moroccans, Tunisians, Algerians, Egyptians, Libyans and desert Arabs joined the Axis forces between 1941 and 1945. About 6,000 of this number passed through the various German military organisations, while the rest served in the forces of Vichy France. They were a minute military contribution to a war that included millions. Their importance, though, lay in the fact that these men played a political role for the German war effort simply because they were Arabs in German uniform. These Arabs in field grey furbished rolls upon rolls of propaganda photographs and films to support the German impression that the Third Reich was fighting for Arab freedom. Their military contribution, however, can be said to have had little significance. This was basically because the purpose for which they were raised – the expected takeover by Axis forces of the Middle East from the United Kingdom – never materialised. Although microscopic in size, these Arab battalions were to have served as the basis for a future pro-Axis Arab army.

There is one instance in which the Axis did begin full-scale recruitment of the local Arabs. This was during the occupation of Tunisia when *Panzerarmee Afrika* (later redesignated as *5. Panzerarmee*), was forced out of Tripolitania, Libya by the British 8th Army. During the brief time the Germans recruited in Tunisia, they managed to raise five battalions – about a small brigade in size of Arab volunteers – and all of it while fighting on two main fronts against the Americans, the Free French, and the British and their Commonwealth allies. They also created these battalions with extreme shortages of all kinds. We can only assume that more recruits and units would have been forthcoming if the Axis (1) had conquered the Middle East, (2) had not been preoccupied with fighting on two fronts, and (3) if supplies had been plentiful.[101]

At the beginning of the Second World War, the Germans had an absence of any organised or pre-determined policy towards the Arab world. This situation pretty much remained unchanged throughout the war. Aside from vague promises of independence and a shared hatred of the former colonial powers (the French and British), and of Jewry, Nazi Germany had very little to offer the Arab world by way of a concrete policy of self-determination and self-rule. The problem was exacerbated by Benito Mussolini, who insisted that no offer of independence or even quasi-independence was to be made to the peoples of North Africa and the Middle East. Mussolini simply wished to replace the current colonial powers with Italian colonial rule and even refused to contemplate the creation of Arab puppet states like Vichy France, Slovakia or Croatia. Mussolini, therefore, proved to be a serious impediment to better relations between Nazi Germany and the Muslim world because *Il Duce* absolutely refused to grant the colonies in North Africa and the Middle East any sort of freedom. The Arab world was aware of this and acted accordingly. They still remembered the numerous 'pacification operations' which caused many massacres perpetrated on the Libyan people by the Italian Army. In that struggle, the Libyan resistance leader, Omar al-Mukhṭār Muḥammad bin Farḥāṭ al-Manifī was eventually caught and executed. But the spirit of resistance that he fostered was never forgotten.

One can say that the Allies courted the Arab people a lot better and obtained far better results. Indeed, this proved to be the case when American forces landed in Morocco and began to arm former Vichy French Arab units with US equipment, on behalf of the Free French. But before this, the Allied interest towards the Arabs was negligible. The use of Arab forces on the Allied side did not come with any promise of Arab independence. On the contrary, it was a continuation of European colonialism. Beginning in 1943, Arab participation on the Allied side proved to be one that would send an Algerian infantry division to fight in Italy as part of the Free French forces. This was the work of pre-war colonial conscription brought back to life. In reality, there were far more colonial troops employed in the Far East than were used in the North African or European campaign. In fact, the Free French under General Charles De Gaulle employed around 400,000 colonial troops during the Second World War. It is interesting to observe that in November 1944, when the defeat of Nazi Germany was all but certain, and newspapers around the world were reporting that the first Allied divisions were entering the Reich, these same colonial conscripts were suddenly withdrawn from Europe and sent home.

Some authors and academics have speculated that the French wished to rid themselves of these colonial units in order to show that it had been French (European) soldiers who had delivered the final blows to Nazi Germany. Of course, this is pure speculation as no one has discovered a document to affirm this theory. By the same token, one can argue that seeing the end of the war in sight, the French simply decided to demobilise its colonial troops and send them back to their respective colonies. I believe the latter answer offers more credence than the former. Suffice it to say that once these Arab, African and Indian forces were no longer needed, this substantial colonial force was reduced and sent home. At the end of the Second World War, many people from Africa, the Middle East, the Indian subcontinent, and the Asia-Pacific rim expressed their desire to expel their former European colonial masters and achieve true independence. After the war, many voices that, as in 1918, had clamoured and demanded independence and self-rule, were also former members of the Allied colonial forces who now had extensive military experience.

For the most part, these European colonial powers resisted granting their colonies independence. Faced with no peaceful way to gain their freedom, many of these former colonial forces went on to take part in the guerrilla and political struggle for their own country's independence. This occurred in Africa, North Africa, the Middle East, Asia, and even in the islands of the Caribbean and Pacific rim. True political freedom was one right the Allies were to deny the Arab world, at least until the war was over, and then only grudgingly. France, for example, fought hard but unsuccessfully to keep its Indochina, Algerian, and Tunisian colonies. The French employed the Foreign Legion and other forces, but these could only partly delay the collapse of the French colonial empire. The French lost Indochina in 1954 after the disastrous battle of Dien Bien Phu (13 March to 7 May 1954), followed by the loss of Tunisia in 1956 and Algeria in 1962. The Dutch, likewise, lost their overseas empire, with the hardest blow being the loss of the oil- and rubber-rich colony of Indonesia in 1949.

The British also resisted the loss of their colonial empire. Palestine and Transjordan were lost because the empire could no longer pay the yearly upkeep in maintaining those mandates. Transjordan obtained its independence in 1946 and Palestine was left for the United Nations to deal with in 1948. Burma (now Myanmar) was also lost in 1948. The jewel in the crown of the British colonial empire, India, was lost in

1947. Nevertheless, the British fought hard to preserve their remaining overseas colonies. The Mau Mau rebellion in Kenya, for example, lasted from 1952 to 1960 and was fought with particular cruelty on both sides. In this struggle, the British defeated the uprising, if only temporarily. For the above listed reasons, we can argue that the Allies did not have much more to offer the Arab people, and to Muslims everywhere, given their resistance to granting their overseas colonies their independence. Many would counter by saying that the Nazis, having racist policies, offered the Muslim world even less. But those who choose to see the involvement of Islam with Nazism in the Second World War in this manner, fail to observe the primary reason for Arab participation with the Axis. For the Arabs, it was not so much *what* the Nazis had to offer them, but rather *what would be destroyed* as a result of a Nazi victory.

Chapter Three

THE 13. WAFFEN-GEBIRGS-DIVISION DER-SS 'HANDSCHAR'

Origins

The creation of the thirteenth division of the *Waffen-SS* was made possible because of the forced conscription that was imposed by the Nazis on the Muslim population of Bosnia and Herzegovina. Some Bosnian Muslims, perhaps inspired by anti-communist, anti-Serbian, or even anti-Semitic views, did volunteer for service in the *Waffen-SS*. However, the overwhelming majority of the men who eventually served in the *13. Waffen-Grenadier-Division der-SS 'Handschar'* were forcibly drafted. The Bosnian Muslims proved to be the most unfortunate group in Yugoslavia during the Second World War. They were ethnically Serbian and spoke Serbo-Croatian, yet were despised by their Orthodox Christian Serb neighbours and were used by the Catholic Croatians to fight the Serbians. They were repudiated by the Albanian Moslems for being so-called closet Serbs, and were exploited by the *Waffen-SS* as a ready manpower source.

The above paragraph, I believe, best describes the situation in which the Muslim community of Yugoslavia found itself during the Second World War. The war in Yugoslavia from 1941-1945 was, in many ways, a war within a war, within a war. That is because the various ethnic and religious groups in this artificially created nation competed and fought one another.[102]

In 1941, the Muslim citizens who lived in Yugoslavia amounted to approximately 900,000 people, mostly concentrated in the provinces of Bosnia and Herzegovina. They accounted for roughly 6 percent of

Yugoslavia's pre-war population. According to the Austro-Hungarian Empire's census from 1910, Bosnia-Herzegovina contained 434,061 Croatians, or 23 percent of the population of those provinces before the First World War. Orthodox Serbs at the time numbered 811,505 or 43 percent of the population, while Muslims numbered 603,910 or 32 percent. This number apparently increased to 40 percent in these two provinces by the start of the Second World War.

The roots of religious hatred in the Balkans

The roots of Bosnia's ethnic-Serbian Muslims lie in the history of a Christian sect known as the *Bogomils*. The *Bogomils,* known in western Europe as the *Cathars,* were despised by both the Eastern Orthodox Christians and European Catholic Christians because their religious practices employed elements of both faiths. The official break between both Catholic and Eastern Orthodox Christianity occurred in the eleventh century. In the beginning of the history of the Catholic faith, the position of Pope did not exist. Instead, each city containing a sizable number of Christians had a bishop. By the middle of the fifth century CE, five Catholic bishops existed: (1) in Rome, (2) in Antioch, (3) in Alexandria, (4) in Jerusalem, and (5) in Constantinople. In 440, Leo I became the Bishop of Rome and in 450 he wrote to the four other bishops of the Christian faith, claiming Petrine Supremacy, based on a passage from the New Testament from Matthew 16:13-20.[103]

> And I say also unto thee, that thou art Peter, and upon this rock I will build my church; and the gates of hell shall not prevail against it. And I will give unto thee the keys of the kingdom of heaven: and whatsoever thou shalt bind on earth shall be bound in heaven: and whatsoever thou shalt loose on earth shall be loosed in heaven.[104]

The bishops of Alexandria, Antioch, and Jerusalem seemed to have accepted the claim of Petrine Supremacy by Bishop Leo I, but the bishop of Constantinople, Anatolius, refused to acknowledge his claim. Thereupon, Bishop Leo I sent the Byzantine Emperor, Theodosius II, a letter explaining his claim that he was the head of the entire Christian Church. Theodosius II backed Anatolius, who stated openly that if Leo I wished to call himself Pope, then he was free to call himself Patriarch of Constantinople. The schism in the Christian faith began as a result of this religious power struggle between both men. Over hundreds of years, the eastern and western Christian churches began to grow apart. Customs developed in each that were different from one another. Even such simple things as the manner in which a monk would cut his hair, or whether the Christian mass should be performed with leavened or unleavened bread became an issue. The final break came in 1054 and is referred to as the Great Schism.

It began when the papal legate sent by Leo IX travelled to Constantinople in order, among other things, to deny the Patriarch of Constantinople Michael Cerularius the title of 'ecumenical patriarch' and insist that he recognise the claim that whoever was Bishop of Rome was the head of the entire Christian Church. Cerularius met with Rome's representative, but the discussion quickly turned angry. It ended with Leo IX of Rome excommunicating Cerularius, and Celarious excommunicating not only Leo IX, but his representative as well.

From this schism developed a long-standing animosity between the Serbians, who are mostly Orthodox Christians, and the Croatians, who are mainly Catholic. In both Christian churches, Muslims were rejected and looked down upon. Because the *Bogomils* practised a combination of both Catholicism and Eastern Orthodox Christianity, they were seen as heretics and were persecuted by both the Catholics and their Eastern Orthodox Christian brothers.

The *Bogomil* beliefs not only shared elements of Catholicism and Eastern Orthodox Christianity, but also encompassed dualism. As such, they were considered heretics. The *Cathars* in France, also known as the *Albigensians,* were viewed similarly. The most famous massacre of the *Cathars* occurred in the French city of Béziers, from 21-22 July 1209, ostensibly during the Albigensian Crusade declared by Pope Innocent III. When the crusaders broke into the city, the Abbot of Cîteaux, who was the representative of Pope Innocent III, yelled out 'Slaughter them all!' As a result, some 20,000 Christian *Cathars* were massacred and the *Cathar* stronghold of Béziers was burned to the ground.

At the end of the thirteenth century, Prince Stefan Nemanja, as well as the entire Serbian Grand Council, issued an edict saying that *Bogomils* were heretics. They also declared that they should be expelled from the Serbian Kingdom. In the ensuing religious strife that followed this declaration, hundreds of *Bogomils* were slaughtered by their Eastern Orthodox Serbian neighbours as they attempted to flee.

Many *Bogomils* who managed to leave Serbia made their way to Bosnia, where a community of *Bogomils* already existed. Bosnia had been an independent kingdom in medieval times and had formed a very distinctive multicultural character under Ottoman rule. Eventually, a substantial portion of its inhabitants converted to the Islamic faith. The majority of these Muslim converts turned out to be members of the much-persecuted *Bogomil* Christian sect. Most of the *Bogomils* that eventually converted to Islam had done so in gratitude for the religious tolerance the Ottoman Turks had extended to them. While the *Bogomils* lived under Ottoman rule in Bosnia and Herzegovina, they had been left unmolested to practise their faith as they saw fit. This was in direct contrast to their Serbian Orthodox Christian brothers who, it seems, continued to persecute and kill them. Is it any wonder, then, that most of these people chose to convert to Islam?

The Austro-Hungarian Empire

Bosnia and Herzegovina had been under Ottoman rule for centuries. However, following the decline of the Ottoman Empire in the late nineteenth century, Bosnia and Herzegovina came under Austro-Hungarian administration through the Treaty of Berlin in 1878. While Austria-Hungary did not initially annex the territories, it was granted the authority to occupy and administer them. In 1908, the Austro-Hungarian Empire officially annexed Bosnia and Herzegovina. This decision sparked international tensions and protests, particularly from Serbia and other Slavic states, as it was seen as a violation of the Treaty of Berlin. The Austro-Hungarian Empire quickly moved to incorporate these two former Ottoman provinces. One way to do this was to conscript the local male population into the Austro-Hungarian Army. In this way, several infantry regiments made up of recruits from Bosnia and Herzegovina were formed. Eventually, four infantry regiments were raised from the Muslim population. According to the Austrians, they were reported to be among the bravest of the Imperial Army. Muslim recruits were allowed to wear a red fez headdress and in addition, each regiment was allowed to have an *imam*, as a way to grow loyalty and military morale. The four regiments raised were located in the following cities:

Bosnia-Herzegovina Regiment No. 1 - Sarajevo
Bosnia-Herzegovina Regiment No. 2 - Banja Luka
Bosnia-Herzegovina Regiment No. 3 - Tuzla
Bosnia-Herzegovina Regiment No. 4 - Mostar

Later, when the First World War broke out and the Austro-Hungarian Army moved against Serbia, these Muslim regiments were used against the Serbian Army, adding to the already high enmity between the Serbian Orthodox Christians and the ethnic-Serbian Muslim community. The end of the First World War saw the formation of the Yugoslav state. It was a byproduct of the Treaty of Versailles and a British-French invention. The Kingdom of the Serbs, Croats and Slovenes, as the nation was known until 1928, was an artificially created state that, from the very beginning, favoured the Serbians at the expense of everyone else. Now the provinces of Slovenia, Bosnia-Herzegovina, Montenegro, Serbia, Croatia, Kosovo, Vojvodina, and Macedonia all came together with their ethnic and religiously diverse peoples to form the Kingdom of the Serbs, Croats, and Slovenes. The country was composed of the following ethnic and religiously varied people:

Table 3. Ethnic & Religious Composition of Yugoslavia in 1941.

Ethnic Group	Population	% of Population
[Orthodox] Serbians	6,500,000	41
[Catholic] Croatians	3,500,000	22
Slovenians	1,500,000	9
Macedonians	900,000	6
Moslem Slavs	900,000	6
Montenegrins	500,000	3
Others: ethnic-German, Hungarians, Greeks, Albanians, Bulgarians, Italians, as well as White Russian exiles.	2,200,000	13

By the time Germany and her Axis partners (Italy and Hungary) invaded Yugoslavia in 1941, these different ethnic and religious groups were ready to fight each other. The Yugoslav government had long been dominated and controlled by the majority Serbs, which of course, many non-Serbs resented. The king was Serbian, and the Yugoslav Army's officer corps was overwhelmingly Serbian. In fact, it was not until 3 April 1941, or three days before the German invasion of Yugoslavia began, that Serbian General Dusan Simovic invited Croatian leaders to join his newly formed government, which had recently toppled the regime of the Yugoslav Regent, Paul Karađorđević.[105] Simovic offered this invitation because he feared that if Germany or Italy invaded, the Croatians in the Yugoslav Armed Forces would not fight. He posited that if the Croatians believed they would have a seat in this newly formed government, then the overwhelming majority of Croatians would support the Yugoslav Army and state. He did not count on the long-standing grievances that Croatians had accumulated over decades, on account of Serbian dominance and abuse in the Yugoslav government.

Most of the people living in pre-Second World War Yugoslavia simply had no desire to live under continued Serbian ascendency.

The past becomes the present

The German invasion of Yugoslavia in 1941 merely accelerated the political, racial and religious differences that caused the eventual breakup of the country, beginning in 1991. This inevitable break would be halted at the end of the Second World War and Yugoslavia would remain together under the strong hand of the communist leader, Josip Broz Tito, who would die on 4 May 1980. The only reason the nation of Yugoslavia remained as an entity after his death was due to the existence of the USSR, which would have invaded the country if any of the provinces at the time had sought independence. But the very same year in which communism fell in the Soviet Union (1991), was the year that saw Yugoslavia beginning to break apart. This struggle for independence ended only nine years later, after almost every former republic went through a bloody struggle to free itself from Belgrade's rule.[106] In every instance, Serbia fought to keep each province in the state. The Serbian nationalist claim that the Serbian minority in these provinces was being abused was simply an excuse for aggression. Serbian men searched the attic at home for the Chetnik caps, field blouses and flags that their grandfathers had used during the Second World War and set out to commit the same horrors that had occurred before. Many Croatians did the same, digging up *Ustaše* symbols and flags. While Serbians massacred Croatians and Croatians massacred Serbians, both groups massacred Bosnian Muslims.

The breakup of Yugoslavia in the 1990s was a complex and violent process that led to significant loss of life. Estimates of the total number of people who died as a result of the conflicts that accompanied the breakup vary widely. It is important to note that the breakup of Yugoslavia involved several interconnected conflicts, including the Croatian War of Independence, the Bosnian War, and the Kosovo War, each with its own death toll. Additionally, there were numerous atrocities committed during these conflicts, including ethnic cleansing and genocide. In Srebrenica, for example, Serbian forces executed around 7,000 Bosnian Muslim men and boys as part of their ethnic cleansing campaign. Estimates of the total number of deaths resulting from these conflicts vary, depending on who is counting. Anywhere from 192,000 to 207,000 Croatians and 86,000 to 103,000 Muslims perished as a result of Serbian nationalism. These conflicts left deep scars on the region and had long-lasting effects on the political, social, and economic landscape of the former Yugoslav republics.

1941: Germany's involvement in Yugoslavia and Greece

In October 1940, Benito Mussolini invaded Greece from Albania. However, the Italians got into trouble almost immediately and their offensive stalled. Eventually, the numerically smaller Greek Army counterattacked and actually pushed the Italian Army back into Albania. Needing to help his faltering ally, Adolf Hitler demanded that Yugoslavia grant Germany transit rights so the *Wehrmacht* could attack Greece. The Prince Regent, Paul Karadjordjević, had warned the Nazi *Führer,* given the animosity that existed between Serbians against Austrians and Germans, saying that Serbians overwhelmingly supported France and the United Kingdom. He prophesied his ouster as head of the Yugoslav government at the hands of his own army, telling Hitler that within three months of his signing the treaty, he would be overthrown.

Nevertheless, Hitler insisted. After more arm twisting by the *Führer,* Karadjordjević signed the pact. The Serbian Regent had requested one of the stipulations in the pact was to be that German troops were not to use the sovereign territories of Yugoslavia for any future invasion of any country. Astonishingly, Hitler had granted this request and it was one right that the minor Axis nations of Romania, Hungary, and Slovakia did not have. Even though this pact had included this and similar stipulations, helping Yugoslavia to keep her neutrality with its neighbouring countries, it was not palatable to the Serbian generals in Belgrade, who still remembered how Germany supported the Austro-Hungarian Empire in the First World War. On 25 March 1941 Karadjordjević was forced to sign a peace treaty with Nazi Germany.

Two days later (Serbian) Yugoslav Air Force officers launched a successful coup that overthrew the Prince Regent's government and immediately annulled the German-Yugoslav pact. Additionally, the Serbs were and continued to be very pro-French and pro-British and therefore anti-German. They resented cohabitation and any form of collaboration with the Third Reich. They also had a chauvinistic attitude towards the other ethnic groups that made up the Yugoslav kingdom. They fully understood that German or Italian influence and meddling in Yugoslavia might one day lead to the independence of many of its regional ethnic groups – most notably, the Croatians. It was only natural, then, that the Germans would support opponents of the Serbian-dominated Yugoslav government, who had long sought their independence from Belgrade.

This desire for independence existed in many Croatians, Slovenians and Macedonians. As for the Muslim population, they appeared to have been indifferent to independence in 1941. Perhaps judging correctly that being ruled by Croatians or Serbians would not alter their status as second-class citizens. The dislike between Macedonians and Serbians, for example, who shared the same basic religion, was such that when Bulgarian troops entered that Yugoslav province as part of the Axis occupation force, they were welcomed by most of the Macedonian population.[107] Similar incidences occurred when German forces crossed into Croatia and when Italian troops entered Kosovo: they were greeted warmly by the Muslims living there.

A Bosnian SS division is proposed

It was not until the autumn of 1942 that *Reichsführer-SS* (National Leader of the SS) Heinrich Himmler and *SS-Obergruppenführer und General der Waffen-SS* Gottlob Berger, who headed the *Waffen-SS* recruiting office, approached Adolf Hitler with the proposal to raise a Bosnian Muslim SS division. This was a significant event, since up until then the *Waffen-SS* had only recruited German, Germanic, or ethnic German volunteers into their units. But the idea of a Muslim SS division was very appealing to Himmler, Berger, and Hitler. For Himmler, it seemed that Muslim men would make the perfect SS soldier, as he believed they made the best soldiers in an ideological struggle against Judaism and communism.[108] The Muslims, he articulated, were all opposed to Judaism. Their religion taught them that if they died in battle, they would immediately be sent up to heaven where their needs would be taken care of by a harem of beautiful women. What better religion could a soldier have? he thought.

For Gottlob Berger, recruiting Bosnian Muslims also made sense. The constantly high losses of men in battle kept him hard-pressed to find replacements for the expanding SS divisions, and the Bosnian Muslims would be another ready source of recruits for Nazi Germany. Finally, Hitler agreed with both Himmler and Berger, and added that the Muslims would help the Germans to garrison Yugoslavia and would therefore spare a German division for employment in Russia or elsewhere, where the need was greater. When Hitler gave his blessing to the project of raising a purely non-Germanic SS division, he forever left the German recruiting door open for the so-called non-Aryans and even those whom the Nazis referred to as *Untermenschen* (subhumans). It would seem that military necessity was slowly but surely whittling away at the German notion of the superiority of the Aryan race. Earlier in the year, the Germans had been successful in raising a volunteer mountain division from ethnic German Serbs from the Banat region of the Yugoslav province of Vojvodina. In fact, this ethnic-German SS division, which contained over 21,000 men at its peak strength, was raised only by the forceful conscription of the ethnic-German population. This was testified under oath by *SS-Obersturmbannführer* Robert Brill, of the *SS Hauptamt* (SS Main Office) during questioning at the Nuremberg War Crimes Trials:

> Herr Pelckmann: Statistics for the earlier years, 1940, 1941, 1942, have not been compiled by the Commission. Perhaps you could give us examples of how non-volunteers were taken into the Waffen-SS at such an early period.
>
> Herr Brill: Yes, I have already mentioned that 36,000 men who were drafted by emergency decrees. In addition, in 1940 we drafted men from the police to set up our field Gendarmerie. We drafted men from the Reichpost to secure our army mail. We drafted the civilian employees of the SS-Verfugungstruppe. In 1941 we frequently drafted personnel from the Army for our cavalry units. I recall further that about 800 Army men were drafted into the Waffen-SS in the summer of 1941… In 1942 we deviated considerably from the volunteer basis. About 15,000 racial Germans were drafted into our Prinz Eugen Division.[109]

SS-Obersturmbannführer Robert Brill's testimony concerning *Waffen-SS* recruitment methods proved to be correct. Brill went on to disclose that with regard to the recruitment of ethnic-Germans, in many cases these men lived outside the borders of the Reich. They thus fell outside of the recruitment authority of the *Wehrmacht,* so the SS was free to draft them. In cases where a recruit could not prove he was an ethnic-German, documents were obtained for them under false pretences. Brill stated that there were numerous cases of this occurring, especially after 1942, when the fortunes of war no longer favoured Germany, and losses continued to mount. One example of this was the use of the local German *Bund* organisation in a particular region or country to obtain replacements for the *Waffen-SS.* These foreign-born ethnic-Germans would be invited to Germany for what was billed as a summer toughening up course. Upon arrival, the men would find out they had joined the *Waffen-SS.* When the recruit would complain, he was put under tremendous mental strain to accept his new lot in life. This also happened to many foreigners who lived in regions outside of the Reich, where ethnic-Germans were predominant

This forceful recruitment of ethnic-Germans and non-Germans outside the borders of Germany helped to slightly relieve the losses being taken by the *Waffen-SS.* However, the recruitment of non-voluntary foreigners into the *Waffen-SS* did not produce the politically fanatical soldier that the *Waffen-SS* represented. In addition, this supply of manpower was neither inexhaustible nor enthusiastic. For the most part, these men proved to be mediocre when it came to fighting quality. This was especially true after many an ethnic-German recruit would write home, bitterly warning his family and his friends to not volunteer and to avoid the draft call. As ethnic-German men in the conquered regions of Europe began to try to evade the Nazi draft, Gottlob Berger began seeking other ways to obtain manpower for the Reich. The Germans, therefore, hoped that the Muslim community of Bosnia and Herzegovina, which Himmler knew was fairly substantial, would supply enough men in order to raise yet another division for the *Waffen-SS*. Heinrich Himmler's knowledge of the Bosnian Muslims went back to the First World War. Himmler himself had very little war experience, having only been an officer candidate who never reached the front lines before the war ended. Nevertheless, he did get to hear about the brave *Mujos* from returning war veterans who had campaigned in the Balkans and had seen firsthand the bravery and ferocity of the Muslim regiments of Emperor Franz Joseph. Himmler would not forget these old war stories and would remember the Muslims from Bosnia and Herzegovina.

The Croatian *Ustaše* had already recruited the Muslim population of Bosnia-Herzegovina, as had the Croatian Army.[110] Now the *Waffen-SS* hoped to do the same. At this stage in the war, most of the Tito partisans were principally composed of Serbian volunteers, with Croatians in the minority. This fact was also taken into consideration by the SS, who hoped to take advantage of the mistrust and hatred between the Muslim and Serbian communities. Herein lay another reason why Hitler, Himmler and Berger wished to raise a Bosnian Muslim SS division. It was expected that the natural animosity which existed between the Muslim and Eastern Orthodox Serb communities would make the unit an effective occupation force. The irony was that both the Muslims and Eastern Orthodox Serbs were from the same Slavic stock. Another irony was that Joseph Broz Tito, the leader of the Yugoslav partisans, was a Croatian. The Orthodox Christian and Muslim communities should have lived side by side as brothers, given that they came from the same ethnic family tree. Their religious differences, however, drove an irrevocable wedge between them that even resurfaced fifty years later, in the 1990s, causing untold horrors and suffering. This animosity still exists today: in this region of Europe, memories are long.

Hitler gives his blessing

On 10 February 1943 Adolf Hitler formally approved of the project and three days later, *Reichsführer-SS* Heinrich Himmler directed that the

The former Iraqi Prime Minister, Rashid Ali al-Gaylani, meeting Adolf Hitler in Berlin. After the pro-German Iraqi uprising, which began on 1 April 1941, British and Commonwealth forces arrived from Palestine and India and crushed the rebellion. Al-Gaylani and other leaders of the plot were able to flee to Iran. However, when British and Soviet forces invaded Iran, al-Gaylani fled to Italy, before making his way to Germany, where he remained for the duration of the war. Throughout the conflict, al-Gaylani worked to secure Arab support for the Axis cause, and Hitler officially recognised him as the leader of the Iraqi exile government. (*Author's collection*)

A bugler in the Arab *845. Deutsche-Arabisches Infanterie Bataillon*. He is wearing the *Freies Arabien* (Free Arabia) arm patch. (*Museum of Modern History, Ljubljana, now known as the National Museum of Contemporary History of Slovenia*)

Another Arab member of the *845. Deutsche-Arabisches Infanterie Bataillon*. This photograph was taken in 1944, when the battalion was stationed in Greece. (*Museum of Modern History, Ljubljana, now known as the National Museum of Contemporary History of Slovenia*)

A German NCO and several North African Arab volunteers. The German NCO is wearing the arm patch of *Sonderstab F*. The Germans raised several battalions of Arab volunteers in North Africa. (*Bundesarchiv*)

This photograph of several Arab volunteers was taken in Greece in autumn 1943. Notice that one of the volunteers is clearly of African descent. (*Bundesarchiv*)

Another photograph of the same African volunteer. (*Bundesarchiv*)

Although this photograph is of poor quality, it nevertheless shows an African volunteer wearing the *Freies Arabien* arm patch, meaning he belonged to the *845. Deutsche-Arabisches Infanterie Bataillon*. When compared with the previous photographs (Nos. 5 & 6), it would appear that all three are of the same volunteer. It is not merely the person is smiling that in both instances, and that his facial features are the same, but the clothing, even down to the civilian sweater being worn underneath the field blouse, is also identical. (*Bundesarchiv*).

These Arab volunteers are wearing the *Sonderstab F* cloth arm patch but were not members of the *845. Deutsche-Arabisches Infanterie Bataillon*. Instead, they formed part of the Arab parachute company under *Major* Rudolf Witzig's *Fallschirm-Korps-Pionier-Bataillon* in Tunisia. (*Bundesarchiv*)

Members of the Arab parachute company practise marching, somewhere in Tunisia. This photograph was taken in the spring of 1943. *(Bundesarchiv)*

The same drill practice for the men of the Arab parachute company. Some of them appear to be singing. *(Bundesarchiv)*

An interesting photograph of two German officers, an Arab officer, and a local official. The Tunisian official appears to be none other than Mohamed Chenik (also known as M'hamed Chenik), the Tunisian nationalist leader. One of the German officers is clearly from the Luftwaffe and likely *Major* Rudolf Witzig, the commander of the parachute battalion the Arab volunteers were attached to. This indicates that Chenik was perhaps inspecting the volunteers of the Arab parachute company. *(Bundesarchiv)*

Three members of the Arab parachute company riding in a motorcycle and sidecar. The Arab volunteers are wearing the *Sonderstab F* cloth arm patch. *(Bundesarchiv)*

An undated photograph of a German *Oberfeldwebel* (Master Sergeant) wearing the *Sonderstab F* cloth arm patch. *(Bundesarchiv)*

An Arab volunteer reading an Arabic magazine. It does not appear to be the Arabic version of the German propaganda magazine *Signal*, given that the word 'signal' in Arabic is *al'iishara*, and we can make out enough of the title of the magazine to know that it is not. The picture was taken in the spring of 1944. *(National Museum of Contemporary History of Slovenia)*

Two members of the Arab *845. Deutsche-Arabisches Infanterie Bataillon* are seen here operating in Greece, autumn 1943. One appears to have binoculars and is acting as a spotter, while the other seems to be holding an MG-34 machine gun. (*National Museum of Contemporary History of Slovenia*)

A poor quality photograph, taken in Tunisia in spring 1943, showing a German NCO leading a platoon of North African Arab volunteers. One volunteer is seen carrying a German machine gun. The white armbands carried the words: '*Im Dienst der Deutschen Wehrmacht*' (In the Service of the German Armed Forces). (*Bundesarchiv*)

Reichsführer-SS Heinrich Himmler bows while shaking the hand of the Mufti of Jerusalem, Mohammed Amin al-Husseini. The Germans referred to the red-bearded al-Husseini as the 'Grand Mufti of Jerusalem' in an effort to elevate his importance in the Muslim world. Al-Husseini was instrumental in helping to establish the Bosnian Muslim *13. Waffen-Gebirgs-Division der-SS 'Handschar'*. (*Bundesarchiv*)

German Order Police personnel post a recruiting poster for the *13. Waffen-Gebirgs-Division der-SS 'Handschar'*, sometime in the spring of 1943. (*National Museum of Contemporary History of Slovenia*)

The Mufti of Jerusalem, Mohammed Amin al-Husseini, gives the Nazi salute as a parade of Bosnian SS soldiers march past, summer 1944. (*National Museum of Contemporary History of Slovenia)*

Members of the *Kaukasischer-Waffen-Verbände der-SS* in the region of Tolmezzo, northern Italy, in the autumn of 1944. (*Museum of Contemporary History of Slovenia)*

The commander of the *Kaukasischer-Waffen-Verbände der-SS, SS-Standartenführer der Reserve* Arved Theuermann, seen here as an *SS-Sturmbannführer* (Major) while serving in the *SS-Totenkopfstandarte. (Bundesarchiv)*

The commander of the *Waffengruppe der-SS Nordkaukasien* of the *Kaukasischer-Waffen Verbände der-SS*, *Waffen-Standartenführer der-SS* Kutschuk Ulagaj, in 1944. (*Bundesarchiv*)

A poor quality image of the commander of the *Waffengruppe der-SS Georgien* of the *Kaukasischer-Waffen-Verbände der-SS*, *Waffen-Standartenführer der-SS* Michael-Pridon Zulukidse, 1944. (*Bundesarchiv*)

Wilhelm Hintersatz, who renamed himself Harun el-Raschid Bey Hintersatz after converting to Islam during the First World War. Promoted to *SS-Standartenführer* on 1 October 1944, he would become the commander of the *Osttürkischer-Waffen-Verbände der-SS*. Here he is seen in a still photograph from a colorised film that was unearthed quite recently. He appears to be at Muslim prayer with his men. (*Bundesarchiv*)

SS-Standartenführer Hintersatz with his translator in a still photograph from the propaganda film. One cannot help but notice the doubt or suspicion on the face of the translator, as his commander is speaking. (*Bundesarchiv*)

Men of the *Sandžak* (Sanjak) militia of Eastern Montenegro under SS command. (*Bundesarchiv*)

The commander of the '*Muselmanengruppe von Krempler*' as the formation was initially called, *SS-Standartenführer* Karl von Krempler. Notice his rather rotund body when compared to the Muslim volunteers. (*Bundesarchiv*)

A German NCO with the Muslim volunteers from the Sanjak. (*Bundesarchiv*)

Tartar volunteers from the Crimea march past their German commander, sometime in autumn 1942. In 1944, these men would later be transferred into the *Waffen-Gebirgs-Brigade der-SS (tatarische Nr. 1)*. (*Bundesarchiv*)

German cadre staff of the Kalmyk formation of the German Army riding on Bactrian camels. This unit is considered the most unique and exotic formation of foreign volunteers employed by the *Wehrmacht*. After various name changes, the unit's final title was *Kalmückisches-Kavalleriekorps*. This photograph was taken in eastern Ukraine in 1943. (*Bundesarchiv*)

A German member of the cadre staff in the *Kalmückisches-Kavalleriekorps*. Here he is seen affectionately stroking his Bactrian camel. (*Bundesarchiv*)

The only known photograph of *Waffen-Obersturmführer der-SS* Gulam Alimov (seen here wearing the rank of a *Waffen-Untersturmführer der-SS*). Alimov would be responsible for the mutiny and desertion of about 500 members of the Turkestani 1st Battalion in the *Osttürkischer-Waffen-Verbände der-SS* on 24 December 1944. Notice that he was a highly decorated volunteer and is seen here wearing the Iron Cross and the Infantry Assault Badge, as well as the Close Combat Clasp among many other awards. (*Bundesarchiv*)

commander of the ethnic-German *7. SS-Freiwilligen-Gebirgs-Division 'Prinz Eugen', SS-Gruppenführer und Generalleutnant der Waffen-SS* Artur Phleps, be charged with raising the Muslim SS division. Artur Phleps was himself an ethnic-German from Romania. The NCOs and officers of the SS 'Prinz Eugen' division were directed to help organise the battalions and regiments of the Muslim SS division. The division was initially referred to as the *Kroatische SS-Freiwilligen-Division* (Croatian SS Volunteer Division). On 19 February 1943 Artur Phleps set to work at establishing a formation staff that would form the basis of the new SS divisional headquarters. Late in February a meeting was held between Ante Pavelić, the Croatian Fascist dictator and Artur Phleps, as well as *SS-Brigadeführer und Generalmajor der Polizei* Konstantin Kammerhofer, who was the Higher SS and Police Leader in Croatia and was, therefore, Himmler's immediate representative.

Kammerhofer represented Himmler in all matters. Pavelić was informed matter-of-factly that the decision had been taken to raise an SS division from what amounted to subjects of the Croatian state. Although Pavelić did not show any outward signs of surprise, anger or indignation, according to the accounts by the Croatian officers that were present at the meeting, he was furious that thousands of his subjects were to be recruited into what was a foreign military organisation. The indignation was doubled since the Germans had not even asked permission as a token of respect and deference to the Croatian fascist leader. Pavelić was teeming with anger at the Germans, who had arbitrarily decided to raise this unit without his consent or blessing. Instead, they were telling the *Poglavnik* of their decision as an afterthought.[111]

Opposition from the Poglavnik

Pavelić resolved then and there to agree to the German *faít acomplí*, for he was in no position to anger the Germans or say no. He was very much dependent on them and the Italians to a lesser degree for military support. Instead, however, he decided he would do his best to undermine and torpedo the entire recruiting effort. German arrogance at not even consulting him prior to their final decision, on what was clearly a matter for the Croatian state to decide, was indicative that the Germans considered Pavelić and his Croatian government as nothing more than a puppet of the Reich. This move clearly infringed on Croatia's sovereignty and Pavelić was hell bent on teaching the Germans a lesson. Pavelić did ask for one thing, however: to name the Muslim division, figuring that the Germans would consent to this relatively insignificant request.

He demanded that this new SS formation be designated as the *SS-Ustaše-Division Hrvatska* (SS *Ustaše* Division Croatia). Both Kammerhofer and Phleps agreed to this request, only to get the formal endorsement on paper from the Croatian Fascist leader. This was tantamount to a rubber stamp of approval and Pavelić knew it. Both of his requests were later ignored by the Germans, whereupon he resorted to further sabotage and subterfuge to cripple the SS recruiting drive. This attempt to disrupt the raising of this Muslim SS division started from the very beginning. Pavelić did this by giving a strict, verbal and written warning that any Muslim who opted to join the *Waffen-SS* would either be drafted into the Croatian Army or be sent to a concentration camp. This campaign increased when the Croatian leader was told that many Muslims in the Croatian Army were deserting to join the new SS division. The reasons for the desertions were many: the Germans were paying the recruits more money than the Croatian state could ever pay; the prestige of belonging to what was then considered an elite German military organisation; to obtain better clothing, equipment and arms; and to serve under better military leadership, not to mention the creation of a special diet for Muslims that the Germans took care to establish.[112]

Yet despite all this effort on the part of the Germans, the number of Muslim recruits began to dwindle to almost nothing by March and April 1943. This had occurred despite Himmler's order to Berger to send Kammerhofer about 2 million *Reichsmarks* to help finance the recruiting effort. It seems that the *Poglavnik* was getting his revenge. If things did not improve, the projected number of 26,000 Muslim recruits would not be reached by the target date of 1 August 1943.[113] Additionally, Kammerhofer and Berger both feared that the entire project was now in jeopardy. An investigation was launched by the staff under Artur Phleps to try to ascertain what problem was causing the recruiting effort to falter. On 19 April 1943 the findings of the staff were presented to the SS leadership involved in the recruiting effort. The principal reason for the failure of the recruiting drive lay squarely on the feet of the Pavelić regime. The findings disclosed that he was doing all he could to undermine the Muslim *SS* recruiting drive. Heinrich Himmler was now the one to become outraged.

He ordered Kammerhofer to remind the *Poglavnik* that Croatians were supposed to be puppets. The Croatians had few friends. The Serbian Chetniks were fighting the Croatian state. The communist Tito partisans were fighting the Croatian state, and the Italians, who initially backed Croatia, were now doing their best to destabilise the Croatian regime for their own ends. The Croatians, therefore, desperately needed continued German support to avoid being overrun by their enemies. For this reason, Ante Pavelić could impede German interests only so far. The *Poglavnik* eventually relented, and the recruiting campaign was allowed to proceed unimpeded. But the damage had already been done and the number of Muslim recruits still remained below requirements.

The Germans now put off all pretences and began the forcible conscription of *unsere Mujos* (slang for 'our Muslims'). The German NCOs who were assigned to accept and train these Muslim recruits had been the veterans of earlier German victories and were, for the most part, indoctrinated into the racist principals and ideals of National Socialism. These theoretical principals espoused the superiority of the *Herrenrasse* (master race) and *Untermenschen* (subhumans). For these German SS men, it was extremely difficult to accept these Slavic Muslim recruits, non-Aryans to be sure, as their equals and partners in the struggle against the Yugoslav guerrillas. The military requirements and necessities of the day were fast superseding political dogma. As will be seen, this was a recipe for disaster and would cause a major problem in the forming of the division. Although Ante Pavelić had done enough damage to cripple the recruitment of these Muslim men, by July 1943 enough recruits had been gathered so that the training of the division could officially begin. The SS-FHA, or *Führungshauptamt* (SS Leadership Main Office) now gave the forming division its first title on 2 July 1943: *Kroatische SS-Freiwilligen-Gebirgs-Division* (Croatian SS Volunteer Mountain Division). Thirteen days later, the divisional staff first mentioned the title 'Handschar' (Scimitar) in its records, as the name that had been bestowed on the division.[114]

Special treatment

A Scimitar was an Arab sword and had a very distinctive look. Given that the division was mostly composed of non-Aryan men, a special right collar tab was devised, because only Aryan men were allowed to wear the double SS thunderbolt runes that were normally worn on the right collar tab. The left collar tab always employed the rank of the person, regardless of whether he was Aryan or non-Aryan. The overwhelming majority of the Muslim recruits came from Bosnia, but the officer corps of the division was principally composed of German or ethnic-German officers and NCOs. There were also numerous cases of racial Germans from Hungary also serving in the division. These served especially as interpreters between the German officers and their Serbo-Croat speaking recruits.

Figure 19. The right collar tab sporting the thunderbolt SS runes. Only Aryan members of the SS were authorised to wear them. The German cadre staff in the division wore this right collar tab. *(Author's line drawing)*

Figure 20. The right collar tab for non-Aryan members of the SS 'Handschar' division. *(Author's line drawing)*

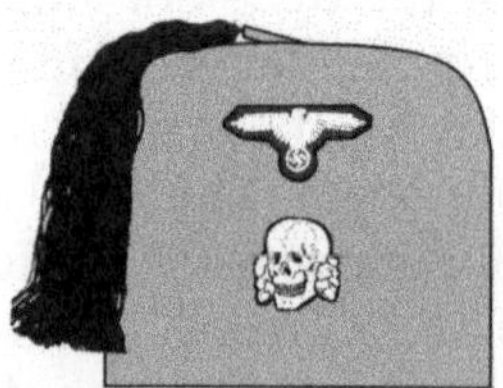

Figure 21. Author's line drawing of a 'Handschar' division red fez cover. The members of the SS 'Handschar' division were allowed to wear this red fez with the SS insignia: the national eagle (SS version), and the death's head emblem. There are photographic examples of both the cloth and metal insignia being used on these special covers. *(Author's line drawing)*

Figure 22. The divisional emblem of the SS 'Handschar' division sported a Muslim scimitar inside a shield. This symbol would be painted in black and white on the vehicles belonging to the division. *(Author's line drawing)*

One such example was *SS-Untersturmführer* Franz Pakos, who began his military career in the Hungarian Army. The German officers assigned to the division varied greatly, from previous serving police officers to even a former concentration camp commandant. One former police official, *SS-Sturmbannführer* (SS major) Karl Liecke, had served in the German Order Police before the war. He later had later been drafted into the *4. SS-Polizei-Division* and fought on the northern sector of the eastern front. Because of his combat experience, he became the fourth officer to lead one of the Muslim SS regiments in the division[115] and was only relieved of this post late in the war. Another officer, *SS-Sturmbannführer* Egon Zill, had the following qualifications before he was posted to the Muslim SS 'Handschar' division:

> Born in Plauen, 1906; Baker and janitor; joined the Nazi Party and SA in 1923, transferred to the SS, 1926; Promoted to SS Major, 1942; Service in Hohnstein, Sachsenburg, and Lichtenberg Concentration Camps, 1934-1937; Protective Custody Camp Leader at the Dachau Concentration Camp, 1937-1941; Staff member of the Concentration Camp Buchenwald, 1938, and Womens Concentration Camps Lichtenburg and Ravensbrueck, 1938-1939; Commandant of the Concentration Camp Hinzert, Natzweiler, and Flossenburg, 1942...[116]

The final title of the division became *13. Waffen-Gebirgs-Division der-SS 'Handschar'*. In July 1944 Egon Zill was listed as the commander of *II. Bataillon,* in one of the SS mountain infantry regiments of the division. However, an SS officer roster dated 1 October 1944 listed him as being transferred into the *23. Waffen-Gebirgs-Division der-SS Kama.* Although SS-*Sturmbannführer* Egon Zill was the exception, his example nevertheless shows us that the division's officer corps had officers that were not considered ideal and properly trained infantry officers. Many had been transferred over from the Order Police, and even administrative posts. It can be said that the most qualified commanders were not sent to this Muslim SS division, since they were kept for the truly elite SS formations. From all of this we can only surmise that the officer corps of the 'Handschar' SS division was composed of diversely qualified and unqualified officers which most likely would have and, as it happened, did produce mixed results in the field of battle. This is after all quite understandable, given the fact that the division was earmarked for occupation duty and anti-partisan operations and not the more strenuous frontline combat duty of the elite SS divisions.

The Germans did try to raise the morale of the Muslim recruits. One way that this was achieved was to allow the Muslims in the division to practice their Islamic faith. Special rations were also accorded the unit.

Each battalion had its own *imam*, each regiment its own *mullah*, and with Hitler's consent, the Muslims were given the same privileges they had in the old Imperial Austro-Hungarian Army: special rations and permission to observe their religious rites *en masse*. The Germans even went to the trouble of establishing two religious schools specifically geared for the Islamic faith in order to train the *imams* and *mullahs* of the Army and *Waffen-SS*. One was located in Göttingen and the other in Dresden. The Dresden school was intended primarily for *Waffen-SS* units, while the one at Göttingen trained religious pupils for the German Army, who also had a large number of Muslims from the Soviet Union in their ranks.[117] The school in Dresden was given the official blessing of the Mufti of Jerusalem, Haj Amin al-Husseini, whom the Germans had elevated by referring to him as the 'Grand Mufti' of Jerusalem. In addition, special insignias were made specifically for the Muslim SS division – one being the right collar tab which depicted a swastika and a hand holding a Scimitar, or curved sword which was favoured by Turkish troops of the old Ottoman Empire. The Muslim recruits were expected to take the oath of allegiance, like other *Waffen-SS* members. A special oath of allegiance had to be devised, however, which would simultaneously make the Muslim SS recruits swear an oath of loyalty to Adolf Hitler and Ante Pavelić, placating the vanity and suspicions of the Croatian leader:

> I swear to the Führer, Adolf Hitler, as Supreme Commander of the German Armed Forces to be loyal and brave. I swear to the Führer and to the leaders whom he may designate, obedience unto death. I swear to God the Almighty, that I will always be loyal to the Croatian State and its authorized representative, the Poglavnik, that I will always maintain the best interests of the Croat people and always respect the state constitution and laws of the Croatian people.[118]

Transfer to France

On 2 July 1943 the SS-FHA decided to shift the forming Muslim SS division to southern France in order to avoid disruption of the unit's training schedule by the partisans, or further Croatian attempts to undermine the formation. The transfer was also made so that this forming SS division could serve as part of the German occupation forces in France. The divisional headquarters staff was now placed in the French town of Le Puy. The divisional forming staff was, as stated earlier, raised and led by *SS-Gruppenführer und Generalleutnant der Waffen-SS* Artur Phleps. While Phleps was in charge of the newly formed divisional staff, some proposals as to who would eventually lead this new division were circulated. One of the choices proposed that stuck initially was *SS-Standartenführer* (SS colonel) Herbert von Obwurzer, who was eventually chosen and given control of the division towards the end of April 1943. While some post-war historians have argued that von Obwurzer was mainly concerned with recruiting and as such cannot be considered as the first true divisional commander, two German authors, including former SS General, Paul Hausser, state clearly that until 8 August 1943, when von Obwurzer was removed from command of the division, he had indeed been the commander of the SS 'Handschar' division.

The fact that he was mainly concerned with the recruiting drive is understandable, given that during this early stage in its development the raising of battalions and regiments was all-important. There was an all-consuming need to recruit men in order to flesh out the division. Finally, on 1 August 1943 a German officer serving in the *Wehrmacht*, *Major* Karl-Gustav Sauberzweig, was inducted into the *Waffen-SS* and given the rank of *SS-Oberführer*, which is the SS rank somewhere between colonel and major general. This induction was voluntary and Sauberzweig did not oppose it at all. In fact, he volunteered.

Sauberzweig could have had many reasons for joining the *Waffen-SS*, but the apparent incentive was most likely that he would be promoted to a much higher rank. Eight days later, on 9 August, he was given command of the division, which had by then been taken from von Obwurzer because of apparently irreconcilable differences between himself and Ante Pavelić. It seems that Obwurzer's recruiting campaign had taken an anti-Croatian stance, which Himmler realised would be detrimental to the already strained German-Croatian relations. He was removed from command for two reasons: (1) to placate the Croatian government and (2) to allow the forming of the division to continue without further Croatian hindrance.[119]

Unsere Mujos

As stated earlier, the placement of the Slavic Muslim SS recruits under the command of German SS NCOs and officers, who were not accustomed to treating Slavic peoples as their equals, led to incidents between the recruits and these German SS trainers. This in turn led to bad feelings, misunderstandings, and callosities between the SS training personnel against the recruits. The Germans would sarcastically refer to the recruits as *Mujos* or *Muselgermanen*, and other pejorative terms.[120] These would range from insults to outright humiliations that were heaped upon the Muslim recruits. To make the tense situation worse for the German war effort, the Muslim SS division had, by then, been infiltrated by a communist cell that was bent on wrecking the training programme and demoralising the unit as a whole. In this, the communists were in agreement with the Croatian fascists: they both wanted to ruin the division.

They planned to do this by (1) magnifying the racist incidents the German training personnel were causing themselves and (2) by a programme of misinformation geared to confuse the recruits, sap their morale, and cause as much friction between them and the Germans as possible. One such example of misinformation was the rumour that began to be circulated by this communist cell that the Germans were planning to employ the division against the western Allies. Given that the division was currently stationed in France, the rumour was given credence, so the Muslim recruits believed it. The gossip went on to say that this had been the reason why the division had been shifted to France. Of course, such a move would have proved disastrous, since the Muslims of Yugoslavia had no quarrel with the western Allies and therefore no desire to fight against them.

The Germans understood this only too well. Unfortunately for the German war effort, this rumour was reinforced as the Muslim recruits found themselves training in France and wondering what they were doing there, so far from home. The Germans could not just explain that they had removed the unit from the Balkans because they feared the partisans would disrupt the training, or that they had done so in order to prevent further Croatian sabotage. This would imply that the Germans were not in control of the countryside and the situation, and thus further demoralise the unit. Another open wound the communist cell worked on was the compulsory service, that is, the outright forceful conscription of the Muslim men into a foreign army. Away from home, not knowing if their families were safe from communist or Chetnik attack, the recruits wondered just what they were doing in southern France. Tensions continued to simmer just beneath the surface until the night of 16-17 September 1943, when weeks of German insensibilities and communist agitation efforts finally boiled over and erupted into what was then thought to be unthinkable: the first ever mutiny within the ranks of the *Waffen-SS*.

Mutiny

The mutiny occurred within the 1,000 men of the division's engineer battalion and was led by *Waffen-Oberjunker der-SS* (SS Officer Candidate) Ferid Džanić. The battalion was stationed in the village of Villefranche-de-Rouergue when it mutinied, killing most of the German officers and NCOs in the unit. One known ethnic German officer who was killed during the uprising was 38-year-old *SS-Obersturmführer* Julius-Friedrich Galantha. There were other plotters in the mutiny, including *SS-Oberjunker* Eduard Matutinović and Nikola Vukelić, and *Waffen-Oberscharführer der-SS* Lutfija Dizdarević. These men, led by Džanić and fourteen other enlisted men, went about systematically forcing each sentry and then each platoon to join the mutiny or die. They thereupon grabbed the Germans in the *1. Pionier Kompanie* and began to kill them. Dr Scheiger, the battalion medical officer, was one of the many Germans caught by the mutineers. He personally begged Sergeant Dizdarević to spare his life, quoting the numerous times he had shown sympathy for the Bosnian recruits. Temporarily, Dizdarević relented, noting that he had no personal quarrel with the good doctor, and that he was one of a few German officers who had treated the recruits with respect.

Dr Scheiger was placed in a room with *Waffen-Obersturmführer der-SS* Halim Malkoč, the battalion's *imam*. Both officers were used as hostages. In spite of this temporary reprieve, both Scheiger and Malkoč were later strangled by Džanić and some of the other plotters. By midday on 17 September, the new divisional commander, *SS-Brigadeführer* Karl-Gustav Sauberzweig, had approached the division's communications battalion, which was the nearest unit to the engineer battalion, and headed towards the village of Villefranche-de-Rouergue and the mutineers in order to put down the revolt personally.[121]

Altogether, twenty German NCOs and officers were killed by the mutineers. It was later learned that the plotters had been in contact with the local French *Maquis* resistance cell. The chief instigator of the revolt, *Waffen-Oberscharführer der-SS* Lutfija Dizdarević preferred to escape into the woods and join the French partisans rather than face the German attack once resistance in the engineer battalion started to fall apart.[122] Attempts by the *Gestapo* to apprehend him eventually yielded results. Džanić and Dizdarević were both killed in battle fighting the Germans. In the days to come, a court martial was convened and fifty Muslim recruits were put on trial. Fourteen out of the fifty were found guilty and shot by firing squad after the court-martial proceedings were concluded.[123] The mutiny, however, caused the intended effect the communist cell had desired: the rank-and-file soldiers of the division were completely demoralised.

The *imams* and *mullahs* tried to restore calm and order, as well as reassure the Muslim recruits. The Germans even sent the Mufti of Jerusalem to the division in the hope that his presence and words of encouragement would restore the morale of the men. In addition to the fourteen recruits who were shot by firing squad, an additional 825

Muslim recruits, almost the entire contingent making up the engineer battalion, were transferred to Dachau Concentration Camp on 27 September 1943. This transfer was done in secret, while the division was enroute to Neuhammer Training Camp in Silesia. The trains carrying the men of the engineer battalion were simply diverted on the way and sent to Dachau instead. It must have been a complete surprise and a surreal moment for the inmates of Dachau to witness hundreds of men arriving as prisoners, but dressed in SS uniforms. After this step, the division was temporarily left without its engineer battalion, which had effectively been dissolved and later had to be rebuilt from scratch.

After some months had passed, 536 of the 825 soldiers sent to Dachau were deemed rehabilitated and sent to work in the *Organization Todt*. The remaining 289 men of the original engineer battalion were sent to a replacement unit stationed in Chlum, which supplied recruits for an SS penal battalion fighting in Russia. This replacement battalion was located in the Protectorate of Bohemia and Moravia (Czech territory). These unfortunate Bosnian Muslim recruits ended the war by serving in the infamous *SS-Sonderregiment 'Dirlewanger'*.

Soon after the revolt, the decision was made to transfer the division closer to Yugoslavia. With this in mind, the entire 21,065-man force was sent to Silesia. The division arrived between September and October 1943 and at the time, was composed of the following:

Table 4. Strength of the 13. Waffen-Gebirgs-Division der-SS 'Handschar' on 1 October 1943.

Officers	NCOs	Men		TOTAL
360	1,931	18,774		21,065

Instruction now resumed anew, and the unit settled down to a daily routine of recruit training. On 9 October 1943 the division was redesignated as: *13. SS-Freiwilligen-Bosnien-Herzegowinen-Gebirgs-Division [Kroatien Nr. 1]*.[124] Up until then, the two Muslim SS Mountain infantry regiments in the division had been initially numbered 1 and 2. Later still, in June 1944, the title was changed so that the title 'Bosnia-Herzegovina' was removed and the name 'Handschar' (Scimitar) was added. Now the regiments were renamed in order to designate their non-Germanic status:

Waffen-Gebirgsjäger-Regiment der-SS No. 27 (kroatische Nr.1)
Waffen-Gebirgsjäger-Regiment der-SS No. 28 (kroatische Nr.2)

On 12 January 1944 a German press release stated that:

> In order to fight Bolshevism, a Bosnian volunteer formation had been raised from the Muslim faithful... The Grand Mufti of Jerusalem was spiritually backing the unit and its purpose.[125]

Of course, no mention was made of the unit's mutiny in France and the delay in training and low morale it had caused to the Muslim faithful. At the beginning of February 1944, 110 trains carried more than 20,000 men and 8,000 mules from the division to Bosnia-Herzegovina. The German 2. *Panzerarmee,* then operating in Yugoslavia, was to receive four divisions as reinforcements that month:

392. Kroatische-Legions-Infanterie-Division
42. Jäger-Division
Panzergrenadier-Division Brandenburg
13. Waffen-Gebirgsjäger-Division der-SS 'Handschar'

Operations in Bosnia-Herzegovina

The return of the Muslim SS division to Bosnia was fraught with politically explosive questions, not merely because of the mutiny, but because the volunteers, most of whom were recruited from Eastern Bosnia, were the target of propaganda by the Bosnian Muslim leaders who sought to gain independence for Bosnia Herzegovina at the expense of the German-sponsored NDH (Croatian) government:

> The return of the 13th Muslim SS Division to eastern Bosnia, the home of most of its recruits, prompted many of its soldiers and commanders to revive their aspirations for autonomy. Their return seriously disturbed the masterminds of official German policy in the NDH. Kasche[126] sided with the NDH government in criticising the Muslim leaders' flirtation with autonomy as harmful to our state policy in this area. He observed that the Muslims were becoming more broadly dissatisfied with the Ustaše state, a sentiment that grew with domestic and international pressure on the NDH. General Sauberzweig, Commander of the 13th Muslim SS Division, disagreed, saying that the NDH existed only because of the presence of German troops.[127]

The Muslim SS division was moved through Vinkovci, Jarmina, Bačinci, Novo Selo, Bojagaci, Kukujevci, Mlasica, and Sid. One source states that the division was placed under the *V. SS-Freiwilligen-Gebirgs-Armeekorps,* but another lists the unit as being at the disposal of 2. *Panzerarmee.*

The 'Handschar' divisional headquarters was initially located in Vinkovci, Syrmia but was eventually shifted south of Brčko, in southeastern Bosnia in March 1944. On 10 March the two mountain infantry regiments were officially renumbered *Waffen-Gebirgsjäger-Regiment der-SS 27 (kroatische Nr. 1)* and *Waffen-Gebirgsjäger-Regiment der-SS 28 (kroatische Nr. 2)*. The divisional reconnaissance battalion, designated *13. SS-Aufklärungs Abteilung,* began its first anti-partisan operation when it took part in *Unternehmen Wegweiser* (Operation Signpost). The operation was aimed at clearing up the Bosut Forest and the area of Županje–Lipovac–Bosna Rača, north of the Sava River, near Brčko. Operation Signpost was conducted by the 'Handschar' division in the region marked '1' on the following map (see Figure 25). During this drive, the German *42. Jäger-Division* was also employed. By 15 March the division's *Waffen-Gebirgsjäger-Regiment der-SS 27 (kroatische Nr. 1)* was moving across the Sava River by Županja, while its sister regiment, *Waffen-Gebirgsjäger-Regiment der-SS 28 (kroatische Nr. 2)*, was located east of Brčko by Bosna Rača. Bijeljina was reached on 16 March 1944.

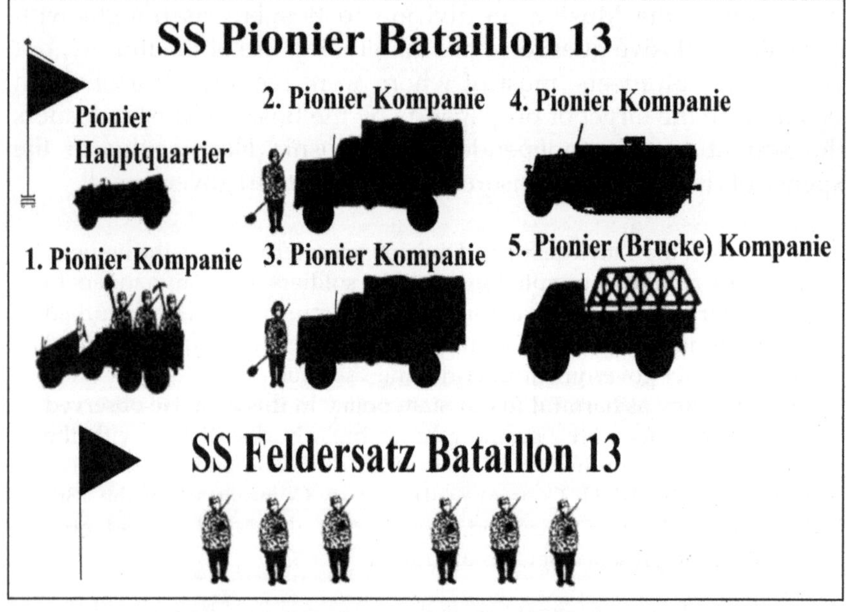

Figure 23. The SS engineer battalion and field replacement battalion of the 13. Waffen-Gebirgs-Division der-SS 'Handschar'. *(Author's line drawing)*

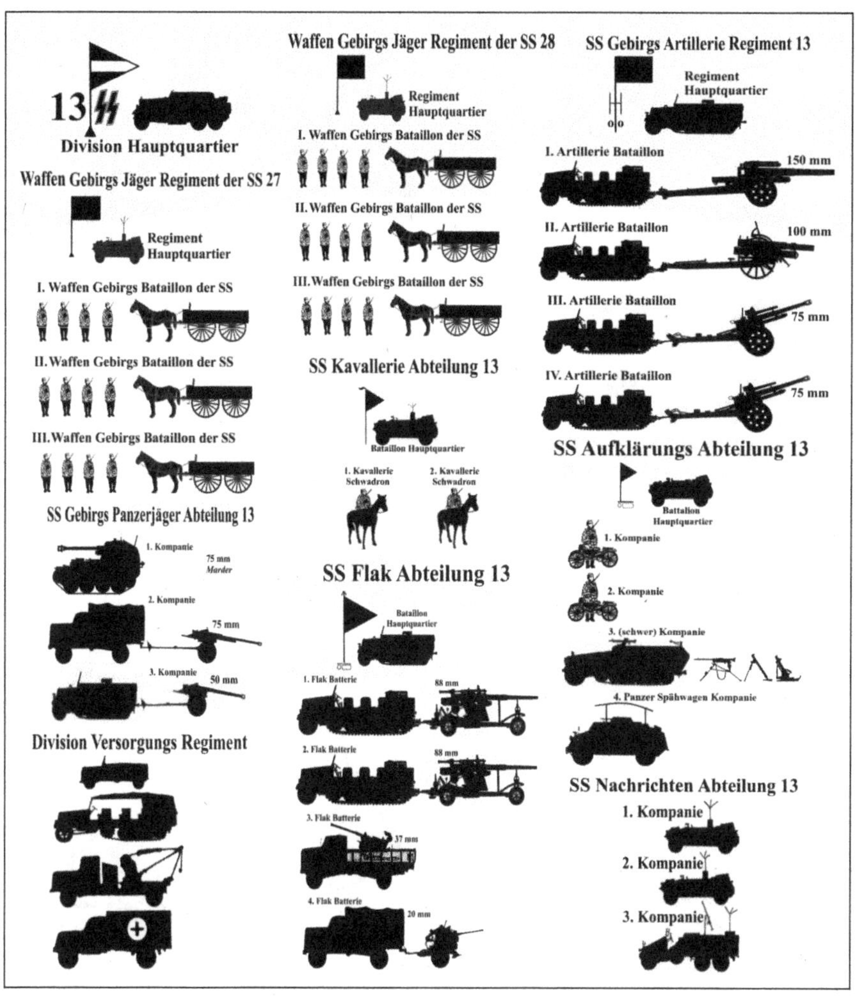

Figure 24. Schematic diagram of the 13. Waffen-Gebirgs-Division der-SS 'Handschar', May 1944. *(Author's line drawing)*

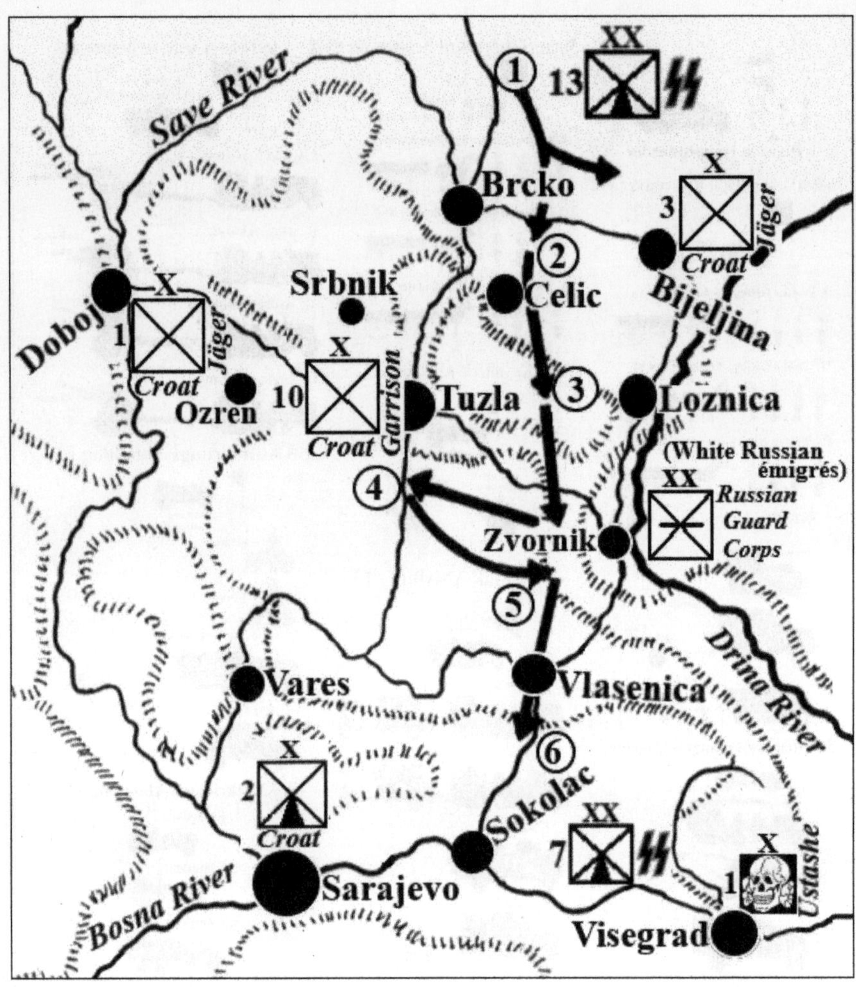

Figure 25. Area of operations of 13. Waffen-Gebirgs-Division der-SS 'Handschar' in 1944. The locations of other Axis forces are also listed. *(Author's line drawing)*

There followed a period of rest where the division established itself mainly in the area bordering Brčko–Čelic–Bijeljina (see the area labelled '2' on the map). The next operation to be launched by the division against the partisans began on 11 April 1944. This manoeuvre was codenamed *Unternehmen Osterei* (Operation Easter Egg). While the operation was in progress, the *I. Bataillon* of *Waffen-Gebirgsjäger-Regiment der-SS 28 (kroatische Nr. 2)*, which was made up purely of Albanian Muslim recruits, was withdrawn from the division and sent to Albania, where the Germans were attempting to raise an Albanian

SS mountain division called *Skanderbeg*. This Albanian unit would contain a mixture of Albanian Muslims and Catholics.

Unternehmen Osterei was quickly followed by *Unternehmen Maibaum I* (Operation May Pole I), which ran from 26 April to 5 May 1944. The area of operations for the division in this action is circled and labelled '3' on the map (see Figure 25). The heart of this drive was the attempted destruction of the partisan 3rd Proletarian Corps, a guerilla formation containing the 16th, 17th, and 36th partisan divisions. The corps was located between Vlasenica and Srebrenica. The 27th Partisan Division, which was located in the region of Romanja–Plannina, was also earmarked for elimination in order to wipe it out as a possible support for the 3rd Proletarian Corps. The SS 'Handschar' division was now under the operational control of the *V. SS-Freiwilligen-Gebirgs-Armeekorps* (5th SS Volunteer Mountain Corps). This corps also controlled the *7. SS-Freiwilligen-Gebirgs-Division 'Prinz Eugen'* (7th SS Volunteer Mountain Division 'Prinz Eugen'). The *V. SS-Freiwilligen-Gebirgs-Armeekorps* ordered the 'Handschar' division to concentrate in the region between Tuzla and Rožanj, while the SS Mountain Division 'Prinz Eugen' would be employed further south in a line between Rogatica and Sokolac (see '4' and '5' on the map).

By 1 May 1944 the 16th Partisan Division, which contained around 2,000 men, had been chased southeast and out of Vlasenica by elements of the SS 'Prinz Eugen' division. Meanwhile, the Partisan 36th Division was in the process of being attacked during Operation Signpost, which was conducted by the 'Handschar' division. The partisans were being pushed into the mountain region northwest of Drinjaca. The operation ended on 5 May and was considered a success. Operation May Pole II began on 14 May and only ran until the 18th. In this action the 'Handschar' division was not directly involved and only the SS 'Prinz Eugen' division took part. The main point of this short operation was to clean out pockets of resistance from the remnants of the 17th Partisan Division just northeast of Sarajevo, around Kladanj (see '6' on the map, Figure 25). It was during this period that members of the *7. SS-Freiwilligen-Gebirgs-Division 'Prinz Eugen'* were accused of killing innocent civilians while searching for members of the 17th Partisan Division. One brigade of the 17th Division managed to make a run for it and escaped by moving through the region east of Sarajevo, and then south to Dobropolje. It was there that elements of the 'Prinz Eugen' division caught up to the partisan brigade and engaged its men.

The month of June 1944 was spent by the Muslims in the 'Handschar' division regrouping and resting. The decision to raise a second Muslim SS division had been made early in the summer of 1944. Another locally raised corps headquarters was now organised that would, in theory, control both Muslim divisions. This was the *IX. Waffen-Gebirgs-Armeekorps der-SS* (9th Armed Mountain Corps of the SS). The title clearly showed its non-Germanic status, since all German or Germanic units were prefixed with the title SS, whereas the non-Germanic formations of the *Waffen-SS* were always referred to as 'armed unit of the SS'. The second Muslim SS division was soon titled 'Kama', even before the official order came through to form the unit, which occurred on 17 June.

Seven days earlier, on 10 June, a large batch of Muslims from the 'Handschar' division were ordered transferred over to 'Kama' in order to form its divisional cadre. Trying to raise this second Muslim SS division outside of Yugoslavia might have proven ruinous' as had already been shown by the mutiny in the 'Handschar' division. Besides, the borders of the Reich were quickly shrinking in the summer of 1944, so the decision was made to begin training and forming the unit in the region bordering the Sava, Spreča and Drina rivers. The entire formation, however, was soon sent to the province of Vojvodina, which was considered relatively free of partisan guerrillas.

The division was specifically sent to the Batschka (Banat) region of Vojvodina, which included a sizable population of racial German Serbs. One sub-unit of the 'Handschar' division was now transferred *en masse* to the forming SS 'Kama' division. This was the *13. SS Aufklärungs Abteilung* (13th SS Reconnaissance Battalion) that was now redesignated as the *23. SS Aufklärungs-Abteilung* (23rd SS Reconnaissance Battalion)[128] by the German SS-FHA (SS High Command). Another unit to be detached from the division was the *13. SS Flak Bataillon* (13th SS Anti-Aircraft Battalion). This unit was redesignated as *SS-Flak-Abteilung 509* and given over to the forming *IX. Waffen-Gebirgs-Armeekorps der-SS* (9th Mountain Corps of the SS). The next anti-partisan drive in which the 'Handschar' division took part in was nicknamed *Vollmond* (Full Moon) and began on 7 July 1944. It centred on the area between Priboj and Loznica (see '6', Figure 25).

This drive was intended to eliminate the newly reconstituted 16th Vojvodina Partisan Division, as well as the 38th Bosnian Partisan Division. These units were reported to have later been defeated by the 'Handschar' division, but remnants managed to withdraw across the Drina River. Next to occur was *Unternehmen Fliegenfänger* (Operation Fly Trap), which began on 14 July and centred on the region south of Tuzla. Later still, on 4 August, the 'Handschar' division took part in *Unternehmen Hackfleisch* (Operation Ground Meat). In the first days of September 1944, the division was ordered by the *V. SS-Freiwilligen-Gebirgs-Armeekorps* to move to the region of Vukovije, Osmaci, and

Srebrenica. It was in this area that the *13. Waffen-Gebirgs-Division der-SS 'Handschar'* battled the 6th Vojvodina Partisan Brigade.

These constant manoeuvres and movements were not without losses. Although the division had begun operations with an effective strength of over 21,000 men, by 20 September 1944 the division had an effective strength of just 14,263 men. This meant that between March and September, the 'Handschar' division had lost 7,000 men killed, wounded, and missing. The numbers of men missing also included deserters, which constituted a significant percentage of those 7,000. This is confirmed by the divisional records, which state that during these seven months of fighting, about 3,000 Muslim soldiers deserted from the unit. The remaining 4,000 casualties were those killed or wounded in battle. This averages out to about 571 men killed and wounded, with an additional 428 men deserting per month. Added together, these two figures come to about 1,000 men per month. If these casualties and desertions would have been allowed to continue, the division would have ceased to exist within the year.

These losses indicate several things. First, it shows that the division was either heavily engaged and/or was roughly handled by its own officers, thus incurring such high casualty rates. This supposition is certainly quite plausible, especially in light of the fact that the division's officer corps contained a good number of men with little or no infantry training or experience. Secondly, it shows us that a large percentage of the Muslim soldiers in the division had no desire to fight for the Germans. This may have been as a result of their mistreatment at the hands of their German training officers, or the communist inspired revolt which demoralised the unit, or both.

The Germans were hoping that the Muslims would fight well to defend their homes in Bosnia and Herzegovina, and this was a belief that should have proved correct, and yet the unit performed from mediocre to poor. It is almost certain that the forced conscription of these men also played a role in the low effectiveness of the division. Conscripted men mainly fight with less enthusiasm than real volunteers. Finally, the efforts by Ante Pavelić to torpedo the recruiting effort probably also played a part. When the Germans began to recruit Muslims for the SS 'Kama' division, they were met with a dismal recruiting effort. The manner in which the division was brought together created the following causes and effects:

> Problems arose in handling of men who formed the ethnically mixed detachments and purely volkish units of completely foreign origin. On top of this, these foreign volunteers were motivated to fight for different

> reasons than their Reich German counterparts. The result of this was that often their deployment could only occur in certain areas and only against certain enemies... These and similar difficulties considerably reduced the military quality of these units. Therefore, cases of mutinies, or refusals to fight appeared even within Waffen-SS formations. This was the case in the SS Divisions Handschar and Skanderbeg as early as the period of basic training.[129]

Yet, despite all these apparent shortcomings, the Germans had decided as early as the beginning of the summer 1944 to raise a second Muslim SS division. There is a general consensus among historians that the 'Handschar' division was not really worth the trouble to form, and that all the pampering and special attention bestowed on it by Himmler and the *Waffen-SS*, which included special Muslim diets, special religious schools, special insignia and clothing, was a wasted effort and a poor investment.[130] Nevertheless, the ever-growing dire military predicament that Germany found itself in forced the decision to create the unit.

Table 5. Strength of the 13. Waffen-Gebirgs-Division der-SS 'Handschar', 20 September 1944.

Ethnic & German Officers	Ethnic German and pure German NCOs	Ethnic German and pure German enlisted men	Total Germans
279	1,611	4,125	6,015
Muslim Officers	Muslim NCOs	Muslim Men	Total Muslims
67	339	7,842	8,248
Grand Total Officers	Grand Total NCOs	Grand Total Men	Grand Total
346	1,950	11,967	14,263

Table 5 lists the numbers of men in the division in September 1944. The list is split up by ethnic background and by rank. Although the Germans had been working on establishing a second Muslim SS division, which eventually reached the stages of early development, that unit had to be aborted for lack of recruits. The decision to disband the 'Handschar' division soon followed in late September, early October 1944. Heinrich Himmler was reported to have realised that the unit's performance, even under the most favourable of conditions, had been mediocre at best and lamentable at worst. The division actually began to lose units and men even before it was disbanded. This was because it was used as a source of recruits for other SS formations, such as the forming 'Skanderbeg' and 'Kama' divisions. When the 'Handschar' division was finally disbanded, the following divisional elements were also assigned to the *IX. Waffen-Gebirgs-Armeekorps der-SS:*

13. SS-Panzerjäger-Bataillon
13. SS-Aufklärungs-Abteilung
13. Waffen-Gebirgs-Artillerie-Regiment der-SS
13. SS-Pionier-Bataillon

These units now became the following corps troops:

SS-Panzerjäger-Abteilung 509
SS-Aufklärungs-Abteilung 509
SS-Waffen-Gebirgs-Artillerie-Regiment der-SS 509
SS-Pionier-Bataillon 509

Das Ende

What remained of the 'Handschar' division was turned into a small battlegroup in the first week of October 1944. The commander of Army Group Southeast requested Himmler's permission to transfer the Muslim SS division from Bosnia to southern Hungary, but apparently the Muslims in the division were unwilling to take any action beyond their native region. The remaining Muslim men from Bosnia and Herzegovina in the division were therefore ordered released from service. The heavy casualties and desertions, low morale and poor fighting quality, coupled by large transfers of units from the division in an attempt to form further questionably competent SS formations, all came together to destroy the 'Handschar' division. The local Bosnians were officially allowed to revert to civilian status, possibly to prevent them from doing so unofficially and potentially taking their weapons with them.

This explains the German attitude towards the Muslim soldiers in the division by late 1944. In fact, in October 1944 an additional 1,000 Muslims deserted the division. The estimated 6,000+ German and ethnic-German personnel of the now-disbanded division were grouped under a reinforced regimental battlegroup. Although there were enough men in this group equal to a brigade in strength, the unit remained categorised as a battlegroup. In October and November 1944 *Kampfgruppe Handschar* (Battlegroup Scimitar) received a reinforcement of 3,000 German sailors who had served aboard vessels operating in the

Aegean and Mediterranean Sea, mainly from Greek ports. In addition, the decision to transfer back to the *Kampfgruppe* all the battalions and the artillery regiment that had been made corps units of the *IX. Waffen-Gebirgs-Armeekorps der-SS* was made in December 1944. It is likely that the German command was hoping to reform the division.

It is reported that *SS-Standartenführer* Desiderius Hampel, who was an ethnic-German Croatian and had previously led *Waffen-Gebirgs-Regiment der-SS 27* in the division, was later given control of the entire divisional *Kampfgruppe* when he was promoted. However, another documentary source states that *SS-Sturmbannführer* Hans Hanke, who initially led *13. SS Signals Bataillon,* and later still was commander of *Waffen-Gebirgs-Regiment der-SS 27,* effectively led the 'Handschar' battlegroup in the last months of the war. German sources list Hanke as having been promoted to *SS-Obersturmbannführer* on 30 January 1945. Another source of information lists Desiderius Hampel as the commander of the 'Handschar' unit until the end of the war. This apparent confusion has been caused by the fact that Hans Hanke led a battlegroup of the 'Handschar' division that had been detached for duty with Army Group South in Hungary in the middle of October 1944, while the remainder of the division (what was left of it) was either in the process of being deactivated or regrouped.[131]

In December 1944 the *Kampfgruppe 'Handschar'*, minus the reconnaissance battalion that was already in Hungary, was located in the town of Barcs on the Drava River under *LXVIII. Armeekorps* of *2. Panzerarmee.* Sauberzweig's command of *IX. Waffen-Gebirgs-Armeekorps der-SS* lasted only until December 1944, when he was replaced by *SS-Obergruppenführer* Karl von Pfeffer-Wildenbruch. This corps was located in Budapest in December, where it was encircled later that month by Soviet mobile forces and eventually destroyed in February 1945. It was in this month that *SS-Flak-Abteilung 509* – the old *13. SS-Flak-Bataillon* – rejoined *Kampfgruppe 'Handschar'* and moved around the towns of Kaposvár and Nagykanizsa, near Lake Balaton in Hungary. The battalion was relegated to the dual role of anti-tank and anti-aircraft defence.

In fact, during its brief history, this SS Flak battalion was responsible for shooting down or destroying fifty-four bombers, five fighters, seven tanks, two guns, forty vehicles, plus other smaller enemy military equipment. *SS-Aufklärungsabteilung 509* had also rejoined the battlegroup in December 1944 when Hanke and his men returned from the front. In January 1945 the remnants of the 'Handschar' division were deemed fit enough to be activated as a division-sized formation once again. This time it lacked any Muslim soldiers and was now composed of ethnic and pure Germans. As such, its effectiveness increased dramatically. On 5 March 1945, just a day before the German Spring Awakening offensive against Soviet forces in and around Lake Balaton in Hungary, the 'Handschar' division was listed as follows:

Two strong infantry battalions
Four medium strength infantry battalions
Three average strength infantry battalions

TOTAL: Nine (9) infantry battalions

Armoured Train No. 64 and Armoured Train No. 79 attached to the division as defensive support.
Anti-tank guns available: 10
Artillery Support: six light and two heavy artillery batteries

TOTAL GUNS: 10 anti-tank and 32 artillery barrels.

Motorisation: 70 percent of the division is motorised
Combat Readiness Status: Category No. 3 – Capable of full defence.

A further troop report for the division dated 17 March 1945 showed that through an influx of personnel from rear area units of the German Army and Air Force, the 'Handschar' division was able to obtain a strength of 9,228 men, of which only 3,601 were combat troops. The combat troops were referred to as the bayonet strength in a division, since this was the actual number of men manning the line companies and other combat units. By 1945 German standards, the division was magnificently manned. The unit remained under *LXVIII. Armeekorps* of 2. *Panzerarmee* for the rest of the war. It withdrew from the region south of Lake Balaton in mid-April 1945 to avoid being encircled by Soviet and Yugoslav forces. Its line of retreat placed the division in the province of *Untersteiermark* (Lower Styria), which was part of Slovenia.

The area in Lower Styria where it was now located was around the city of Marburg (Maribor), on the Drava River. Actual capitulation of the unit did not occur until 7 May 1945 in the region just south of St. Vieth, on the Glau River, where it surrendered to members of the British Army. The men of the division hoped that their surrender to Allied troops would prevent their capture by the Tito partisans, who were surely going to judge them for their actions in Yugoslavia. The 'Handschar' division had operated in Bosnia between March and October 1944, a span of just eight months. The post-war Yugoslav government accused some German and Muslim members of the division of committing war crimes during that eight-month period. A total of thirty-eight German nationals who served in the division were extradited to Yugoslavia after the war, including the leadership of the division, such as the divisional, regimental and battalion commanders.

The final military analysis of the SS 'Handschar' division was that it was not worth forming and could be considered a failure of the Germans to exploit the manpower resources of the Muslim population in Yugoslavia. There had been various reasons why this had occurred, some of which had been outside of the control of the Germans, such as (1) Ante Pavelić's successful undermining of the German recruiting drive, and (2) the communist cell that infiltrated the division then initiated the revolt while the unit was in France. However, the German SS command was also at fault for (3) supplying the division with officers who lacked proper combat experience and mediocre leadership, and (4) sending to the division training officers and NCOs who showed nothing but arrogance and contempt towards the Muslim recruits.

The use of the Mufti of Jerusalem to try to play the religious card with the recruits proved lukewarm at best. This was because the Muslim recruits from Bosnia were less connected to the Muslims in the Middle East and therefore the admonitions and urgings of the Mufti of Jerusalem did not count as much. The history of the *13. Waffen-Gebirgs-Division der-SS 'Handschar'*, then, is a perfect example of everything that was wrong with the manner in which Germany often attempted to exploit foreign manpower resources. It also showed that just because two groups (the Germans and the Muslim community at large) shared certain things in common, this did not always guarantee cooperation or success.

The Huska Legion

Muslims were also employed in the Croatian Army. Two important formations that were established were the Huska Legion and the Hadžiefendić Legion. In 1943 Hussein (Huska) Miljković created a legion in the Cazin region of northwest Bosnia and Herzegovina. It was officially called the Muslim militia (*Muslimanska milicija*) and consisted of eleven Muslim militia battalions. In February 1944 the Huska Legion deserted to the partisans and was redesignated as the 1st Muslim Brigade of the Una Operational Group, 4th Croatian Partisan Corps. Legion personnel had no special uniforms and wore a mixture of former Croatian *Ustaše*, and *Domobran* uniforms, with the crescent and star on their fez covers. Special rank insignia was worn on the sleeves.

The Hadžiefendić Legion

In 1941 Major Muhamed Hadžiefendić proposed to Field Marshal Kvaternik, the Croatian Defence Minister, that a volunteer Muslim militia be raised in the northeast Bosnia. His plan was quickly approved and in late 1941 Hadžiefendić had formed the *Dobrovoljacki zdrug narodnog ustanka* (People's Uprising Volunteer Brigade), unofficially called the Hadžiefendić Legion. It comprised at least four to five People's Uprising Volunteer Detachments, each divided into several companies. Interestingly, one source states that (at least) the NDH police in Bosnia had not been aware of the formation:

> In late April 1942, NDH military and political centres received a report from the Tuzla police precinct, which informed the authorities that in the Usor and Sol region, a volunteer legion of the popular uprising had been formed under the command of Reserve Major Muhamed Hadžiefendić, and that it numbered between 5,000 and 6,000 men. According to the assessment of the Tuzla police, the legion was a riotous, plundering band that did not recognise NDH rule. For this reason the Tuzla authorities demanded that the legion be disbanded and its members diverted to Home Guard units. In fact, the legion had been formed by Muslim military conscripts who refused to serve as Home Guard. This was proof that the NDH military machine was disintegrating. By separating from the NDH armed forces, the Muslim militia units did not sever their relations with them. On the contrary, they continued to receive arms and ammunition from Croatian troops whose commanders counted on the militia's participation in combat against the partisans and Chetniks. The Muslim militia seemed to gain popularity among the Muslims as a force for Muslim self-defence, so its cooperation with the individual warring sides was often transitory. Surrounded by three enemies with competing military goals, the Muslim militia survived precisely because the Ustaše, Chetniks and partisans each treated them differently. The Ustaše considered them a passing occurrence and expected their members to return to their former Croatian units. The Chetniks continued to perceive them as part of the Ustaše army, while the partisans tried to recruit militia members to their own ranks.[132]

The officers and some of the NCOs of the legion wore standard Croatian Army uniforms and insignia, whilst the volunteers wore civilian clothes. Many NCOs attached army rank insignia to the collars of their civilian jackets and some companies were equipped with ex-Yugoslav helmets of the French Adrian model. In December 1942 the German Plenipotentiary in Croatia, General Glaise-Horstenau, demanded that the personnel of the legion be disciplined and uniformed, but it is not known if that order was carried out.

Chapter Four

THE KAUKASISCHER-WAFFEN-VERBÄNDE DER-SS, 1944–1945

Muslim volunteers from the Caucasus

As the fortunes of war turned against Nazi Germany, the Third Reich found itself lacking sufficient military forces to hold back the Allied onslaught. Political ideology quickly turned to pragmatic military expediency, as the *Wehrmacht* and *Waffen-SS* began to form combat formations made up of non-Aryan men in its ranks. One such example was the *Kaukasischer-Waffen-Verbände der-SS* (Caucasian Armed Brigade of the SS), a Muslim SS cavalry brigade which was organised from 1944–45. The formation never took part in combat operations, as the war came to an end shortly after it was established, but its story, however, is typical of many volunteers who served *an deutscher Seite* (on the German side).

Creation

The origins of the *Kaukasischer-Waffen-Verbände der SS* date back to the *Freiwilligen-Stamm-Division* (Volunteer Cadre Division), which was made up of people from the USSR and was initially located in France in 1944. This was the unit that supplied trained volunteers to the eastern volunteer battalions, Russian and Cossack units, and even the *162. (Turkestanische) Infanteriedivision.* The division was a conglomeration of several training regiments that were merged together in early 1944 and stationed in France.

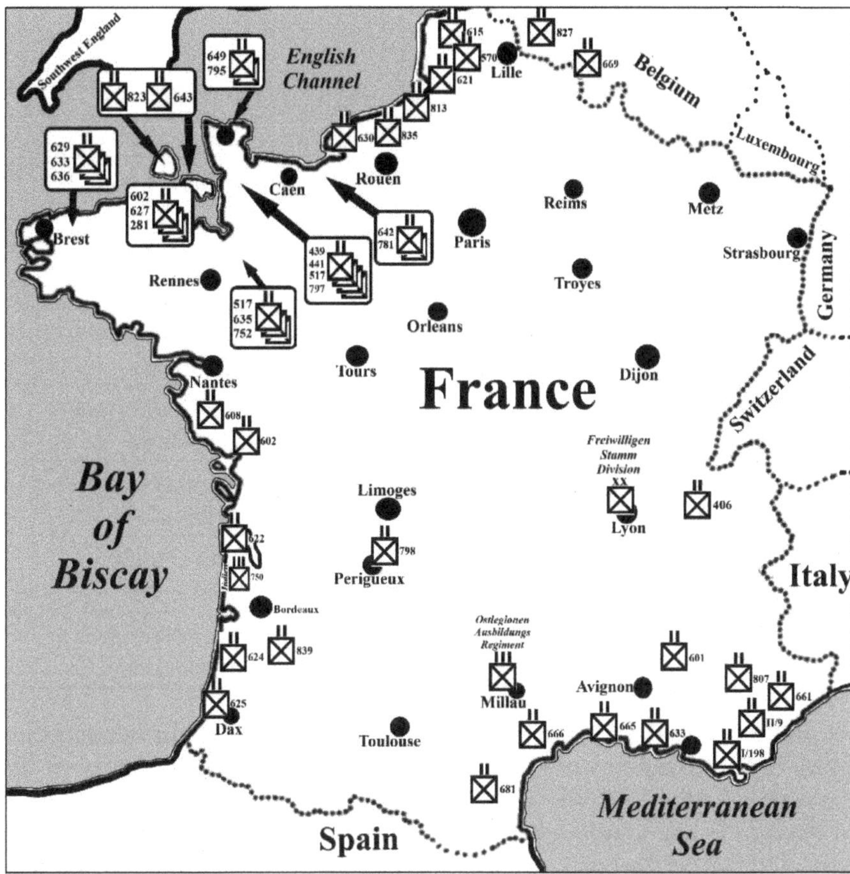

Figure 26. Location of volunteer formations from the USSR. The Volunteer Cadre Division, which supplied recruits to various volunteer units, was located near the city of Lyon. *(Author's line drawing)*

The divisional headquarters was raised on 1 February 1944 and stationed in the French city of Lyon. This headquarters would administer the various regiments, of which there were five in all, made up of differing nationalities. The regiments were split up along these racial and national lines. The order of battle for the Volunteer Cadre Division and its regiments was as follows:[133]

Table 6. Location of the Eastern Volunteer Cadre Division, 1944.

Location	Formation	Nationality
Lyon	Divisional Headquarters	Various ethnic groups
Lyon	School for volunteer formations	Various ethnic groups
Castres	Volunteer Cadre Regiment 1	North Caucasians, Turkestani, and Georgians
Mende	Volunteer Cadre Regiment 2	Azerbaijanis, Armenians, and Volga Tartars
Mende	Volunteer Cadre Regiment 2[134]	After April 1944: Ukrainians and Russians
Macon	Volunteer Cadre Regiment 3	Turkestani Volunteers for 162nd Infantry Division[135]
Namur	Volunteer Cadre Regiment 4	Russian and Ukrainian Volunteers[136]
Langres	Volunteer Cadre Regiment 5	This Regiment supplied Cossack volunteers.

At the end of 1944 General Andrey Andreyevich Vlasov, the head of the ROA, or Russian Army of Liberation, attempted to assert control over all the peoples of the USSR that were fighting on the German side. The leaders of the Caucasian peoples protested bitterly about this. They were said to accept Vlasov as the head of a liberation movement against Stalin, but his control should be kept strictly to the Russian peoples. The importance of the document for our purposes lies in the fact that the Caucasian SS Cavalry formation was mentioned, alongside other Caucasian units:

Table 7. Number of Caucasian Volunteers in 1944.

Ethnic Group	Number	Grand Total
In legion and reinforcement battalions:		
Armenians	11,000	
Azerbaijanis	13,600	
Georgians	14,000	
North Caucasians	10,000	
Total		48,600

In construction and supply units:		
Armenians	7,000	
Azerbaijanis	4,795	
Georgians	6,800	
North Caucasians	3,000	
Total		21,595
In German units:		
Army	25,000	25,000
In the *Waffen-SS and Luftwaffe*		
Waffen-SS	4,800	
Luftwaffe	2,200	
Total		7,000
Grand Total		77,195

In addition, their comments specifically mentioned the Caucasian SS formation:

> In 1942 almost all the battalions were committed to frontline service. In spite of errors and abuses, they served well and frequently earned recognition from the highest German command headquarters. There are engaged in battle in Croatia at the present time: *I. Georgisches Bergsteigerbataillon, II. Nordkaukasisches Bergsteigerbataillon, 842. Nordkaukasisches Bataillon* and *843. Nordkaukasisches Bataillon*. The abovementioned units participated in the difficult withdrawals from Greece. In Italy there are the Azerbaijani regiment of the *162. (Turkestanische) Infanteriedivision, Georgisches Bataillon II/198* and the *Kaukasischer-Waffen-Verbände der SS* presently being organised.[137]

The commander assigned to this new SS cavalry force was *SS-Standartenführer der Reserve* Arved Theuermann, who was born to a German family on 4 August 1892 in Zabela, Russia. He served in the Tsarist Army as an officer, which included a stint with the Russian 16th Hussar Regiment during the First World War. During the Russian Civil War he had served in Lithuania from 1919 until 1920 as a member of the Baltic *Landwehr-Division* (Territorial Defence Division). His military awards included the Baltic Cross 1st and 2nd Class, the Maltese Cross and the Russian Order Cross. Fluent in Russian, German and French, after the Civil War his family moved to Germany. His SS personnel file at the Berlin Document Centre (now the *Bundesarchiv* in Berlin) states that his SS number was 273,804 and was dated 10 October 1935. Before joining the SS, he had served in the SA (*Sturmabteilung*, Storm Troopers) from 1930 until 1935:[138]

> 14 December 1930 – 18 December 1931:
> Commissioned under the leadership of the SA regiment in Greifswald.
> 18 December 1931:
> Leader of the *42. SA-Regiment* (Greifswald).
> 12 March – 14 November 1933:
> Leader of the *49. SA-Regiment* (Greifswald).
> 15 November 1933 – 19 April 1934:
> Commissioned under the leadership of 10th SA Brigade 'Pomerania-West'.
> 20 April – August 1934:
> Leader of *10. SA-Brigade.*
> 8 December 1934:
> Transferred to the staff of the Chief of Training.

Strangely enough, below this listing his file also had another SS number for him, Nr. 273,509, which was dated 1 July 1930.[139] His Nazi Party membership number was 3,703; a very low Party number. The file states he received his promotion to SS lieutenant colonel on 10 October 1935. As the father of four children, initially three girls and then finally a boy, it seems he was trying very hard to raise a large family, just as the National leader of the SS, Heinrich Himmler, had requested of his men. It might have also been that Theuermann was simply chasing for a boy.

After graduating from high school, Theuremann had attended a higher education school in Hannover before joining the SA. After joining the SS in 1935, he went through the SS Officers' Academy at Bad Tolz and was assigned to Higher SS District West from 1 May to 1 October 1937.[140] He next served on the staff of the XXth SS Military District (Kiel) from 1 October 1937 until 1 April 1940. His next tour of duty was on under Command Staff East from 27 June 1941 until 1 April 1942, before being assigned as commander of the Legion Nederland from 1 April to 11 July 1942. After this he was placed on Himmler's Personal Staff for one month, while being attached to *SS-Ersatzbataillon Ost* East between 11 July and 12 August 1942. It was then that Theuermann was assigned to the staff of the *Höhere-SS und Polizeiführer-Kaukasien,*[141] a post he held from 1 December 1942 until 9 April 1943. His next post was on the cadre staff of the forming Latvian volunteer SS division, which he held from 9 April until 1 November 1943. His next assignment was on the reserve list of the SS-FHA from 1 November 1943 until 20 December 1944. He was then posted as the local SS leader at Bad Saarow from 20 December 1944 until 1 January 1945, when he was assigned as commander of the forming Caucasian SS cavalry formation. The actual order sending him to command the unit was dated 25 January 1945, although the official date of his posting was 20 December 1944.[142]

Preparations for organising the *Kaukasischer-Waffen-Verbände der SS* however, had begun even earlier. *SS-Obersturmbannführer* Walter Blume, of the SS-FHA was assigned to help organise the Caucasian Armed Brigade of the SS.[143] Records show that as early as 31 October 1944, the regimental commanders for the unit had been chosen and were:[144] Colonel Israfil Bey, Colonel Kutschuk Ulagaj, Colonel V. Sarkisjan, and Colonel Michael-Pridon Zulukidse. Colonel Israfil Bey, as well as the other regimental officers, was offered the rank of *Waffen-Standartenführer der-SS* (colonel of the armed SS).

Bey was in charge of the Azerbaijani volunteers, while Ulagaj (also spelled Ulagay) was the assigned commander of the North Caucasian soldiers. *Waffen-Standartenführer der-SS* Michael-Pridon Zulukidse, a Georgian prince, was to lead the Georgian contingent. Each regiment would contain two cavalry battalions, with the North Caucasian and Azerbaijani cavalry battalions being trained and organised by the Replacement Battalion of the *22. SS-Freiwilligen-Kavallerie-Bataillon*, while the Replacement Battalion of the *8. SS-Freiwilligen-Kavallerie-Bataillon* trained the two Georgian cavalry battalions.

The first regiment to be ready for employment was the Georgian SS cavalry regiment, which completed training in November 1944.[145] However, several battalions of Caucasian peoples were already assigned to the unit in September. The *Nordkaukasisches Bataillon 836*, which had 6-700 men left, was earmarked for the Caucasian SS cavalry unit although it was still withdrawing from France and was presently located in Belfort. On 20 January 1945, Cadre Regiment 1 of the Volunteer Cadre Division,[146] was at Neuhammer Training Camp, in Germany.[147] Unfortunately, the unit only had 375 men left; barely half a battalion to work with.

The head of the North Caucasian people, Kasi Kasbek, was located in Paluzza, northern Italy. It was there that he had a leadership school plus a hospital for wounded Caucasian volunteers, run by Professor Dr Ketschkarov.[148] The decision to send the forming SS cavalry unit to northern Italy was partly made by *SS-Standartenführer* Fritz Arlt, the head of the *Leitstelle-Ost* (Control Centre East) staff, who was responsible for ethnic groups from the Soviet Union.[149] He was also in charge of the *Flüchtlings-Leitstelle* (Refugee Coordination Centre).

A document dated 21 October 1944, and written by Arlt, listed the recruiting potential for the forming *Kaukasischer-Waffen-Verbände der SS*.[150] In the letter, Arlt stated that he estimated there to be 30,000 potential Caucasian volunteers in German-held PoW camps, with an additional 10,100 more likely recruits in German work and construction units. Furthermore, his statistics showed that 60,000 more Caucasian recruits were already in the hands of the *Wehrmacht*, and that of this number perhaps 10-20,000 had already been either killed, wounded, captured, or had deserted. This still left a large pool of possible volunteers with which to raise the formation, a good number of which were in the legion volunteer battalions.[151]

German author Joachim Hoffman, an expert on the Russian volunteer movement, states clearly that the Armenian, Azerbaijani, Georgian, North Caucasian, and Turkestani volunteers were earmarked for the *Kaukasischer-Waffen-Verbände der SS* and the *Osttürkischer Waffen-Verband der SS*.[152] This means that any units made up of these people in late 1944–1945 were earmarked for these two SS brigades. However, there were always exceptions as to why some of these units never made it to their assigned formation. For example, as late as 15 March 1945, the *644. Ukrainische Gardekompanie* and the *825. Wolga-Tatarische Kompanie* were performing railway security duty under the German 2. *Armee* in Prussia.[153]

Another example was the 1,600-man *822. Georgische Infanterie-Bataillon* (the 'Tamar' Battalion), stationed on Texel Island off the Dutch coast. On 6 April 1945 it mutinied, and in the process, killed all 400 Germans in the battalion. It took the Germans until the end of April before they finally put the revolt down.[154] Only a few Germans, including the battalion commander, *Major* Klaus Breitner, managed to escape to warn the German command of the mutiny.

The formations that have been tentatively identified as having helped to form the *Kaukasischen Waffen-Verbände der SS* included the following units:[155] *835. Nordkaukasische Bau-Bataillon,*[156] the *837. Wolga-Finnische Bataillon,*[157] the *781. Turkestanische Bataillon,* the *783. Turkestanische Bataillon,* the *786. Turkestanische Bataillon,* the *789. Turkestanische Bataillon,* the *795. Georgische Bataillon,* the *797. Georgische Bataillon,* the *799. Georgische Bataillon* and the *815. Armenische Bataillon.*

In addition, there were several battalions that were dissolved in early 1944, with the personnel from these units being transferred to other active battalions. It may well be that these men were processed through the newly created Volunteer Cadre Division in France. Those battalions included the following formations: 792nd Turkestani Battalion, *792. Turkestanische Bataillon,* the *793. Turkestanische Bataillon,* the *794. Turkestanische Bataillon,* the *820. Aserbaidschanische Bataillon,* the *839. Turkestanische Bataillon, das 840. Turkestanische Bataillon, das 841. Turkestanische Bataillon* and the *842. Turkestanische Bataillon.* As stated previously, the *Kaukasischer-Waffen-Verbände der SS* was formed with the remnants of the *Freiwilligen-Stamm-Regiment 1* (1st Volunteer Cadre Regiment).

The *Freiwilligen-Stamm-Division* was raised from the following battalions: *Freiwilligen-Stamm-Regiment 1* (North Caucasian volunteers), *I./370. Turkestanische Bataillon,* the *II./4. Georgische Bataillon,* the *I./9. Georgische Bataillon* and the *II. /4. Nordkaukasische Bataillon.* These battalions were all disbanded and sent to Castres, in southern France, in February 1944: *Freiwilligen-Stamm-Regiment Nr. 2* (Volunteer Cadre Regiment No. 2), the *804. Aserbaidschanische Bataillon,* the *806. Aserbaidschanische Bataillon,*[158] the *II./9. Armenische Bataillon,*[159] the *832. Wolga-Tatarische Bataillon,* the *833. Wolga-Tatarische Bataillon* and the *834. Wolga-Tatarische Bataillon.*

The following units were all disbanded and sent to Mende, southern France, in February 1944: *Freiwilligen-Stamm-Regiment Nr. 3,* the *792. Turkestanische Bataillon,* the *794. Turkestanische Bataillon,* the *839. Turkestanische Bataillon,* the *841. Turkestanische Bataillon* and the *842. Turkestanische Bataillon.* The *Freiwilligen-Stamm-Regiment Nr. 3* was to provide replacements for the *162. (Turkestanische) Infanterie-Division.* As for *Freiwilligen-Stamm-Regiment Nr. 4,* this regiment was formed in March from Ukrainian and Russian volunteers and was to serve replacements for units made up of these two Soviet peoples. At first the unit of Caucasian cavalry volunteers in northern Italy was referred to as the *Freiwilligen-Brigade-Nordkaukasien,* we know that it contained around 5,000 men with 2,000 dependants.

The title of the *Kaukasischer-Kavallerie-Brigade der-SS* was eventually changed to *Kaukasischer-Waffen-Verbände der-SS.* One source says that the brigade began with 4,800 men, then was raised to 5,000. The German liaison officers for the brigade were *Hauptmann der Polizei* Paul Theurer, *SS-Obersturmbannführer* Hubert Ritter von Aichinger and *SS-Standartenführer der Reserve* Arved Theuermann.[160] There was also *SS-Obersturmführer* Josef Werner, who led the communications battalion (two companies).

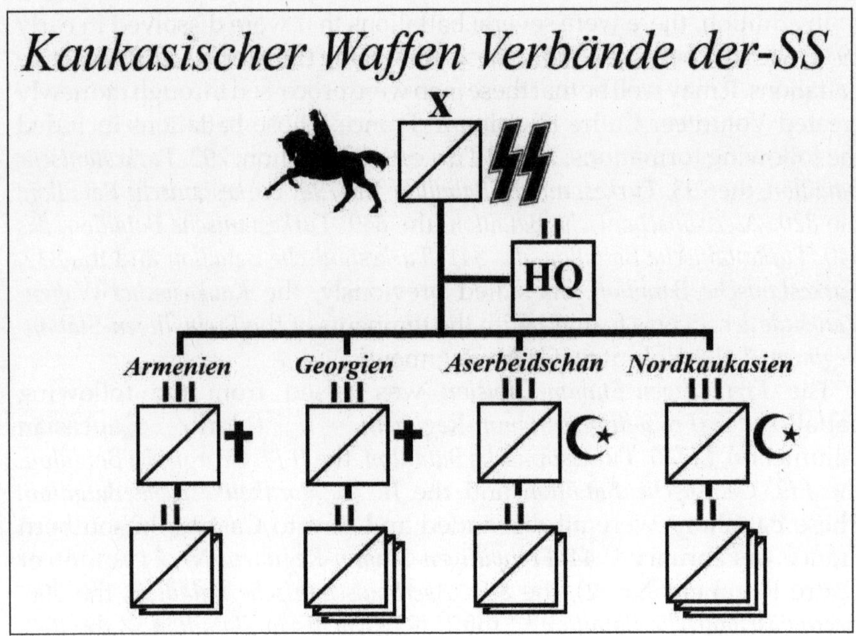

Figure 27. Schematic drawing of the organisation of the Kaukasischer-Waffen-Verbände der-SS in December 1944. *(Author's line drawing)*

National insignias and organisation

On 24 November 1944 *SS-Hauptsturmführer* Dr Rainer Olzscha, of *Amtsgruppe D* of the *SS-Hauptamt* submitted a report detailing the insignia to be worn by the men in each regiment of the *Kaukasischer-Waffen-Verbände der SS*. The regiments were named *Waffengruppe der-SS* (Armed Group of the SS), and the *Waffengruppe der-SS Georgien* would continue to wear the national insignia on their left sleeve. The others, the *Waffengruppe der-SS Armenien, Waffengruppe der-SS Nordkaukasien,* and *Waffengruppe der-SS Aserbeidschan,* would also continue to wear their national insignia. In addition, each *Waffengruppe der-SS* would be entitled to wear a black cuff band on the lower left sleeve, with the title of the regiment sewn in silver thread lettering.[161] Each *Waffengruppe der-SS* was the equivalent of a regiment in size and contained two or three cavalry battalions. Each cavalry battalion contained four cavalry squadrons, one of which was considered a heavy squadron because they had more machine guns and mortars. A German *Kriegsgliederung* (organisational structure of military forces) for 1944 contained a detailed outline of how an Kaukasischer-Waffen-Verbände der SS was organised.[162]

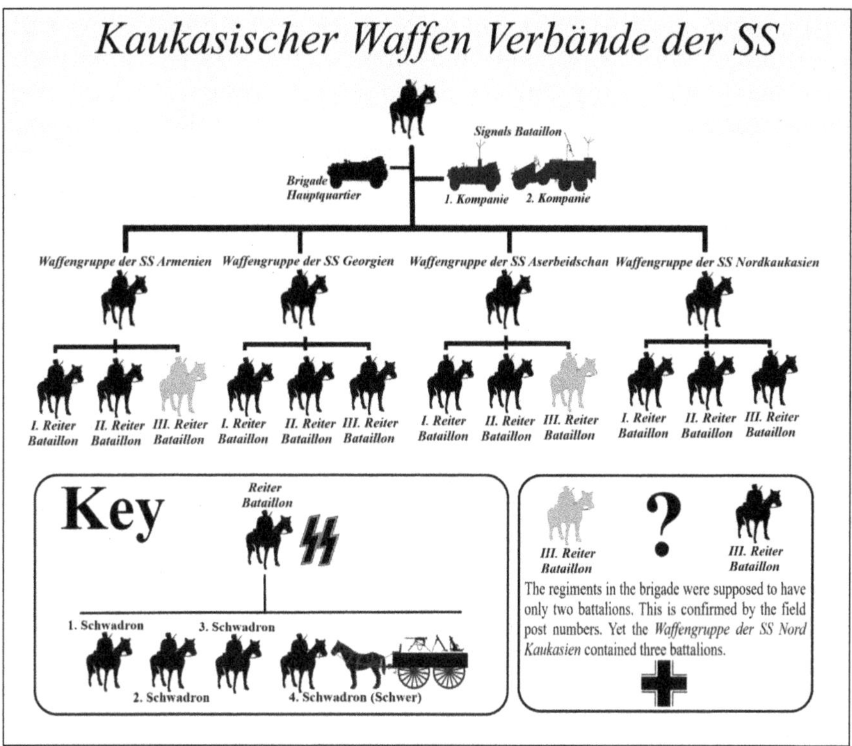

Figure 28. Schematic diagram of the Kaukasicher-Waffen-Verbände der-SS. *(Author's line drawing)*

It appears that the main reasons why Arved Theuermann had been chosen to command the *Kaukasischer Waffen Verbände der SS* was (1) his knowledge of the Russian language and (2) his service on the staff of the *Höhere-SS und Polizeiführer-Kaukasien*. This tour of duty in the Caucasus, however, had been brief. Other officers who had served with Theuermann in that command included:[163] *SS-Sturmbannführer* Otto Böttcher, *SS-Hauptsturmführer* Otto Krumbein, *SS-Hauptsturmführer* Willi Krueger, *SS-Hauptsturmführer* Otto Thorbeck, *SS-Obersturmführer* Hans-Otto Jäger, *SS-Untersturmführer* Werner Schmidt, and *SS-Untersturmführer* Hugo Isebarth.

Personnel

While Theuermann was the typical ethnic German from Russia, the regimental commanders of the brigade had some interesting careers and similar backgrounds. Kutschuk Ulagaj, for example, who was the commander of the *Waffengruppe der SS Nordkaukasien*, was born a Circassian and was a Muslim by faith. He had graduated from an academic school in Krasnodar and on 6 August 1913 had graduated from the Tsarist Army Cavalry School at Yelisavetgrad. Ulagaj had served in the Tsarist army and had won numerous medals, including the Dagger of St. George, which had an inscription describing his bravery in combat.[164] He had served as a cavalry officer and by 1917 had been promoted to captain. He returned to the North Caucasus Mountains in 1917 and helped to organise a White Russian cavalry formation. His cavalry unit fought in the North Caucasus Mountains until 1 October 1920, at which time they withdrew and fought their way to the Crimea, where Ulagaj joined Wrangel's White Russian forces. He served there as commander of the 3rd Kuban Cossack Cavalry Regiment and ended the war as a colonel. He and his family then left the Soviet Union and immigrated to Poland after losing the civil war.

He continued his activities in the cavalry by next serving as an officer of the Polish Army. When the Bolshevik government tried to take lands that belonged to Poland, a war broke out between the USSR and Poland in the early 1920s. In this short-lived war, Ulagaj served on the Polish side with distinction. In 1924 he and his family moved to Albania, where Ulagaj was able to obtain a commission in the Albanian Army as a cavalry officer. He served in the Albanian Army from 1924 until 1937. Ulagaj's father was a career public advisor who spoke Russian, Albanian, Italian, and Croatian. The first mention of Ulagaj serving in the German Army was a note in his personnel file that stated he had been on the staff of the German command in Belgrade, Yugoslavia in 1942. It is likely that he might have served initially in the *Russisches Schutzkorps* and then been placed on the permanent staff of the German command in Belgrade.[165]

On 12 December 1944 Ulagaj was inducted into the *Waffen-SS* and sent to the *SS Panzergrenadier Ausbildungs und Ersatz Bataillon 1,* where he would be clothed and outfitted. On the same date he was given the rank of *Waffen-Standartenführer der-SS.*[166] This was different to the rank of *SS-Standartenführer,* in that it denoted that the person holding the rank was a non-Aryan. At this time, Ulagaj's wife and children were staying at the Hotel Aschgan in Villach, in southern Austria, just across the border from Slovenia.

What is fascinating about Ulagaj's history towards the end of 1944 is his connection to *Waffen-Untersturmführer der-SS* Tscherim Soobzokov, a Circassian whose affiliation with the Germans had begun in 1942. Soobzokov had actually got into trouble in 1941 when he had struck the judge who had sentenced his brother to a term in a Soviet prison. He had hence been placed in a Red Army penal battalion and had been wounded in the shoulder in 1941. After this, he was sent to rehabilitate in a military hospital in his home region, although he stated that he received little medicine or medical care. When the Germans arrived in his native land in July 1942, it was not long before the 18-year-old Soobzokov volunteered for service. It is not surprising that as a Circassian, Soobzokov would volunteer to serve on the German side against the Russians. In fact, even today, most Circassians hold Russians with disdain and resentment given what Russia did to the Circassian people under the rule of Tsar Alexander II, when a genocide was perpetrated between 1860 and 1869.[167] A month after volunteering, Soobzokov became a junior clerk in the local German police station. However, he eventually won the disfavour of the local German police officer in charge of the station, and so in the autumn of 1942 he joined a frontline unit to avoid serving under him:

> The Germans had formed a battalion, the 800th Battalion,[168] of our people to fight with their army. I don't know where they got all the people. Some were probably prisoners of war who joined to keep from starving. In late September, this battalion passed through our town to fight the Red Army 30 miles away, and I asked to go with them. To me were given two carts and horses, and my job was to supply the battalion horses with hay. I was only in one fight – some Red Army troops attacked us once from the forest and I didn't run away. I deserted from the battalion in February of 1943 and lived with a group of refugees. In June of 1943, in the town of Partizani, in Ukraine, one person who is now living here in New Jersey pointed me out to the Germans. I was picked up by the German military police and they told me I would be shot within 48 hours. But some of our elders talked them out of it, and I was taken back into the armed forces and sent to the front in the Kuban sector.[169]

Soobzokov managed to get himself out of the battalion by claiming that his shoulder wound was giving him trouble. He was sent to a legion hospital in Poland where he says he received little medical care – much like he had experienced while under the Red Army. He managed to escape from Poland and was in Hungary in 1944 when the German military field police caught up to him:

> In November 1944, I was taken into custody again in Hungary and accused of hiding Soviet partisans, which was totally untrue. They put me through a tough interrogation… they beat me around the head a lot, on and off, for about two weeks. I was released with the help of an elderly man who was an officer with Vlasov. He was able to talk the Feldgendarmerie [German Military Field Police] out of shooting me. By this time the land was shrinking, you could not move around anymore.[170] I told the whole truth to a professor I knew, and he took me

> to meet General Kutschuk Ulagaj, who was recruiting Circassians for the Germans. He had been a Colonel in the Tsarist army, and his name was known to all Circassians. My wife's grandfather had once hidden him from the communists, around 1920. He escaped from the Russians and had been living in Berlin. He told me that I was in a lot of trouble but that he would try and help me. [171]

Thus, it was *Waffen-Standartenführer der-SS* Kutschuk Ulagaj, the commander of the *SS-Waffengruppe-Nordkaukasien* (North Caucasus Armed Group of the SS), who offered Soobzokov a way to avoid being shot: join his regiment and avoid execution. It was in this way that Soobzokov came to be posted to the Caucasian Armed Brigade of the SS on 4 January 1945, thus saving himself from a Red Army or German Army firing squad, or at the very least, from a Soviet Gulag or German concentration camp. It should be noted that there is no way to verify Soobzokov's story about deserting the 800th North Caucasian Battalion and almost being shot by the Germans, if not for the intervention of the Circassian elders.

The commander of the *Waffengruppe der SS Georgien* was *Waffen-Standartenführer der-SS* Michael-Pridon Zulukidse. He had been born on 8 October 1894 in Tiflis, Georgia, and had served in the Georgian Army, earning the Kaiser Wilhelm Order of Anna medal (3rd and 4th class), and the Stanislaus Medal (3rd and 4th class) with laurel crowns. He graduated from high school in Elisaethpol in 1912 and then attended the Tsarist cavalry school in St. Petersburg. He received his commission as a second lieutenant in October 1914 and was assigned to the Russian 7th Uhlan Regiment. He later attended law school in St. Petersburg but only completed three semesters. While serving on the Romanian front as a battalion commander in the Tsarist 7th Cavalry Division, Zulukidse was captured when the division was decimated.

The Austro-Hungarians and Germans were keen on sowing division in Tsarist Russia. To that end, they convinced Zulukidse and eight other Georgian officers and 120 other ranks from the destroyed 7th Russian Cavalry Division, to help the Austro-Hungarian military by forming a Georgian cavalry regiment which was intended to help form the core of a Georgian Army that would help give Georgia its independence. It was in Georgia that Zulukidse's unit was merged with the Georgian 2nd Hussar Regiment on 28 March 1918. His cavalry formation eventually ended up becoming a part of the White Russian forces and as a result, was instrumental in helping to defeat the Red Army holding Akhaltsikhe. His regiment was later sent to Tiflis to assist the city commandant in clearing the capital of Bolshevist Anarchists.[172] Zulukidse described quite fully his service in those days:

> With my same two squadrons I was ordered to Letschmum under General Shobataschvilli to fight the rebels. After this operation on July 28th 1918, I received the order to free the town of Abastumani which was being held by the Turks. Besides my two squadrons I was given an infantry battalion. After the battle of Sekari Pass on August 4th I occupied the town the next day and was commandant until August 15th. By the outbreak of the Georgian-Armenian war I was called to Tiflis and named the commander of the 2nd Hussar Regiment after which we were sent to the Armenian front. Here I was a group commander to the left flank. The war ended with the destruction of the Armenian troops and I successfully took part in all the operations. On January 5th 1919 I was promoted to colonel. On May 1st I was sent to Ossetia to put down a Bolshevist rebellion. After clearing this place of the Bolshevist bandits on May 27th I was named commandant of the government district of Arthvili. I remained here until the Bolshevist army invaded Georgia, upon which I formed a special cavalry formation to be used on the Tiflis front. On February 25th 1921 Tiflis fell and my unit was sent to defend the town of Batum from the Turks. With my cavalry unit and a few infantry units under my orders, the town was freed of the Turks, who lost 2,000 men and 60 officers. After the full occupation of Georgia by the Bolshevists I began my illegal actions, which were carried on in contact with Colonel Kaichorso, the famous leader of the Georgian rebellion of 1924. In 1923 I had to break off my fight against the Bolshevists under special circumstances and flee to Turkey. [173]

From Turkey, Michael-Pridon Zulukidse immigrated to France, where he made his living by first being a factory hand and then working as a truck driver. On 8 April 1922 his wife gave birth to a son, Konstantine Gleimuras Zulukidse. His days as an officer and prince were now behind him. For many years he worked in low-paying jobs while attending a local school at night to learn the French language. In 1936 he volunteered to join the nationalist Spanish Falange to fight the Republican Spanish government. The Spanish republic consisted of people who supported democracy, but also contained people who believed in communism, socialism, and even anarchism. Even after so many years in exile, the resentment Zulukidse held over the loss of his country to the Bolshevik revolution was deep enough in his convictions to want to oppose it, even if that meant opposing it in Spain.

When France fell in July 1940, the new Vichy French government needed to reorganise its army. The problem Philippe Pétain's government had in 1940 was one of loyalty. A segment of French society was opposed to any kind of coexistence with the Nazis. That French camp was led by Colonel (later General) Charles De Gaulle. Prime Minister Pierre Laval made it a necessity to infuse men who would be loyal to the Vichy French government, and the best way to do that was to recruit men with known anti-communist sentiments. This was especially true after 22 June 1941, when the Soviet Union became a part of the Allies fighting the Axis powers. Zulukidse was approached and asked if he would accept a commission in the Vichy French Army in Syria.

He was told that in the future there may be a chance the French Army might enter the Caucasus against the Russians, and the French General Staff needed officers who knew the countryside and its people. This was a blatant lie or, at best, wishful thinking. Nevertheless, Zulukidse accepted the offer. His regiment saw action in Syria and was sent against the British forces advancing from Palestine. On 1 January 1941 he had been made commander of a Vichy French cavalry in the Spahi Regiment in Algiers, where on 25 January 1941 he and his squadron put down what he termed as a communist inspired rebellion in a Vichy French infantry regiment. From March through to September 1941, he took part in Vichy French army manoeuvres in North Africa.

In September 1941 he was told that the French were forming a regiment of volunteers to fight in the Soviet Union, and so, he and forty other ex-Tsarist officers travelled to Versailles, the home base of the *German-sponsored Französisches Infanterie-Regiment 638* in order to join them.[174] He and his comrades remained in the regiment for three weeks until the German command told them that they had to be withdrawn because they were not French born. In those heady days of late 1941, the Germans were still arrogant and full of bluster, believing that these Tsarist-era officers were not needed. However, in October 1942 Zulukidse and others like him were recalled to Germany and were sent to the Reich Ministry for Eastern Affairs in Berlin and offered the opportunity to fight in Russia. After signing on and swearing fealty, Zulukidse and his comrades were sent to Kielce, Poland to a Russian PoW camp run by *SS-Sturmbannführer* Geibel.

In Kielce, he was entrusted with forming a Caucasian unit from Soviet prisoners of war and served as officer and training officer in this unit throughout 1943. The volunteers were initially tasked with guarding other prison camps. This was likely a battalion of eastern volunteers, one of many, that served to occupy Poland during the war. The men also took part in anti-partisan operations. In 1944 the formation was disbanded and he and 100 other men were sent to France where they served as *Waffen-SS* guard personnel.[175]

Between 1 August 1944 and 1 February 1945 *Waffen-Standartenführer der-SS* Michael-Pridon Zulukidse served as a reserve officer in the *8. SS-Kavallerie-Ausbildungs- und Ersatz-Bataillon*. From 1 February 1945 he was a part of the forming *Kaukasischer-Waffen-Verbände der SS*. It was no coincidence that NCOs and officers from the *8. SS-Kavallerie-Ausbildungs- und Ersatz-Bataillon* helped to train and organise the *Waffengruppe der SS Georgien* and its two cavalry battalions. The *22. SS-Kavallerie-Ausbildungs- und Ersatz-Bataillon*, meanwhile, helped to train and organise the *Waffengruppe der SS Nordkaukasien* and the *Waffengruppe der SS Aserbeidschan*.

The personnel file that remains of Muhammed Israfil Bey is quite small. What few documents there are state that Bey had a wife, Fatima Beyraschenska, and the couple had two children. His daughter was born in 1929 and his son in 1932. In 1944 the boy was aged 12 and daughter was 15.

The following officers were in command of the *Kaukasischer-Waffen-Verbände der-SS* as of 6 March 1945:[176]

Table 8. Command Roster of the Kaukasischer-Waffen-Verbände der-SS, December 1944.

Brigade Commander	*SS-Standartenführer der Reserve*	Arved Theuermann
Ia	*SS-Obersturmbannführer*	Hubert Ritter von Aichinger
Ic	*SS-Hauptsturmführer der Reserve*	Emanuel von Jaskiewicz
Commander Armed Group of the SS Armenian	*Waffen-Standartenführer der-SS*	V. Sarkisjan
Commander I. Battalion, Armed Group of the SS Armenian		
Commander II. Battalion, Armed Group of the SS Armenian		
Commander Armed Group of the SS Azerbaijani	*Waffen-Standartenführer der-SS*	Muhamed Israfil Bey

Commander I. Battalion, Armed Group of the SS Azerbaijani		
Commander II. Battalion, Armed Group of the SS Azerbaijani		
Commander Armed Group of the SS Georgian	*Waffen-Standartenführer der-SS*	Pridon Zulukidse
Commander I. Battalion, Armed Group of the SS Georgian		
Commander II. Battalion, Armed Group of the SS Georgian		
Commander III. Battalion, Armed Group of the SS Georgian		
Commander Armed Group of the SS North Caucasus	*Waffen-Standartenführer der-SS*	Ulagaj Kutschuk
Commander I. Battalion, Armed Group of the SS North Caucasus		
Commander II. Battalion, Armed Group of the SS North Caucasus		
Commander III. Battalion, Armed Group of the SS North Caucasus		

Other officers in the Caucasian Armed Brigade of the SS:		
	Waffen-Hauptsturmführer der-SS	Akaki Barkalaja
	Waffen-Obersturmführer der-SS	Abdul Abubakarov
	Waffen-Obersturmführer der-SS	Misost Dzhido
	Waffen-Obersturmführer der-SS	Ramasan Dujakulov
	Waffen-Obersturmführer der-SS	Chaibulla Magomayev
	Waffen-Obersturmführer der-SS	Anatolie Schakmann
	Waffen-Obersturmführer der-SS	Tscherim Soobzokov
	Waffen-Obersturmführer der-SS	Magomed Uschano
	Waffen-Untersturmführer der-SS	Achmet Dikayev
	Waffen-Untersturmführer der-SS	Ismail Dscharimov
	Waffen-Untersturmführer der-SS	Georg Kordsachia
	Waffen-Untersturmführer der-SS	Harun-Raschid Magomayev

By 3 November 1944, the armed groups of the SS Georgian, Armenian, Azerbaijani and North Caucasus were in different stages of development. While each regiment was to contain about 1,200 men, some were over strength. One of these was the Armed Group of the SS North Caucasus, which had a strength of 1,538 officers and men.[177] The average strength of each of the three battalions was just over 500 men. The full distribution of officers and men in this group as of 3 November 1944 was as follows:

Table 9. Strength of the North Caucasus Armed Group of the SS.

Formation	Officers	NCOs	Men	Total
Regimental Staff	20	15	12	47
1st Cavalry Battalion Staff	16	8	21	45
1st Cavalry Squadron	7	17	64	88
2nd Cavalry Squadron	8	18	60	86
3rd Cavalry Squadron	10	20	97	127
4th Cavalry Squadron	6	17	72	95
Total:	47	80	314	441
2nd Cavalry Battalion Staff	5	6	3	14
5th Cavalry Squadron	5	12	79	96
6th Cavalry Squadron	4	13	57	74
7th Cavalry Squadron	4	13	44	91
8th Cavalry Squadron	4	10	69	83
Total:	22	54	282	358
3rd Cavalry Battalion Staff	6	15	38	59
9th Cavalry Squadron	3	18	131	152
10th Cavalry Squadron	3	17	101	121
11th Cavalry Squadron	1	17	93	111
12th Cavalry Squadron	1	24	119	144
Total:	14	91	482	587
13th Cavalry Squadron	5	15	72	92
14th Cavalry Squadron	-	-	-	-
GRAND TOTAL	108	255	1,162	1,525

The existence of the III. Battalion has been verified but not for the other regiments. The field post numbers confirm that the regiments in the brigade were supposed to have only two battalions. Therefore, it is not clear if only the North Caucasus regiment was the only regiment with three battalions, or if any of the other regiments in the brigade also contained three cavalry battalions. The commander of Armed Group of the SS Armenian was a certain *Waffen-Standartenführer der-SS* V. Sarkisjan. No data is available on this officer. We know that this SS cavalry brigade remained stationed in northern Italy for the rest of the war. The actual transfer of the unit from Neuhammer Training Camp to Paluzza occurred in early January 1945. The date for the transfer order was 30 December 1944.

The End

In late April 1945 a Cossack officer reported to the combined Cossack-German headquarters of General Pyotr Nikolayevich Krasnov in Tolmezzo. He announced that the Osoppo Partisan Brigade, which was not communist, had captured the Georgian prince Michael-Pridon Zulukidse, and his entire 3rd Battalion. Although, initially at least, the story was accepted, it was not true. In reality, Zulukidse had surrendered his command after the guerrillas had promised to spare his life and that of his men.[178] What is notable about this event is not so much that it shows how discipline was breaking down as the war was coming to an end, but that the battalion that surrendered alongside Zulukidse was the '3rd Battalion'. Again, each regiment in the brigade was supposed to contain only two cavalry battalions. This episode, therefore, pretty much affirms the existence of a 3rd Battalion in the Georgian regiment of the *Kaukasischer-Waffen-Verbände der SS*.

Like Zulukidse, General Krasnov was now offered the same choice, but he chose to refuse to surrender and moved his men and horses to southern Austria. In the beginning of 1945, the *Kaukasischer-Waffen-Verbände der SS* was still located in northern Italy. It was not used against the Red Army or the western Allies but continued to remain 'forming' until it meekly surrendered to British forces in early May 1945. Tscherim Soobzokov's story described the attitude he had shortly after the war ended and even decades later, when he was accused of being a war criminal. While his particular case may or may not be prevalent throughout the history of the unit's volunteers, it is nonetheless a fitting end to the story of this *Kaukasischer-Waffen-Verbände der-SS*.

> I never had anything to do with fighting in the SS, because this division had not completed its formation. Actually, I think the idea was to keep PoWs out of combat and out of the hands of the Russians. We were almost disconnected from Berlin. Nobody was under my command, and I wasn't under anybody's command. What stupid person is going to join the SS at the end of 1944?[179]

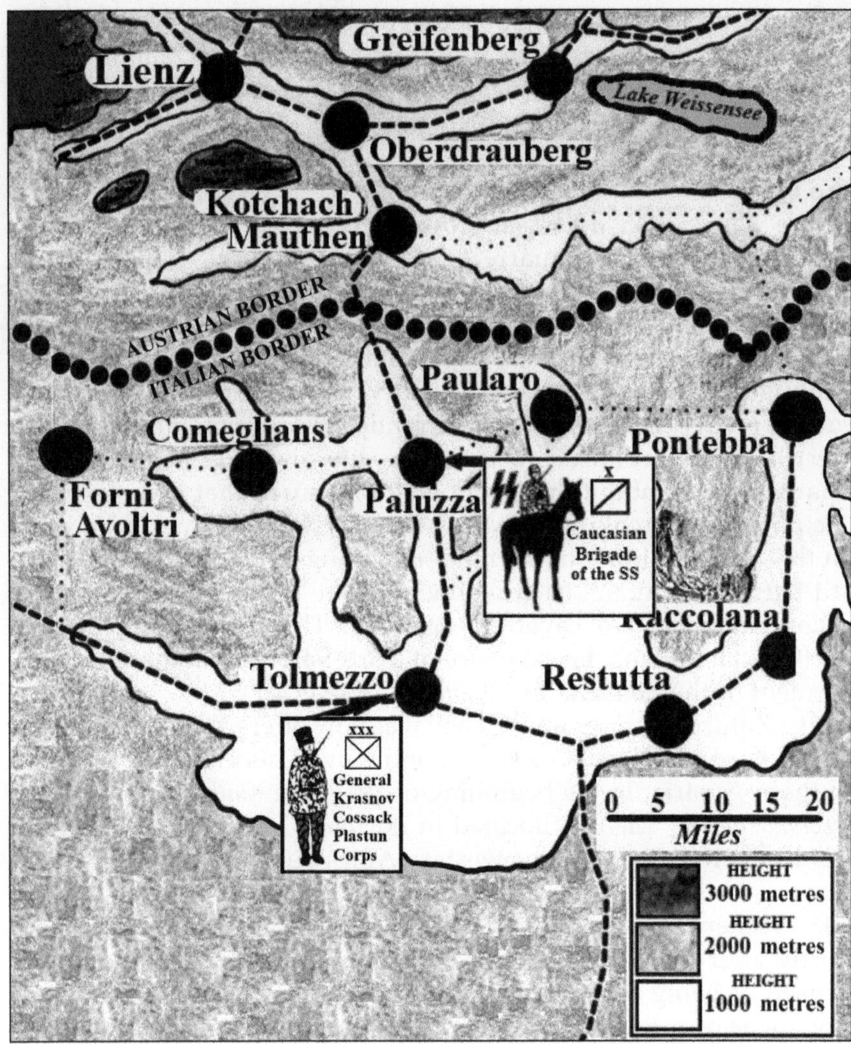

Figure 29. General location of the *Kaukasischer-Waffen-Verbände der SS* and General Peter Krasnov's Cossack Infantry Corps, January 1945. *(Author's line drawing)*

It should be noted that in 1985, Soobzokov was under inquiry by the United States Office of Special Investigations for alleged crimes against the Jewish population in the Caucasus region. Therefore, during his interview with the FBI, he may have been trying to over-simplify the matter in order to put an innocent spin on his brief service with the German Order Police. However, it appears from all available data that he did not join the *Waffen-SS* until December 1944 and that the

Kaukasischer-Waffen-Verbände der-SS committed no crimes against the Soviet Army, the western Allies, or even the Italian partisans. Most likely because it was never deemed as combat ready and was still undergoing training when the war came to an end. By his own admission, however, Soobzokov did serve in one capacity or another under the SS and Police Command in the Caucasus and so this is the basis for the charges levelled against him. Insofar as the question of whether the regiments in the brigade contained two battalions instead of three, the field post numbers were finally assigned to the unit in February 1945. It only recorded two battalions per regiment, but we know that in at least two out of the four regiments, three battalions existed:

Table 10. Field Post Numbers for the Kaukasischer-Waffen-Verbände der-SS.

Kaukasischer-Waffen-Verbände der-SS	Field Post No.
Divisionsstab	13360
Regimentsstab - Waffengruppe Nordkaukasien	02439
I. Bataillon / Waffengruppe Nordkaukasien	20358
II. Bataillon / Waffengruppe Nordkaukasien	15518
Regimentsstab - Waffengruppe Armenien	12443
I. Bataillon / Waffengruppe Armenien	19309
II. Bataillon / Waffengruppe Armenien	16927
Regimentsstab - Waffengruppe Georgien	21345
I. Bataillon / Waffengruppe Georgien	23251
II. Bataillon / Waffengruppe Georgien	00628
Regimentsstab - Waffengruppe Aserbeidschan	21771
I. Bataillon / Waffengruppe Aserbeidschan	22213
II. Bataillon / Waffengruppe Aserbeidschan	01793

Soobzokov died on 9 September 1985 from the effects of a pipe bomb that had been placed on the porch of his home in Patterson, New Jersey. The culprit, or culprits, was never found. Soobzokov had been the target of an earlier assassination attempt, when a mail bomb was sent to him in 1979, but as before, no culprits were ever discovered. The FBI did learn that the same type of bomb killed another former member of the *Waffen-SS*, Elmars Sprogis, who at the time was living in Long Island, New York. It may not have been a coincidence that Sprogis was killed by a pipe bomb on the same day that Soobzokov passed away (9 September 1985). In 2016 Aslan T. Soobzokov, who was the son of Tscherim Soobzokov, brought a defamation lawsuit against the author, Eric Lichtblau and his publisher, Houghton, Mifflin and Harcourt. The previous year, Lichtblau had written a book entitled *The Nazis Next Door: How America Became a Safe Haven for Hitler's Men,* in which Tscherim Soobzokov was painted as a war criminal. The case was initially dismissed, but Aslan T. Soobzokov, who was a lawyer, appealed the decision. His appeal was denied a year later, in 2017.

Chapter Five

THE OSTTÜRKISCHER-WAFFEN-VERBÄNDE DER-SS, 1944–1945

Origins of the Turkic Muslim SS

Towards the end of 1943, the project of raising a Turkic Muslim SS division began to take form within the SS-FHA (SS High Command). For more than two years the SS-FHA had been working with the RSHA (the Reich Main Security Office) on a plan to raise such a division. *Reichsführer-SS* Heinrich Himmler had been informed about the tenacious fighting qualities of the Turkic volunteers, including how three Turkic battalions had fought to the last man at Stalingrad and how other Turkic battalions had been destroyed but not routed during the fighting withdrawal from the Caucasus. He had been impressed when told how another Turkic battalion had broken out of a pocket near Kharkov and re-entered it just to rescue the body of their beloved German commander. This German officer had been an enlightened commander who had treated his Turkestani volunteers with respect, and the men of his battalion had repaid him with great devotion to duty.

One of the chief architects of the Turkic-SS programme was Dr Reiner Olzscha, a physician and member of the SS whose interest in the East had been aroused by his own professional investigation of epidemics and who later co-authored a book on Turkestan. At a time when the *Waffen-SS* was grasping for more manpower, *SS-Hauptsturmführer* Dr Olzscha of *Amtsgruppe D* in the SS-FHA, was trying to sell his pan-Turkic ideas.[180]

The one uniting element tying all the men who were pushing for a Turkic-SS unit was the desire to use the innate hatred felt by the people of Turkestan for Stalinism, after Turkestan had disappeared from Soviet maps in 1924.[181] The Soviet Union had banned all languages except Russian, suppressed religion, and imposed collectivisation methods. The people of Turkestan hated these communist attempts to destroy their personal, religious and ethnic freedoms, and it therefore should be no surprise that more than 50,000 Turkestani people died fighting on the German side and an additional 12,000 were wounded. This belittles the estimated 3,000 Turkestani volunteers who deserted the German military during the war. Of these 3,000 deserters, only about 300–500 joined the communist partisans, while the rest deserted to anti-German / anti-communist partisan forces.

Himmler's mind was finally made up about raising a Turkic Muslim SS when a German army officer by the name of Andreas Meyer-Mader convinced him of the possibility of using such a Turkic formation. *Major* Meyer-Mader had contacted *Reichsführer-SS* through the SS-FHA, offering to help raise and command such a Turkic SS unit. Himmler was impressed with Meyer-Mader's credentials. Not only had Meyer-Mader been commanding a Turkic battalion for quite some time, but he had also seen foreign service in China while attached to the German embassy before the war. As such, *Major* Meyer-Mader was considered an expert on 'Eastern peoples.'

In November 1943, *Major* Meyer-Mader had his meeting with Heinrich Himmler. One month later Himmler requested Gottlob Berger, the head of the SS-FHA to arrange a meeting between the Grand Mufti of Jerusalem, *Major* Meyer-Mader, and a representative of the SS-FHA. The meeting was to be arranged to obtain the approval of the Grand Mufti to raise a Turkic Muslim SS division, whose political and military goal was the fight against Bolshevism. Himmler and Meyer-Mader had agreed that the presence and the 'blessing' of the Grand Mufti, Haj Amin al Husseini, would be needed so that his 'spiritual leadership' (religious and political influence among Muslims) would help facilitate the setting up of a division.

Meanwhile, Himmler decided to appoint *Major* Meyer-Mader as head of the proposed *Muselmanische SS-Division 'Neu-Turkistan'*. Meyer-Mader was transferred into the ranks of the *Waffen-SS* and promoted to the rank of *SS-Obersturmbannführer* (SS lieutenant colonel), effective from 1 January 1944. On 14 December 1943, another meeting was held in Berlin. Present at that meeting were the Grand Mufti of Jerusalem, *Major* Meyer-Mader, and three Turkestani officers from Mader's *480. Turkestanisches Infanterie-Bataillon*. At the end of this meeting, they all declared themselves ready to support the formation of a Turkic SS unit.

Three weeks later, on 4 January 1944, another meeting was attended by the same men and *SS-Sturmbannführer* Schulte, who was deputy head of the SS-FHA, and therefore Gottlob Berger's immediate subordinate. They finalised details of raising the proposed Turkic SS division, and decided to disband the German Army *450., 480.*, and *I./94 Turkestanisches Infanterie Bataillone* and transfer the men into the *Waffen-SS*. These volunteers formed the regimental cadre for the division. Among other decisions made, all men agreed that the unit would begin assembling in an SS work camp near Poniatowa, Poland. Approximately 30,000 potential Turkic recruits existed in the form of Red Army prisoners of war and men from Turkestan who were working in Germany. The divisional formation staff was headquartered in Lublin, also located in the *General Generalgouvernement*.[182] The new division used the *SS-Truppenübungsplatz* (SS Troop Training Ground) near Trawniki for organisation, equipping and field exercises.

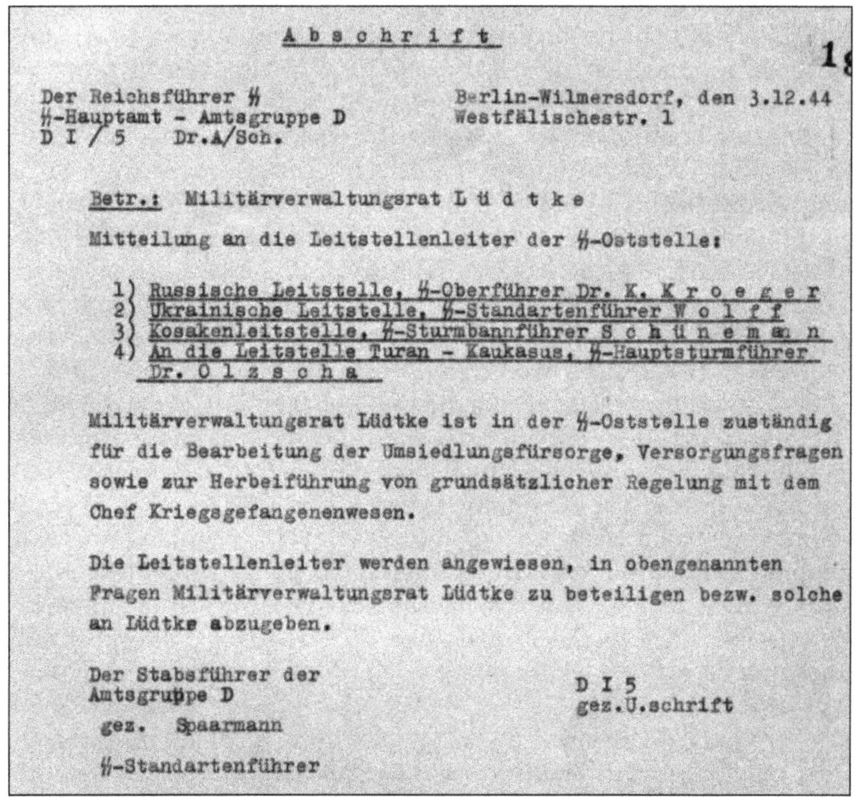

Abschrift

Der Reichsführer SS
SS-Hauptamt - Amtsgruppe D
D I / 5 Dr.A/Sch.

Berlin-Wilmersdorf, den 3.12.44
Westfälischestr. 1

Betr.: Militärverwaltungsrat Lüdtke

Mitteilung an die Leitstellenleiter der SS-Oststelle:

1) Russische Leitstelle, SS-Oberführer Dr. K. Kroeger
2) Ukrainische Leitstelle, SS-Standartenführer Wolff
3) Kosakenleitstelle, SS-Sturmbannführer Schünemann
4) An die Leitstelle Turan - Kaukasus, SS-Hauptsturmführer Dr. Olzscha

Militärverwaltungsrat Lüdtke ist in der SS-Oststelle zuständig für die Bearbeitung der Umsiedlungsfürsorge, Versorgungsfragen sowie zur Herbeiführung von grundsätzlicher Regelung mit dem Chef Kriegsgefangenenwesen.

Die Leitstellenleiter werden angewiesen, in obengenannten Fragen Militärverwaltungsrat Lüdtke zu beteiligen bezw. solche an Lüdtke abzugeben.

Der Stabsführer der
Amtsgruppe D
gez. Spaarmann
SS-Standartenführer

D I 5
gez.U.schrift

Figure 30. A message from SS-Standartenführer Spaarmann of Amtsgruppe D of the SS-FHA, dated 3 December 1944, making it clear that Military Administrative Councillor Lüdtke would be the liaison between the German prisoner of war system and the SS Eastern Office. The message reads: 'Military Administrative Councilor Lüdtke is responsible in the SS Eastern Office for dealing with resettlement welfare, supply issues and for bringing about fundamental settlements with the head of the prisoner of war system. The control centre managers were instructed to involve Military Administrator Lüdtke in the above-mentioned questions. Give these to Lüdtke.' This had to do with the recruitment of volunteers for the Osttürkischer-Waffen-Verbände der-SS from German military prison camps. *(Author's collection)*

The 1. Ostmuslimisches SS-Regiment

By 6 December 1943, the *I./94 Turkestanisches Infanterie Bataillon* had been disbanded and its men transferred into the Waffen-SS. On 18 December the men of *450. Turkestanisches Infanterie Bataillon* were transferred, and the *480. Turkestanisches Infanterie Bataillon* soon followed. By the middle of January 1944, the Turkic SS division was taking shape. *SS-Obersturmbannführer* Andreas Meyer-Mader began making the rounds of German PoW camps, recruiting men from Turkestan for his SS division. He recruited not only volunteers from Turkestan, but also Azerbaijani, Kirghiz, Uzbek, and Tadzhik volunteers.

All were of the Muslim faith, although it is not known how many Muslims volunteered from a direct appeal by the Grand Mufti of Jerusalem to their religious or political beliefs. Certainly, many volunteered because of him, but many also joined to escape the harsh life that the SS work camps offered them. Those chosen from PoW camps most likely did so not out of some religious or political belief, but purely out of the desire to survive. These German PoW camps were designed to slowly starve men to death. It was no surprise, therefore, that soon enough Meyer-Mader had assembled enough men to form three reinforced infantry battalions into the *1. Ostmuslimisches SS-Regiment* (1st Eastern Muslim SS Regiment).

Typical of these Turkic volunteers was *Waffen-Untersturmführer der-SS* Alichan Kuliev. Born in Turkestan on 3 June 1921 and conscripted into the Red Army in 1939, Kuliev attended Flight Leader School but was taken prisoner at Brest-Litovsk on 24 June 1941. He was an early volunteer of the Turkestani legion formed by the German army and spent three months in Warsaw undergoing an officer's training course. Later, Kuliev helped to raise two companies of Turkestani volunteers. He was attached to the *3. Kompanie, 783. Turkestanisches Infanterie Bataillon* as a platoon leader but was later transferred to the battalion staff as ordnance officer.

Wounded at Rostov, he was taken to a field hospital in Dnepropetrovsk, but later returned to *783. Turkestanisches Infanterie Bataillon,* which had been reconstituted to a strength of about 500 men. The *783. Turkestanisches Infanterie Bataillon* participated in the fierce fighting around Stalino in 1943 and later fought Russian partisans 12 kilometres (7.5 miles) east of Bryansk. After this, the battalion was transferred to the Nikolai bridgehead, where 300 of the battalion's 500 men lost their lives in its defence. While he and the rest of the survivors of the *783. Turkestanisches Infanterie Bataillon* were in southern France for rest and refitting, Kuliev heard the request for Turkestani volunteers and offered himself. He was soon on his way to Poland.

By the end of January 1944, Meyer-Mader had brought a force of some 3,000 men into the regiment. The formation of the division began to slow, mainly because of a shortage of equipment of every type, including such elementary items as uniforms and boots. Photographs aptly illustrate the extent of these shortages and the plight of the soldiers. The pictures show men of the *1. Ostmuslimisches SS-Regiment* in an assortment of mixed German Army and *Waffen-SS* uniforms. In the beginning of February 1944, the regiment was transferred to Belarus for further training and for anti-partisan duty. Meanwhile, the SS-FHA made an attempt to introduce a sizeable German cadre into the proposed division, while recruitment of volunteers continued. In late January 1944, the SS-FHA had requested the German Army to release *Hauptmann* Billig from duty with the *Wehrmacht* Welfare Office in Rostock for assignment with the *Waffen-SS*. This occurred on 5 February 1944. Unknown to the SS-FHA, Billig had a serious drinking problem which would adversely affect his performance in the *1. Ostmuslimisches SS-Regiment*.

During the first half of March 1944, the *1. Ostmuslimisches SS-Regiment*, under *SS-Obersturmbannführer* Meyer-Mader, was conducting anti-partisan operations from their base at Yuratsishki (also spelled 'Juraciški'), near Minsk, when Meyer-Mader was killed at the hands of a lucky partisan sniper on 28 March 1944, apparently shattering the morale of the regiment. Transferred into the *Waffen-SS*, perhaps against his wishes, it is quite possible that the newly appointed *SS-Hauptsturmführer* (SS captain) Billig resented his new duties, which took him far away from his comfortable post in Rostock, Germany.

Meyer-Mader's death unleashed the unreliable elements in the regiment, who began to foment trouble. Though unsubstantiated, there is speculation that the *1. Ostmuslimisches SS-Regiment* had been infiltrated by Red Army agents for the express purpose of destroying the morale of the unit and, if possible, causing the desertion of its men. One example of this involved a unit of the German Brandenburg commandos operating in Russia that had trouble with its native contingent. A well-known anti-communist in the battalion identified a recent recruit as the culprit in all of the unrest. This newcomer, a Ukrainian, staunchly denied his guilt. Still, the German officers decided to keep an eye on him. When the battalion later mutinied, killing most of the Germans, the real instigator was revealed to be the so-called 'anti-communist' all along. Of course, the falsely accused Ukrainian had been killed during the uprising by the real culprit.

It was into this environment of resentment and mistrust that *SS-Hauptsturmführer* Billig made his appearance at Yuratsishki at the end of March 1944. He began his tenure as regimental commander by exacerbating the already volatile situation with his inept handling of his initial encounter with the troublesome elements in the regiment. Completely drunk, he removed the problem by shooting seventy-eight suspected mutineers. Though he probably believed this would rid the regiment of its mutinous mood, it only had the effect of alienating the volunteers and inspiring a hatred for this 'drunken newcomer'. After this incident, Billig's command was short-lived. He was transferred on 6 April, but his replacement did not show up until 27 April. Even though the regiment had no official commanding officer, volunteers for the unit continued to arrive, including a large contingent between 7 and 12 April.

On 27 April, *SS-Hauptsturmführer* Emil Hermann arrived to take control of the demoralised SS regiment. Hermann's first step was to take stock of the situation. He soon found out that, as a result of Billig's actions, hundreds of volunteers had deserted and so immediately began to defuse the situation and soon regained control by making concessions and employing sensible decisions. However, on 2 May 1944, just a week after his arrival, Emil Hermann was removed from command. He was not transferred, however, but remained on the regimental staff until the SS-FHA could find another commander. The unit would again be without a commanding officer until June 1944.

In July 1944 *1. Ostmuslimisches SS-Regiment* was ordered back to Poland and removed from the control of the Higher SS and Police Leader Minsk. That month, it was located in Łomża, before being moved to Białystok. Towards the end of July, it was attached to the *SS Sturmbrigade Dirlewanger,*[183] an SS unit made up of paroled criminals, poachers, murderers and rapists. In August that year, this SS brigade would send one of its regiments to help crush the Polish uprising in Warsaw. In the meantime, the search for a suitable commander continued. One officer for the SS unit was presumedly found when the name of *Major* Harun el-Raschid Bey was presented to *Reichsführer-SS* Himmler in July 1944. Born in Senftenberg as Wilhelm Hintersatz on 26 May 1886, he was renamed Harun el-Raschid Bey while serving as a colonel in the Austro-Hungarian army in the First World War. He had been attached to the Turkish general staff, working with the famous Enver Pasha during most of the conflict. During his stint in Turkey, he converted to the Islamic faith and took the name of Harun el-Raschid Bey, which had been officially given to him by the sultan of Turkey.

His most recent position before being transferred to command the Turkic SS brigade was that of liaison officer between the RSHA (*Reichssicherheitshauptamt,* Reich Main Security Office) and the Grand Mufti of Jerusalem, Haj Amin al Husseini. He had recently come over from the army, receiving the rank of *SS-Sturmbannführer* (SS major) on 24 August 1944. On 1 September, just eight days later, he was promoted to *SS-Obersturmbannführer.* Thirty days later, on 1 October, he was once again promoted and became an *SS-Standartenführer* (full SS colonel).

The formation of the *Ostmuselmanische SS-Division-Neu-Turkistan* was on the mind of the *Reichsführer-SS* throughout the summer and autumn of 1944. On 2 May, a directive by Himmler had stated implicitly that 'the formation of an eastern Muslim division, from members of the Turkish race, is to be carried out this year'. By autumn 1944, that prospect had disappeared as not enough recruits were forthcoming to raise the proposed Turkic-SS division. Thus, on 1 October, Himmler implemented the changes described as follows:

> To the SS-FHA and from the RFSS:
> Effective immediately -

> As of 1 October [1944], I order the formation of the *Osttürkischer-Waffen-Verbände der-SS.*
> The *Osttürkischer-Waffen-Verbände der-SS* will gather all useable Eastern Turkic volunteers (Turkestani, Volga and Ural Tatars, Crimean Turks, Azerbaijanis, etc.) for the military and political training of these volunteers to make the formation a purposeful fighting unit...
> Makeup:
> The staff of the *Osttürkischer-Waffen-Verbände der-SS* is to consist of the following units, as per the accompanying order of battle; the responsibility of the formation will be with the commander, *Waffen-Standartenführer der-SS* Harun-el-Raschid.
> The formation of the fighting units will be found in the special orders from the SS-FHA.
> Formation:
> The *Osttürkischer-Waffen-Verbände der-SS* is to be subordinated to the SS-FHA in all matters of formation, training, supply, as well as leadership, directly to *Amt-II.* The SS-FHA is responsible for all political and cultural questions, also for any propaganda tasks.

Formation to take place in Slovakia, particulars to follow.
Personnel:
The German officers in the *Osttürkischer-Waffen-Verbände der-SS* will be briefed by the commander, in direct agreement with the SS-FHA. *Amt-II, Abteilung Ie.* Necessary NCOs and other ranks will be supplied by the SS-FHA, *Amt-V, Abteilung IIa.*
Material: Information about weapons, equipment, and vehicles will come from the SS-FHA, *Abteilung lb.*

Signed

H. Himmler
RFSS[184]

The *1. Ostmuselmanisches SS Regiment* remained under the control of the SS Dirlewanger Penal Brigade during the rest of the summer of 1944, although *SS-Hauptsturmführer* Hermann had been killed in action on 11 July 1944. Apparently, after the fighting in Warsaw, the Dirlewanger Brigade had been sent to Radom for rest and refitting. It is not known whether the *1. Ostmuselmanisches SS-Regiment* followed the *SS-Sonderregiment 'Dirlewanger'*, but on 12 October, on the advice of *SS-Obergruppenführer* Gottlob Berger, the brigade was transferred to Slovakia. As per Himmler's order written on 20 October 1944 (but backdated to 1 October), the formation of the *Osttürkischer-Waffen-Verbände der-SS* would take place in Slovakia. If indeed the Turkic-SS regiment was detached from the Dirlewanger Brigade before that unit's transfer to Slovakia, it nevertheless found itself in that country by the end of October 1944. The three battalions of the *1. Ostmuselmanische SS-Regiment* were divided on racial lines, featuring battalions of Turkestani, Azerbaijani, and Tatar volunteers from the Idel and Ural Mountains. Each battalion had a staff company headquarters plus five rifle companies, while the regiment also had a regimental staff company.

Political events outside the *1. Ostmuselmanisches SS-Regiment* began to take a turn for the worse. While in the process of forming into a brigade, elements in the RSHA began to make overtures about the eventual transfer of the brigade to General Vlasov's Russian Army of Liberation, which was contradictory to the Turkestani National Committee's aims for an independent state. This committee, sponsored by the *Ost-Ministerium* and headed by Veli Kayyum Khan, the head of the Turkestani 'government in exile', had been in charge of the political and national leadership of the Turkestani volunteers.

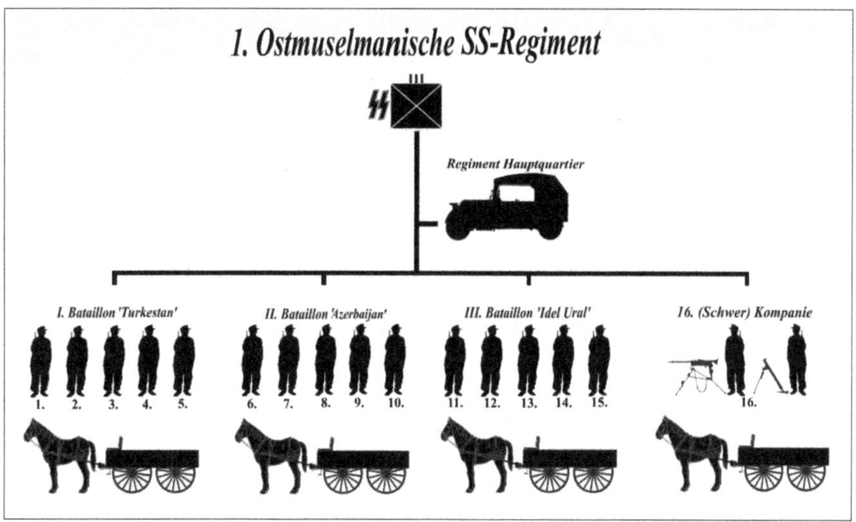

Figure 31. Schematic diagram of the 1. Ostmuselmanische SS Regiment. At peak strength, the regiment contained 1,800 officers, NCOs and enlisted men divided into sixteen companies. *(Author's line drawing)*

It had successfully raised the morale of the Turkestani volunteers by supporting independence for Turkestan and, with the aid of Veli Kayyum Khan and the SS-FHA, had set up schools at Dresden and Gottingen to train religious *imams* for the military units. The Dresden school mainly trained priests for the Turkestani *Waffen-SS,* while the school at Gottingen taught *imams* for the Turkic units in the *Wehrmacht.* The teachings of both schools centred on pan-Turkic / pan-Islamic beliefs. Slowly, the news of the infighting within the SS about the fate of the Turkestani men filtered down through the ranks of the forming brigade, which resented the thought of being transferred to a Russian-controlled organisation. This resentment would eventually lead to a mutiny.

The Osttürkischer-Waffen-Verbände der-SS

On 2 November 1944 (and again on 2 December), the forming *Osttürkischer Waffen-Verband der SS* was listed under the control of the *Höhere-SS und Polizeiführer-Slowakei.* Other formations under this command included the *178. Reserve-Panzer-Division, SS-Sonderregiment 'Dirlewanger',* the *14. Waffen-Grenadier-Division der SS (ukrainische Nr. 1), 18. SS-Freiwilligen-Panzergrenadier-Division 'Horst Wessel',* and *SS-Kampfgruppe Schill.* The brigade had been reorganised into three regiments: Turkistan, Azerbaijan, and Idel-Ural, but events in December proved disastrous for the morale of the Turkestani volunteers, when a mutiny occurred at the end of the month.

A Christmas party had been organised by the German and Turkestani men of the Turkestani regiment. Though they were Muslims, the Turkestanis went along with their German comrades, if only because free gifts were offered. It was during this Christmas party that the men of the Turkestani 1st Battalion, led by *Waffen-Obersturmführer der-SS* Gulam Alimov, deserted the brigade. *Waffen-Untersturmführer der-SS* Alichan Kuliev, who was a witness to the mutiny, later testified as to what occurred on the night of 24 December 1944:

> Waffen-Obersturmführer der-SS Alimov, Waffen-Untersturmführer der-SS Dr Dschaparow, Waffen-Hauptscharführer der-SS Safajew, SS-Oberscharführer Futtermeister, and Waffen-Untersturmführer der-SS Asatpalvan were in Alimov's room for the Christmas gathering. Five minutes later, SS-Untersturmführer Lampa and SS-Oberscharführer Flamek arrived. Both Germans had numerous Christmas packages that contained cigarette packs, candy, and even games, Alimov gave them a very cheerful welcome. The Germans then presented the gifts to the men present. Thereafter, soup and cognac were drunk at the table. The cognac was brought by Waffen-Untersturmführer der-SS Asatpalvan, the company commander of the 3rd Company. Asatpalvan proceeded to distribute the cigarettes that were in the packages. After this, Asatpalvan turned to the Germans, telling them that their superior [SS-Hauptsturmführer Furst] was very bad in nature and by race. He also said to them that he had no doubt that Furst thought bad of him (Asatpalvan), and accused him by noting that two other Turkestani officers had been sent to the officers' course at Myjave instead of him. Alimov interrupted the conversation, telling the Germans that he did not understand why Furst had not first consulted with him about the transfer of the two officers. SS-Untersturmführer Lampa replied that he did not understand all of this. Then the Germans were roughly dismissed from the room. Alimov then gave the order to leave the battalion, calling for the horses in order to withdraw. They went over to the area of the Azerbaijani Battalion, but its men would not leave with him. He then took his men into the forest, shooting myself and SS-Untersturmführer Spiese, who happened to be coming back from Myjava. The order to prevent his escape was received too late. SS-Standartenführer Harun el-Raschid Bey received news of the mutiny by Waffen-Unterscharführer der-SS Alim. Bey took the report and pounded himself on the shoulder. He then proceeded to the high mullah's room and there slept the night. That same evening Bey awoke and telegraphed Pressburg [Bratislava, Slovakia] for an aircraft to take off and drop leaflets in the wooded area where Alimov was supposed to be. The leaflets asked Alimov to return and that all would be forgiven. Waffen-Obersturmführer der-SS Alimov disregarded the offer and remained in the town of Propat. A part of the

men who went with him by force, were then force-marched toward Nove Mesto and returned to their barracks. Alimov was arrested by Slovaks friendly to the partisans.[185]

Approximately 450 to 500 men of the 1st Battalion deserted that Christmas night; about 300 eventually returned to the battalion, while the other 200 joined the Slovak partisans. No doubt the reason given by Alimov and Asatpalvan was an excuse. The mistrust spawned over the RSHA's handling of the proposed transfer of the brigade was probably the real cause for the desertion. The virtually complete desertion of a Turkestani battalion of the *Osttürkischer-Waffen-Verbände der-SS*, led by its Uzbek leader, *Waffen-Untersturmführer der-SS* Gulam Alimov on 24 December 1944, was crucial to the organisation's eventual reorganisation. While some soldiers who managed to flee were captured by German forces, others chose to return on their own.

It was determined from the accounts of a number of these returnees that they were not apprised of their battalion commander's intentions. The precise motivations of Alimov were the subject of the main SS investigation. Personal reasons prevailed, despite the German commander of the *Osttürkischer-Waffen-Verbände der-SS*, Harun el-Raschid, attempting to clarify in his report to *SS-Hauptsturmführer* Dr Reiner Olzscha that 'the whole process was not a Turkistan issue', but instead was a problem with 'Alimov and his clique'. In truth, there is some indication that Alimov felt betrayed in his role as an Uzbek commander, given the practice of some German officers to purposefully promote non-Uzbeks in the *Osttürkischer-Waffen-Verbänd der-SS*.

Alimov addressed a letter to Harun el-Raschid on 24 December 1944, the day before he deserted to the Slovak partisans, requesting that the officer candidates – who were plainly not Uzbek – who had been sent by the SS Main Office, be returned due to their 'ineffectiveness'. Furious, *Reichsführer-SS* Himmler, through the offices of the SS-FHA, ordered the *Osttürkischer-Waffen-Verbände der-SS* to be reorganised on 30 December (but he backdated the order to 15 December). The SS-FHA pointed the accusing finger for the Christmas Eve desertions at the brigade's commanding officer, Harun el-Raschid Bey. A report dated around the middle of January 1945 from *Amtsgruppe D* of the SS-FHA stated the following:

> After the present commander unilaterally and against orders of the SS-FHA placed command in the hands of untrustworthy men, a group of the Turkestani volunteers under the command of Waffen-Obersturmführer der-SS Alimov murdered some NCOs and went over to the partisans.[186]

The report went on to say that since the behaviour of the commander showed that he could not or would not take the necessary steps, he should be relieved of his command and *SS-Hauptsturmführer* Fürst given the leadership of the brigade, especially regarding the *Waffengruppe der SS Turkistan.* By this time, the removal of Harun el-Raschid Bey was a forgone conclusion. Someone had to take the fall for the mutiny, and Harun el-Raschid – whether guilty or not – was the most likely candidate. He left the *Osttürkischer-Waffen-Verbände der SS* in February 1945, and Fürst took command. Fürst was promoted to *SS-Sturmbannführer* one month later. The command and formation of the *I. Bataillon* of *I. Bataillon of Waffengruppe der SS Turkistan* had consequently been severely depleted. Gulam Alimov had deserted with all of the company commanders and most of the *I. Bataillon.*

The ordnance officer of the battalion, *Waffen-Untersturmführer der-SS* Dr Dschaparov, was acquitted of any involvement in the mutiny, as was the company chief of the battalion, *Waffen-Untersturmführer der-SS* Safayev. Replacing the company commanders was not easy, but it is known that *Waffen-Obersturmführer der-SS* Nasarov, who had been attached to the SS-FHA, was transferred to the 1st Battalion, possibly taking over command of the unit. Reorganisation of the *Osttürkischer-Waffen-Verbände der-SS* began in January 1945.

Conforming to the SS-FHA orders of 30 December, the Azerbaijani regiment in the brigade was withdrawn and transferred to the *Kaukasicher-Waffen-Verbände der-SS,* which was then forming in northern Italy. The 3rd Battalion of the old *1. Ostmuselmanische SS-Regiment* formed the basis of the *SS-Waffengruppe Idel-Ural,* while the 1st and 2nd Battalions of the regiment formed *SS-Waffengruppe Turkistan.* The men who formed *SS-Waffengruppe Krim* came from another *Waffen-SS* formation that had been disbanded on 31 December 1944, the *Waffen-Gebirgs-Brigade der-SS (Tatar Nr. 1).* The origins of the Tatar [SS] Brigade date back to the summer of 1944, when all of the Crimean Tatar Schuma battalions were gathered together and formed into a volunteer mountain regiment of the Waffen- SS. In May 1944, the regiment began to take form at Moorlager Training Camp when it was transferred to the Ostturkischen- Waffen-Verbände der- SS:

> To the Ostturkischen- Waffen- Verbände der- SS:
>
> From the SS- FHA With effect from 15 December 1944, the Osttürkischer- Waffen- Verbände der- SS is to be reorganised as follows:
>
> Staff, Osttürkischer-Waffen-Verbände der-SS
>
> Staff SS-Waffengruppe Idel-Ural, Staff SS-Waffengruppe Turkestan, Staff SS-Waffengruppe Krim, formed as battalions.

In the framework of the personnel at its disposal, the following units are to be formed first:
Staffs for the three SS-Waffen-Gruppe (abridged regimental staffs to be worked out in the Osttürkischer-Waffen-Verbände der-SS) and approved by the SS-FHA, Amt-II, and Organization Abteilung Ia.

Each SS-Waffengruppe will have:
Two infantry battalions with five infantry companies per battalion. Formation of other units will be notified by the SS-FHA.

Formation of the unit is to take place around Mlava, Slovakia.

The commander is to be responsible for the formation of the fighting units.
The Ostmuselmanische SS-Regiment forms part of the Osttürkischer-Waffen-Verbände der-SS and is thereby considered dissolved.
Any Azerbaijanis are to be separated out of the Osttürkischer-Waffen-Verbände der-SS and delivered directly to the Kaukasicher Waffen-Verbände der-SS.

Chief of the SS-FHA
Signed Juttner
SS-Obergruppenführer and General der Waffen-SS[187]

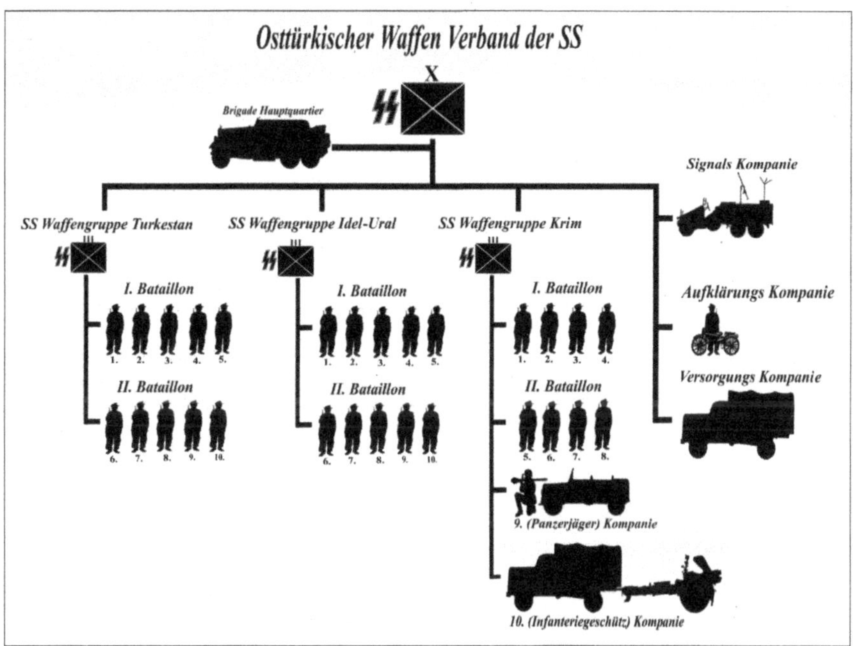

Figure 32. The Osttürkischer-Waffen-Verbände der-SS, March 1945. *(Author's line drawing)*

At that time only a battalion had been formed, but by June a sufficient number of men had been gathered to form a regiment or small brigade. The SS-FHA decided in late June to expand the unit into a brigade and issued an order outlining such an expansion on 8 July 1944. That month, the forming brigade left Moorlager for Hungary for training under the Replacement Army and for garrison duty. *SS-Standartenführer* Wilhelm Fortenbacher received command of the *Waffen-Gebirgsjäger-Brigade der-SS (tatarische Nr. 1)*. Unfortunately for the unit, Fortenbacher believed that his post was a sort of demotion, since the unit was not considered a first-class formation. Because of this, he took little interest in his command, and the brigade made little headway. Another reason for the brigade's stilted development was that many weapons and equipment were yet to arrive because the *Waffen-SS*'s higher priority was arming the more elite *Waffen-SS* divisions. The order to disband the forming brigade finally came in December 1944, and the men were ordered to join the *Osttürkischer-Waffen-Verbände der-SS*.

The brigade had at this time a sizeable number of men: 11 officers, 191 NCOs, 2,219 men, plus 1,097 ethnic Germans – in all some 3,518 men. The German Field Post numbers illustrate the transfer of Tatar personnel into the *Osttürkischer-Waffen-Verbände der-SS*. It was not until February 1945 that the Tatar personnel from the disbanded *Waffen-Gebirgsjäger-Brigade der-SS (tatarische Nr. 1)* joined the *Osttürkischer-Waffen-Verbände der-SS*. The Tatar 2nd Battalion as described above contained four infantry companies (5th through to 8th Company). This means that its 1st Battalion contained the 1st through to the 4th companies.

The order of battle of the *SS-Waffengruppe Krim* differed from the other two *SS-Waffengruppe* in that its battalions had four rifle companies instead of five. Another difference was that it had two independent companies not under the control of either the 1st or 2nd battalion, but rather directly controlled by the *SS-Waffengruppe* company headquarters. This was the separate 9th Company, which was the anti-tank unit, employing the disposable single-shot *Panzerfaust* anti-tank projectile and the *Panzerschreck* reusable bazooka. The 10th Company was also independent of the two infantry battalions and contained three infantry howitzers.

This was the last listing of the *Osttürkischer-Waffen-Verbände der-SS* in the German situation maps, indicating that it transferred to northern Italy. I cannot confirm this movement. Certainly, it sounds suspect, since the German Army was in the process of withdrawing from northern Italy, beginning in April 1945.[188] One of the last and few remaining documents from the brigade were written from Austria, which leads me to believe that the *Osttürkischer-Waffen-Verbände der-SS* was moved into Austria sometime in April. If indeed it had never been ordered to northern Italy, it is almost certain that it never reached there. The end of the war in early May 1945 put an end to the brigade. Whether it was committed during those last days of the war is not known. My belief is that it continued to train but was never used in combat. Had the war lasted another six months, it is highly likely that the brigade would have been used, but its effectiveness would still have rated it as a second- or third-class fighting formation. German military reversals had sapped the morale of the brigade. One final note should be made about this unit. The brigade was one of the more exotic *Waffen-SS* formations, and its distinctive cuff-band insignia marked it as such. Most of the *Waffen-SS* formations had personalised insignia, among them the unit cuff-band worn on the lower left sleeve of the tunic. All the other formations had black cuff-bands with white lettering spelling out the unit's name; the cuff-band of the *Osttürkischer-Waffen-Verbände der-SS*, however, had the Islamic colours of white on a green background.

Chapter Six

THE MUSLIM MILITIA AND LEGION OF THE SANJAK, 1943–1945

Origins

It is generally agreed that among those countries either allied with or occupied by Germany during the Second World War, none produced a greater variety of hodgepodge military and paramilitary formations than the former Soviet Union and the former Yugoslavia. This was usually based on some ethnic differentiation, and almost always took the form of legion, militia, guard, police or auxiliary police units. More often than not, they had a German commander and a small German cadre. This chapter will attempt to cover what may have been one of the most obscure of the irregular units formed in Yugoslavia: the Muslim militia of the Sanjak.

Although it is occasionally mentioned in the literature, few details concerning it survived the war. The Sandžak (Sanjak in Serbo-Croatian and Sandschak in German) is a mountainous region in eastern Montenegro with a large Muslim population that dates back to the conquest and occupation of much of what became Yugoslavia by the Ottoman Turks nearly five centuries ago. Hated, frequently harassed and occasionally attacked by their Serbian Orthodox neighbours, the Sanjak Muslims had usually found it necessary to maintain some sort of a community protective association to keep watch over their villages and safeguard their property.

Immediately following the Blitzkrieg invasion of Yugoslavia on 6 April 1941 by German, Italian, and Hungarian forces, Yugoslavia's defeat and capitulation followed barely twelve days later. With the central

Yugoslav government knocked out, the Sanjak Muslims strengthened their protective organisation because of the growing Chetnik and communist partisan threat in eastern Montenegro. Discarded Yugoslav weapons and equipment left over from the war in April, plus a few Italian rifles and numerous volunteers, transformed the protective association by the end of 1941 into something more akin to a village guard or militia. Given the history of the Balkans, the Muslims in the Sanjak were taking no chances of being caught by surprise.

Employment

In February 1942 the militia was used offensively for what is believed to be the first time, and is credited with helping to drive the partisans out of Sanjak. On 1 February the Muslim militia from Sjenica and villages in the Pester Mountains to the south, together with Chetniks and Nedic collaborator troops from Serbia, attacked Tito partisan units in Nova Varos but were thrown back. A week later, on 7 February, Muslim militia from the village of Komarani near Nova Varos, which were operating with elements of the Italian 19th Division 'Venezia' from Prijepolje, engaged in a running fire fight with partisan units withdrawing across the Lim River into western Sanjak.

By the end of February, the partisans had cleared eastern Sanjak and the region remained relatively peaceful until the beginning of 1943. However, a completely unexpected horror befell the Sanjak Muslims between 5 January and 7 February. Acting on a carefully prepared plan to seize the Sanjak by cleansing it of its Muslims, strong Chetnik forces descended on the area in two separate actions and massacred in the most bestial fashion all those they could lay hold of in the districts of Prijepolje, Pljevlja, Priboj and Čajniče. No one was spared. The Chetnik report also stated that around 500 armed Muslim self-defence militiamen were encountered during the raid on 5 January and some 1,200 during the second action on 7 February. The Muslim militia killed or wounded ninety-four Chetniks, according to the after-action report.[189]

Regrouping and reorganisation

Recovering from the battering and heavy losses suffered during January and early February, the Sanjak militia did not actively participate in the second largest anti-partisan operation conducted by the Axis occupiers in Yugoslavia during the war, even though much of the action occurred in the Sanjak. This was *Unternehmen Schwarz* (Operation Black), which was also known to the partisans as the Fifth Enemy Offensive. The total number of victims ran between 5,000 and 10,000, mostly women and children. The lower figure is from postwar Muslim sources and is probably closer to the true offensive in Yugoslav history, which pitted 127,000 Axis troops against the weakened remnants of Tito's main line divisions that numbered around 19,700 men.

The operation ran from 15 May to 15 June, and two units, the *Infanterie-Regiment 724* of the German *104. Jäger-Division* and the Italian 19th Infantry Division 'Venezia', held positions for more than two weeks right in the heart of the Sanjak militia's home territory. However, they were not employed in closing the ring around Tito's forces even though they were reported to be in considerable strength. In a top secret *(Geheimkommandosache - Chefsachen)* operation's order dated 25 April 1943, just a few weeks before *Schwarz* was scheduled to begin, division commanders and chiefs of staff were instructed:

> They [the Muslims] are to be treated as allies and are not to be disarmed. The Muslims in Sanjak have formed a Muslim self-defence militia, which is essentially an armed village guard. It supposedly comprises 8,000-10,000 men.[190]

On 9 September 1943, the date Italy capitulated, the German *118. Jäger-Division* handed over the town of Pljevlja to the Sanjak militia. The divisional commander, *Generalmajor* Josef Kübler, wanted to maintain the militia at a strength of around 5,000 men because his own troop strength was too weak to fight both the Tito partisans and the Chetniks, while simultaneously keeping the supply roads open. Kübler viewed the militia of the Sanjak as a local defence force and as a counterweight against the partisan and Chetnik bands in the region. However, he did not feel that he could supply and equip them and wrote to higher headquarters for their immediate assistance.[191]

Meanwhile, strong Chetnik forces began concentrating in the area for a planned assault on Pljevlja. To prevent the town from falling into the hands of the Chetniks, Tito's 2nd Proletarian Division opened an offensive against them on 20 September and then entered Pljevlja on 22 September without any opposition from the Muslim militia. In wartime Yugoslavia, towns changed hands frequently and it was more the norm than the exception for the defenders to strike an agreement with the attacking force that left the town unharmed with few, if any, casualties on either side.[192] In September 1943, an SS officer named Karl von Krempler was made commander of a new SS headquarters, the *Höhere SS und Polizeiführer Sandschak* (Higher SS and Police Leader Sanjak). About five weeks later, on 30 October, the Sanjak militia is mentioned for the first time in connection with Karl von Krempler.[193] The unit was referred to in an operations order as *Muselmanengruppe von Krempler* (Muslim Group von Krempler). The official title, however, would eventually be *SS Polizei Selbstschutz Regiment 'Sandschak'*.

SS-Sturmbannführer der Waffen-SS und Oberst der Polizei Karl von Krempler was considered something of an authority on the Muslims of Yugoslavia, having been involved in recruiting large numbers of them in East Bosnia for the *13. Waffen-Gebirgs-Division der-SS 'Handschar'* during the spring and summer of 1943. In a rare photograph taken during the summer of 1944, Krempler is shown as a portly, sloppily dressed older officer of average height with the *Edelweiss* sleeve insignia on his right sleeve, above which is sewn the special badge for the single-handed destruction of a tank.

Where he managed to destroy a tank is unknown, but he may have been in Russia prior to being reassigned to Yugoslavia. In any case, he was sent to Sanjak in early October 1943 and given the task of rebuilding the militia into what the Germans hoped would eventually be a legion.[194] Sjenica, now the principal seat of German authority in Sanjak and headquarters of Krempler's militia and other units, became a target of the partisans. The partisan 2nd Proletarian Division began assembling forces in the area on 10 November 1943 for a planned assault on the town.

Before it could be launched, however, some five battalions of German troops, supported by Krempler's militia, counterattacked over the next two days and forced the partisans to withdraw from the area. Later in the month, as the Germans made preparations for a major anti-partisan operation (*Unternehmen Kugelblitz*), which was to take place to the south of Tuzla in East Bosnia, agreements were signed with most Chetnik units. The Chetniks promised to cease hostilities against all German-allied forces throughout Yugoslavia, beginning on 21 November 1943. The Sanjak Muslim militia was specifically named in at least several of these agreements. On the same date, *2. Panzerarmee* issued orders to *Kampfgruppe Siegfried*. This battlegroup was composed of *2. Regiment Brandenburg (motorisiert), Grenadier Regiment 524, Muslimische Legion von Krempler* a battery of artillery and a platoon of tanks. *Kampfgruppe Siegfried* was to secure the Sjenica area to allow for the unhindered movement of *1. Gebirgs-Division,* which was to pass through Sjenica en route from Greece to East Bosnia for *Unternehmen Kugelblitz.*[195] By the end of 1943, Krempler's Muslims were beginning to take shape along more formal (and more German) lines, although even their kindest critics could never in practice consider them a legion. Instead, they remained simple peasants who disappeared for days and weeks without notice to till or harvest their land. German plans to provide uniformed and other equipment were never completed, and only a handful received *Wehrmacht* alpine trousers, tunics and boots. Nearly all of them, however, wore a fez, some of which were red while others were white. One German ad-hoc company, composed of some members from the *Höhere SS und Polizeiführer Sandschak* command and a few local German police, existed on a temporary basis only. Drill, discipline and training were sadly deficient, no matter how hard Krempler and his team tried.

These were the same problems the Germans faced six months later in their mistaken attempt to form and train *21. Waffen-Gebirgs-Division der-SS 'Skanderbeg' (albanische Nr. 1)* in nearby Kosovo, using Albanian Muslims. Finally, the Muslim commander and leader of the Sanjak militia Hafiz Sulejman Pačariz, is identified in the literature for the first time. How long he had held that position is not known. Described as a colourful character and a respected religious figure, Pačariz is said to have led his men while riding a black stallion.[196]

1944

In January 1944 the war resumed in the Sanjak region following a prolonged lull. From 16-17 January the militia supported a local offensive by German and Chetnik forces southwest of Sjenica against the 7th Partisan Brigade and 4th Proletarian Brigade, aimed at opening up the north–south roads through central Montenegro, which were firmly held by Tito's rapidly growing and increasingly well-armed forces. The effort proved unsuccessful and the Sanjak militia returned to Sjenica. Another attempt was made between 6 and 8 February by the Germans, Chetniks and Muslim militia to open a road or two through central Montenegro, but this too failed even though some headway was made and the town of Meljak was taken from the partisan 4th Sanjak Brigade.

The lack of progress, the strength of the enemy and the weather forced a halt to further efforts until reinforcements could be brought up, and a general lull once again fell over Sanjak for the next month and a half. Meanwhile, the Sanjak Muslims were granted a certain degree of autonomy by the Germans, and Krempler helped them set up an administration in Sjenica. On 21 February 1944, in response to an inquiry, the *Höhere SS und Polizeiführer Serbien* (Higher SS and Police Leader in Serbia), *SS-Gruppenführer* August Meyszner, informed the *Militärbefehlshaber Südost* (Military Commander Southeast), *General der Infanterie* Hans Felber, that Krempler's forces in Sanjak consisted of two battalions of Muslims, totalling around 800 men.

However, an element of confusion exists here, because a message sent by the Military Commander Southeast to *2. Panzerarmee* on

28 February stated that from Krempler's force of around 4,000 to 5,000 Muslim militia, 2,000 were to be taken away to provide for the organisation of a Muslim legion. The legion, it continued, was to be similar in type and manner to the *13. Waffen-Gebirgs-Division der-SS 'Handschar'*, and was to be uniformed, equipped and supplied by the Germans. Furthermore, the legion would be provided with a scale of rations identical to that for German troops.[197]

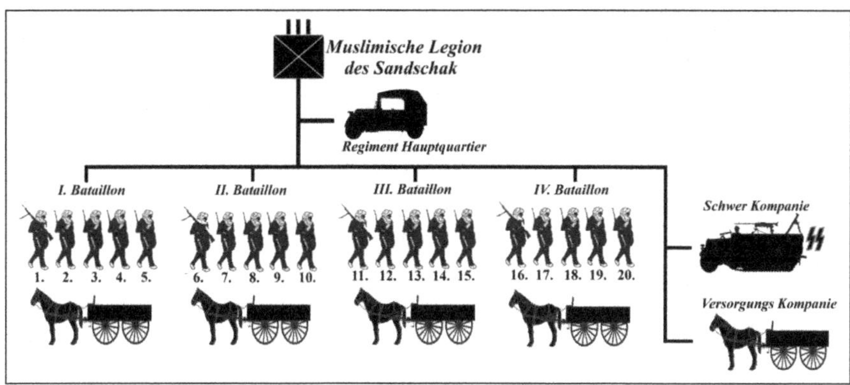

Figure 33. The Muslim Legion of the Sanjak in SS service in the autumn of 1943. The German cadre troops within the militia included the headquarters staff plus a company of SS troops from the Höhere SS und Polizeiführer Serbien command, acting as the heavy weapons unit. This heavy weapons company was withdrawn in the spring of 1944. *(Author's line drawing)*

March 1944 brought further fighting and clarification of the militia's chain of command. On the 18th, militia forces from around Priboj, as well as German troops and Chetniks garrisoned in the town and elements of *4. Regiment Brandenburg (motorisiert)* from Prijepolje, fought an eight-hour battle with elements of the partisan 4th Krajiski Border Brigade and the 2nd Proletarian Brigade that had been threatening Priboj and the immediate area. The enemy was driven off and the town held, but the Germans were forced to strengthen its garrison.

On 26 March, the Military Commander Southeast cabled the *Reichsführer-SS* in Berlin stating that Krempler's Muslim militia together with elements of the Muslim legion, then forming in Sanjak, were to be immediately subordinate to *2. Panzerarmee* (whose headquarters was located in Niska Banja near Nis, in Serbia) and for troop services to *Höhere SS und Polizeiführer Serbien*. This proposed chain of command was approved by Himmler on 30 March, who at the same time appointed Krempler *SS-Führer im Gebiet Sandschak* (SS Commander in the Sanjak Region).[198] Beginning in April, Krempler's Muslims were, in whole or in part, in almost continuous anti-partisan operations over the next five months.

From their base camps in large, liberated areas of central and parts of eastern Montenegro, guerrilla forces were ordered by Tito to begin moving into Serbia, which until the spring of 1944 had been relatively free of them. The Germans, of course, wanted to block this movement and keep the enemy bottled up in Montenegro. On 4 April, Krempler's militia was alerted for the first of these large, coordinated anti-partisan operations, *Kammerjäger* (Exterminator), which continued for nearly seven weeks. On 11 April Krempler's men moved along the Brodarevo–Bijelo Polje road, around 25-40 kilometres (15-25 miles) southwest of Sjenica against the 37th Partisan Division, together with thousands of Germans and Chetniks. The fighting seesawed back and forth for weeks up and down the Tara and Lim valleys, with town and villages in many cases changing hands several times.

The breakout into Serbia eventually failed, and Tito ordered his divisions to pull back into their Montenegro–Sanjak bastion, regroup, and then initiate a buildup of forces pending a second attempt.[199] By the end of May, most of Krempler's Sanjak Muslims had returned to Sjenica to rest and refit. Between 18 and 24 June, two battalions of German troops supported by 400 Sanjak militiamen began an advance along a narrow dirt track toward Bijelo Polje, a distance of about 50-60 kilometres (30-37 miles) as it wound its way across the Pester Mountains. But unexpectedly strong resistance from elements of the partisan Garibaldi Division[200] and several brigades from other divisions prevented the column from reaching Bijelo Polje after a week of fighting that cost each side around 150 casualties.

A week later, Krempler's legion carried out a nocturnal attack during the night of 1-2 July across the Lim River, near the village of Stitari, just east of Bijelo Polje. A small bridgehead was gained on the west bank, but formations of Tito's 2nd Partisan Division held good positions and Krempler's men could go no further. The bridgehead was eventually given up because it was difficult to supply and there were inadequate fresh troops available to expand it. The legionaries were therefore forced to pull back across the river to their prepared positions on the east bank.[201]

On 28 April the *Höhere SS und Polizeiführer Serbien* (now *SS-Gruppenführer* Hermann Behrends) in Belgrade reported to *Reichsführer-SS* Himmler in Berlin that the formation of Legion Krempler was in the process of being completed, and that *Hauptamt Orpo*[202] in Berlin had been most helpful in the effort. In July 1944 the legion was formalised and re-designated as *SS Polizei Selbstschutz Regiment 'Sandschak'* (Police Self-Defence Regiment 'Sanjak'). Its field post numbers were as follows:

Regimentshauptquartier (Regimental Staff Company) – 21,095
I. Bataillon (1st Battalion) – 22,118
II. Bataillon (2nd Battalion) – 23,051
III. Bataillon (3rd Battalion) – 24,125
IV. Bataillon (4th Battalion) – 24,983

Postwar Yugoslav sources, based on prisoner of war interrogations, maintain that three of these four battalions were in existence at the end of July 1944, and together with the remaining Sanjak Muslim militia, not included in the regiment (formerly legion), the total strength ran to approximately 4,000 men – all of whom came under the command of *SS-Standartenführer und Oberst der Polizei* Karl von Krempler. Yet a carefully constructed order of battle layout of all German forces in the Balkans prepared by *Oberbefehlshaber Südost/ Heeresgruppe F* (Commander-in-Chief Southeast) and forwarded to OKH in Berlin, shows the new regiment as only having a headquarters staff and the 1st Battalion, with the 1st to 4th companies, the latter marked in training.

So, it would appear likely that *SS-Polizei-Selbstschutz-Regiment 'Sandschak'* never matured past a single battalion, and the remaining Muslim forces under Krempler were all militia. It may be, as stated earlier, that the Germans at this point in the war simply could not provide the uniforms and equipment to outfit more than one battalion. There were just too many new units in and outside Germany competing for too few resources.[203]

The second major anti-Partisan operation, *Daufgänger* (Daredevil), began on 18 July and ran until the 28th. The operation was intended to smash Tito's second breakout attempt from Montenegro into Serbia but only succeeded in slowing down three of his divisions, although they eventually forced their way through into western Serbia. By 2 August, the 2nd Proletarian, 5th Shock, and 17th Partisan Division had evaded the German net and crossed over the Ibar River, which forms the border between Montenegro and Serbia.

The operation involved a large mixed force of German, Bulgarian, Serbian collaborator, Chetnik, Albanian, and Sanjak Muslim troops spread over a large area. Krempler's men were deployed around Bioče on the east bank of the Lim between Bijelo Polje and Berane. Holding this sector, they were instrumental in delaying the movement of the 5th Shock and 17th Partisan Division across the Pester Mountains toward the Ibar for eleven days.[204] The Germans now directed their efforts toward preventing the three remaining divisions in Montenegro, the 1st Proletarian, 3rd Shock, and 37th Partisan Division, from following the same course. If these forces, which comprised the partisan 1st Corps, could be sealed off between the Tara and Piva rivers, they could be crushed on the field of battle and their infiltration into Serbia prevented.

This, the third of the large anti-partisan operations, was called *Ruebezahl*, and began on 12 August and concluded on the 30th. It involved elements of the *7. SS-Freiwilligen-Gebirgs-Division 'Prinz Eugen'*, *21. Waffen-Gebirgs-Division der-SS 'Skanderbeg'*, *1. Gebirgs Division*, Albanian Army units, Chetniks and numerous other formations. Krempler's unit began playing their role on 14 August when, in company with *SS-Freiwilligen-Gebirgs-Regiment 14* of *7. SS-Freiwilligen-Gebirgs-Division 'Prinz Eugen'*, and *Jäger Regiment 2 'Brandenburg'*, they attacked toward Bijelo Polje and then along the road toward Prijepolje, forcing back elements of the 1st Proletarian and 37th Partisan Division. In the intense fighting that ensued, the partisans suffered heavy losses, even though they had been ordered by Tito to avoid contact with the enemy and move to the southeast. By the last week of August, the weakened, but still intact, divisions of the partisan 1st Corps broke out of Montenegro and pushed into southwestern Serbia. A large-scale linkup with the oncoming Soviet forces was now inevitable.[205]

At the beginning of September 1944, the main body of Krempler's regiment was deployed along a line following roughly the towns of Priboj, Prijepolj, the Pester Mountain range, and the town of Rozaj. It was at this time that the regiment was attached to *Kampfgruppe Bendel*. This battle group contained two battalions of Muslim light infantry from the rapidly dissolving Albanian Army, with German officers and trainers in overall command. During the first half of the month, many of the better German formations throughout central Yugoslavia were rushed to take up defensive positions in the Banat and along the Serbian–Bulgarian border to block the Red Army's rapidly moving spearheads through western Romania, and so prevent these from cutting off the line of withdrawal of *Heeresgruppe E* from Greece.

Consequently, Krempler's forces found themselves overextended and were forced to pull back to Sjenica. Aware of Army Group E's planned withdrawal from Greece and the Aegean through Macedonia, Kosovo, Sanjak and into Bosnia, the 2nd Partisan Corps in Montenegro issued orders on 9 October for the 7th Brigade of the 3rd Partisan Division, along with two battalions from the 3rd and 5th brigades of the 37th Partisan Division, to move on Sjenica and either take the town and hold it, or destroy all communications targets (i.e., bridges, telephone lines, rail lines, etc.) leading into and out of the town.

The partisan force arrived in the area on 14 October and that very night, launched a strong attack on Sjenica and its principal garrison: *SS Polizei Selbstschutz Regiment Sandschak*. Krempler's Muslims were taken by surprise and were forced back to Duga Poljana, some 23 kilometres (14 miles) to the east. Although German forces retook Sjenica on 15 October, this was the end of Krempler's Muslim militia forces in the Sanjak. Now scattered and demoralised, with many of their villages in partisan hands, nearly all of the older militiamen deserted or simply went into hiding. Tito had issued a general amnesty in September 1944 and many collaborator personnel were able to switch sides safely.

The several hundred younger men who remained in uniform and managed to evade Tito's partisan units arrived in Sarajevo at the beginning of November, well-armed and in good order. With them was Hafiz Sulejman Pačariz and his Chief of Staff, *Major* Ramiz Sipilovic. They rested and refitted for several months before being placed under the authority of *Ustaše* General Vjekoslav Maks Luburić, who had been sent to Sarajevo by the Croatian *Poglavnik* (leader) Dr Ante Pavelić, to take command of *Ustaše* forces in East Bosnia and Herzegovina, and to round up and impress the small bands of Muslim and non-Muslim militia withdrawing to the Sarajevo area. The *SS Polizei Selbstschutz Regiment Sandschak* was allowed to retain its identity and Pačariz was given the rank of *Ustaše Pukovnik* (colonel in the *Ustaše* militia). In the meantime, *SS-Standartenführer der Reserve und Oberst der Polizei* Karl von Krempler and the German training cadre who had severed all contact with the Muslim militia after it departed the Sanjak, were reassigned.

The end of the legion

In early March 1945 after five months of inactivity, the Sanjak militia was ordered to the front along the Ivan Sedlo (Ivan Saddle), just 25 kilometres (15.5 miles) southwest of Sarajevo, through which the road from Mostar ran (and still does to this day). Heavy fighting prevailed here over the next month, but the German-Croatian defenders could not hold out and Sarajevo fell to the partisans on 6 April. Of the militiamen from the Sanjak, some were killed in the defence of Sarajevo, some were captured in the city itself and then executed by the Tito partisans, but the majority made their way to Sisak, southeast of Zagreb, where they were incorporated into General Luburić's Obrana Brigade, considered by many Croatians to have been their most elite combat unit of the Second World War.

In mid-April the Obrana Brigade was reorganised and renamed the 30th Assault Regiment, becoming part of the newly formed Croatian 18th Assault Division, which at the time was stationed and undergoing training in Sisak. The remnants of the Sanjak Muslim militia were grouped into this regiment. Tito's partisan offensive to end the war moved very rapidly during the second half of April 1945 and the component elements of the new 18th Croatian Assault Division were forced to retreat toward Austria before the formation of the division could be completed. Only a handful of the Sanjak Muslims were able to reach safety. *SS-Polizei-Selbstschutz-Regiment Sandschak* was formally disbanded in Graz, Austria in 1945. The others who were unable to flee were hunted down and murdered in Zagreb after the city fell to the partisans on 8 May. Several Sanjak Muslims perished in the fervent defence of Zagreb, others fled into Austria together with other *Ustaše* troops. Some also fell in battle along the route of withdrawal into Austria or were handed over to Tito after the war by the United Kingdom and subsequently perished on forced death marches, or in death camps.

The Sanjak Muslims in Italian Service, 1941-1943

The Sanjak Muslims had an earlier sponsor before their collaboration with the Germans. While Italy still maintained control of Montenegro, an all-Muslim legion was formed for service in the Sanjak under the sponsorship of the Italian MVAC *(Milizia Voluntare Anti-Comunista),* or Anti-Communist Volunteer Militia. As of 28 February 1943, the total number of Muslim men from the Sanjak who were serving in this legion was 780. It is ironic to note that the same Chetnik forces that launched a series of punitive expeditions in the Sanjak in January and February 1943 – expeditions whose purpose was to kill all Muslims – also belonged to the Italian MVAC. This mean that during February 1943, MVAC Chetniks were killing MVAC Muslims. This blood feud between the Orthodox Serbians and Muslims never ended and explains what the Germans called a 'pointless gun battle' between the Serbian State Guard and about 200 Muslim militiamen near the town of Ivanjica Gust, across the border from Sanjak and Montenegro on 15 July 1943.

Chapter Seven

THE WAFFEN-GEBIRGS-BRIGADE DER-SS (TATARISCHE NR. 1), 1944–1945

Origins

The origins of the *Waffen-Gebirgs-Brigade der-SS (tatarische Nr. 1)* goes back to the initial batch of Crimean Tartar volunteer auxiliary companies that began to be raised in the Crimean Peninsula in autumn 1941. Even before the German invasion of the Soviet Union in 1941, there were groups and individuals in the mostly Muslim areas of the country who opposed the communist system. These came from the various races such as the Uzbeks, Kazaks, Kirghiz, Tajiks and Turkmen, as well as Crimean Tartars, and the peoples of the Caucasus: the Kalmyks of the Volga Steppe, the Azerbaijanis, Georgians, Armenians, and North Caucasians. Most of these émigré refugees had escaped the USSR before 1923, after which, it became increasingly difficult for those people who opposed the Bolsheviks to escape the Soviet Union.[206]

Most of the refugees were of the older generation, such as Mustafa Chokai and Osman Khoja (also called Togan), but also included younger men like Kayum Khan, who would become one of the leading proponents of a Turkestan free of Russian or Turkish control. Two other exiles were a Crimean intellectual leader named Jafar Krimer and Cafar Seydahmet. They too, like the others, were hoping not for the restoration of the Romanov monarchy like the White Russian exiles, but sought independence for their region and basically distrusted any Russian government, whether it was communist, monarchist, or even democratic.

The attitude of the White Russian armies during the Russian Civil War had borne this out. These leaders sought no less than complete independence from Moscow. Nothing less would suffice. This attitude lasted even through the Second World War. While General Andrey Andreyevich Vlasov sought to gain the control of all anti-Stalinist forces, these leaders did their best to oppose this plan. In fact, even though a special effort was made in late 1944 to find non-Russian peoples to join Vlasov's KONR movement, of those that accepted, most were figureheads without political clout. Therefore, of all the committees formed by Rosenberg for the non-Russian peoples of the USSR, only the Kalmyks actually merged with the KONR units.[207]

It was thus not strange that when the Germans reached some of the regions where these people lived, they would be stirred into action by German promises of self-determination and independence. Former émigrés who were aided in forming so-called independence committees under the guidance of Alfred Rosenberg and his *Ostministerium* (Ministry for the East) backed up these promises. Of course, the Germans were giving false hopes and aspirations when, in truth, they had no desire to free the people of the Soviet Union and establish independent states. In fact, on 16 July 1941 Adolf Hitler himself had declared that the Crimea was to be emptied of its entire people and populated by transplanted Romanian ethnic Germans from Transnistria.[208] *Reichsführer-SS* Heinrich Himmler convinced Hitler, however, that the current military situation called for this plan to be postponed until after the war was over. He stated clearly that:

> For the duration of the war, touching on the question of the Tatars and their transfer to consolidated areas by all means must be avoided. We must not bring the least unrest to these people who incline towards us and have faith in us. This would be a catastrophic error.[209]

The very first Crimean volunteers were formed in October 1941 under the auspices of the German 22. *Infanterie-Division*. This German unit organised a militia that was armed with rifles but initially did not carry any ammunition. The militia was to act as the local police in the villages and towns in the region of the 22. *Infanterie-Division*. Things began to become more organised in January 1942 when the German SD began raising Tartar self-defence companies:

> A Tartar Self-Defence Company about 100 strong will be formed by the SD for the fight against partisans in the following localities: (1) Karassubasar, (2) Bacht-schissaraj, (3) Simferopol, (4) Yalta, (5) Aluschta, (6) Sudak, (7) St. Krim, and (8) Evpatoria.[210]

Eventually, these SD-sponsored companies were expanded into six battalions. *Einsatzgruppe D,* which had units operating in the Crimea, initially supplied the officers and direction, as well as the logistics to arm and clothe these Crimean Tartar volunteers in army attire. That the SD was directly involved in the creation of these Tartar units is borne out by another account:

> Six Crimean Tatar battalions were recruited for police and anti-partisan duties largely under the direction of the SD. While the German command found them helpful, the extreme nationalists looked upon them as the nucleus of a future Crimean Army. Among the rank and file their formation appears to have evoked neither enthusiasm nor violent hostility.[211]

However, although six battalions were originally raised, the eventual number would reach eight. When the recruitment of these volunteers reached battalion-level, the *Ordnungspolizei* (Order Police) assumed responsibility. The battalions were listed as the following:[212]

Schutzmannschaft Bataillon 147
Schutzmannschaft Bataillon 148
Schutzmannschaft Bataillon 149
Schutzmannschaft Bataillon 150
Schutzmannschaft Bataillon 151
Schutzmannschaft Bataillon 152
Schutzmannschaft Bataillon 153
Schutzmannschaft Bataillon 154

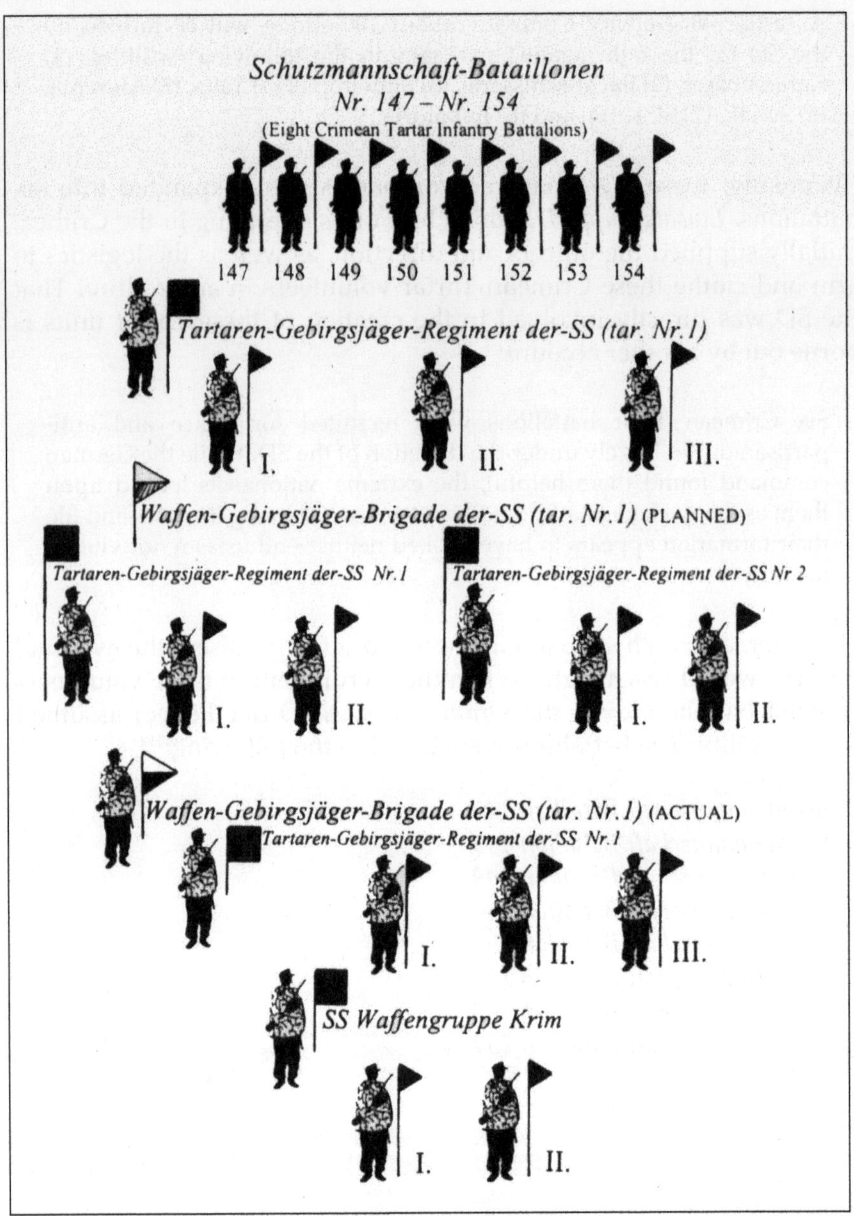

Figure 34. Evolution of the Tartar volunteers in German service, 1942-1945. *(Author's line drawing)*

The Waffen-Gebirgsjäger-Regiment der-SS (tatarische Nr. 1)

The initial creation of a *Waffen-Gebirgsjäger-Regiment der-SS (tatarische Nr. 1)*, or 'Armed Mountain Infantry Regiment of the SS (Tatar Number 1)' was made in late March, early April 1944, when the German Order Police Command in Crimea gathered what effective Tartar battalions still remained and merged them into a three-battalion Tartar SS Mountain regiment. This unit took part in the German defence of the Crimea and was withdrawn shortly before the fall of the peninsula. The first instance of the regiment being employed against the Russians was on 11 April 1944, when the unit was situated in Dzhankoi and used to bolster the Romanian defences of that Crimean city.[213] The regiment's main line of resistance was in the city itself, while the Romanian 10th Infantry Division, with about 4,500 men, covered its left flank, and the Romanian 19th Infantry Division, with an equal number of troops, covering its right flank.

Unfortunately for the Axis forces, by 14 April the combined German, Romanian, and Tartar troops had been pushed back south, halfway to Simferopol and the regiment was now holding the town of Barangar.[214] The Tartar Mountain regiment next served north of Simferopol, and again, was located between the trenches of 10th and 19th Romanian Infantry Divisions. The unit was withdrawn to Romania in the beginning of May 1944. Postwar Soviet accounts mention that of the approximately 228,000 Tartars in the Crimea, 15-20,000 served in the German military. The actual number was probably around 5,000. In fact, the Germans managed to evacuate 36,000 Germans, 3,800 enemy PoWs, 16,000 Russian volunteers of the Eastern Legions, 1,600 Crimean civilians, and 9,600 Romanians.[215]

The Waffen-Gebirgs-Brigade der-SS (tatarische Nr. 1)

Reichsführer-SS Heinrich Himmler instructed the commander of the *Höhere SS und Polizeiführer Schwarzes Meer* (Higher SS and Police Command Black Sea), *SS-Brigadeführer und Generalmajor der Polizei* Konrad Hitschler to supply 200 ethnic-German men of the *Ordnungspolizei* (Order Police) for the forming Tartar SS brigade.[216] Hitschler had previously held the command of *SS Polizei Ausbildungs Bataillon Oranienburg* (SS Police Training Battalion Oranienburg),[217] and later in the war would be posted as Commander of the Order Police in Hungary.[218] The Germans assigned a brigade medical officer for the unit: *SS-Sturmbannführer* Dr Heinz Thumstäder. Born on 26 April 1907, Thumstäder's SS number was 314179. He was later promoted to *SS-Obersturmbannführer* four months after the brigade was disbanded, with the actual date of promotion being 30 April 1945.[219] According to one source, the unit was to contain more than 600 auxiliary *Hilfswilliger* who were not actual combat troops but support personnel. The actual strength of the brigade on 20 September 1944 is hereby compared with its authorised strength:[220]

Table 11. Strength of the Tartar SS Brigade on 20 September 1944.[221]

	Officers	NCOs	Men	Auxiliaries	Grand Total
Authorised	67	440	2,927	614	3,434
Actual	11	191	2,219	-	2,421

Of the above 2,421 men, exactly 1,097 men were *Volksdeutsche.* The morale of the unit was low, given that they had been withdrawn from the Crimea and all the volunteers knew that Germany was on the defensive and losing ground. In addition, the poor and lack-lustre administration and management of the Tartars at the hands of their German masters had a permanent negative and demoralising effect on the volunteers.[222] This was borne out by the defection of men from the Tartar battalions beginning in late 1942. The unit had received the remnants of the *1. Ostmuselmanisches SS Regiment* (1st Eastern Muslim SS Regiment), a unit that had operated in Belarus and had taken part in the crushing of the Warsaw uprising.[223] At the end of 1944, the decision was made to disband the SS brigade and reform the Tartar volunteers into a two-battalion regiment that would become part of the *Osttürkischer-Waffen-Verbände der-SS* (Eastern Turkic Muslim SS Brigade). An attempt had been made earlier in the summer to absorb the *Kalmückisches Kavalleriekorps* (Kalmyk Cavalry Corps), but this move was opposed by the German officers and Kalmyks in the unit and they were eventually transferred into the *XV. Kosaken-Kavalleriekorps* in 1945.[224] The Tartar volunteers now became part of *SS-Waffengruppe Krim.* The group had two infantry battalions of four companies each, plus a separate anti-tank company and infantry gun company attached to the regimental (*Waffengruppe*) headquarters. To that end, it appears that the brigade was moved from the rear of Army Group South to the Reich in mid to late December 1944 and placed in *SS Truppenübungsplatz 'Kurmark'* (SS Troop Training Ground 'Kurmark') near the city of Frankfurt. In autumn 1944, the unit had a total of 2,421 men (eleven officers, 191 NCOs, and 2,219 enlisted personnel). Of that number, 1,097 were ethnic-Germans, mostly from the USSR. When the brigade was disbanded and the men sent to join the *Osttürkischer-Waffen-Verbände der-SS,* the ethnic Germans in the brigade remained at *SS Truppenübungsplatz 'Kurmark'* and were used to flesh out other *Waffen-SS* units.[225]

Chapter Eight

KALMYK VOLUNTEERS IN THE GERMAN ARMY, 1942–1945

In the snowy expanses of Siberia large trees grow, and exiled Kalmyks suffer from the cold

- Alexei Balakaev

Why tell their story?

Although the Kalmyk people are not Muslim, these Buddhist volunteers were nevertheless a unique formation within the German Army. Their story deserves telling within the confines of the exotic formations fielded by the *Wehrmacht* – of which the Muslim units were definitely some of the most unusual. The Kalmyk formation that served in the *Wehrmacht* however, is considered the most unique force of foreign volunteers the Germans ever assembled. During the German invasion of the Soviet Union and subsequent occupation of captured territories, the German Army encouraged the establishment of some form of auxiliary police or self-defence formation raised from the local indigenous population. The minority non-Russian groups, especially the Kalmyks, Cossacks and Tartars, were given special consideration and treatment by the Germans and were permitted to establish self-defence units. One of the most interesting would eventually become known as the *Kalmückisches Kavalleriekorps;* a formation destined to become the most exotic foreign volunteer unit in the *Wehrmacht.*

Introduction

The Kalmyks are a Mongolian race of people, scattered throughout Central Asia, and extending westward into southern Russia. They were nomads, possessing herds of horses, cattle, and sheep,[226] who migrated to the Volga Steppes a little before 1700, and then again in response to a Chinese 'invitation' seventy-one years later (1771). The resistance of the Kazaks on the northern steppe was greatly weakened by this Kalmyk migration. The story of the Kalmyks has been forever immortalised in De Quincy's classic essay, *Revolt of the Tartars*.[227] The word 'Kalmyk' literally means, 'to remain' in the Turkish language.

The Kalmyks refer to themselves as *mana khalyamik emtn* ('our Kalmyk people') but they have accepted the westernised versions of 'Kalmuk', 'Kalmuck', or 'Kalmyk'. The forebears of the Kalmyks came from the pasturelands of Jungaria (also spelled Dzungaria), between the Altai and the Tien Shan ranges in western inner Asia. The Kalmyk people were a remnant of the Oirat Mongol Confederacy, which had stubbornly fought over control of Peking (Beijing) between 1450 and 1650. Later they were used as pawns in the inevitable power struggles between China and Russia. Surprisingly, the Kalmyks were never absorbed into Turkdom, nor did they embrace the Islamic faith. They were, in fact, the only German Army military unit made up completely of Buddhists of the 'Greater Way'.

During the Russian Civil War, Lenin had promised the Kalmyks and other Asiatic races in Russia more freedom from the central government in Moscow in exchange for their help in defeating the Tsarist armies. Instead, the Kalmyks and other peoples had formed 'republics', which the Bolshevik government quickly crushed. The lack in a belief in God, forced collectivisation methods, and other restrictions on the lives of these people by the communists is what drove a greater wedge between the Soviet government and the Kalmyk nation. Resistance to communist rule quickly followed. However, it was not until the summer of 1941 that the NKVD (Soviet Secret Police) had finally been able to gain the upper hand in the Kalmyk Steppes. By then, this guerrilla war had caused the population to be reduced to some 80-90,000 people.[228] This was in stark contrast to a population that had reached 190,600 by 1887. In 1959, seventy-two years after this census, the Kalmyk nation only had 106,100 souls.[229] It seems that decades of fighting Moscow, famines caused by collectivisation methods, and deportation to Siberia as punishment for having assisted the Germans, had taken a heavy toll.

The summer of 1942 brought the German invasion to the Kalmyk homeland when Hitler's panzers roared towards Stalingrad along the Volga bend and moved against the Caucasus Mountains. The further Army Group's 'A' and 'B' advanced between the Caucasus and Stalingrad in those autumn days of 1942, the wider the gap between their offensive spearheads north and south of the Kalmyk Steppe grew. The Germans realised that they needed assistance from the local population in patrolling this important lynchpin of the front lines. Unlike other parts of the Soviet Union, the Germans actually made an attempt at granting semi-autonomous rights to the Kalmyks and other Caucasian peoples. Buddhist temples were reopened and local indigenous authorities were chosen, which enjoyed great autonomy. In December 1942 agrarian reforms began, and the lands began to be restored to the Kalmyk people.[230]

The Caucasian peoples had suffered greatly under communist rule. For example, of the 4,000 mosques, 2,000 *madrassahs* (religious schools), and 10,000 *mullahs* (religious leaders) that existed in the region in 1920, fewer than 150 mosques, 80 *madrassahs,* and 150 *mullahs* remained by 1939.[231] The religious buildings had simply been destroyed, and the Islamic leaders killed or sent to a Siberian Gulag. In return for their newfound freedoms at the hands of the Germans, the Kalmyks and other peoples of the Caucasus reacted extremely favourably to the Axis occupation. For their support of the Germans, the entire Kalmyk population would eventually be exiled in 1946. This support is borne out by several accounts, including some Russian and German post-war histories:

> The situation was particularly bad in the Caucasus region, where the Kalmyks and a number of the Caucasian peoples, including the Chechens, Ingush, and some other peoples, served the Germans willingly.[232]

And from the German point of view, the same results were seen:

> In some areas, such as the Cossack and Kalmyk lands in the North and in the Muslim areas, the welcome was truly enthusiastic.[233]

This assistance to the German military initially began with the selection of a number of *Panje* horses, which were small but sturdy Russian mounts to replace the losses of European horses that the Germans had lost by the tens of thousands. Of the total number of horses used by the Germans in the Russian campaign, 17 per cent died of heart failure brought about by the exertion of towing guns or vehicles stuck in the *rasputitsa* (mud), as well as other cases causing lameness and stomach ulcers. On the open steppe, the European horses would die if the temperature fell to -15.5°C or below. The *Panje* horses used by the Kalmyks, however, could survive in these temperatures and seemed to have as much if not more stamina and energy than their larger, European counterparts.[234] These Kalmyk cavalrymen also used Bactrian camels, though the *Panje* horse was preferred. The successful cooperation between the Germans and their benevolent policies netted great accomplishments in recruiting these native nomadic horsemen into more squadrons.

By August and September 1942, the front lines between those Axis units fighting in and around Stalingrad and the Axis forces fighting in the Caucasus was stretched to breaking point. In the summer of 1942, the German *16. Infanterie-Division (motorisiert)*, under *Generalmajor* Sigfrid Henrici, took Elista, the capital of the 'Kalmyk Autonomous Soviet Socialist Republic', which Joseph Stalin had established in 1935.[235] The division had been assigned the task of keeping a link between German forces fighting in the Caucasus and those German units in and around the city of Stalingrad. The division quickly set up shop in this Kalmyk capital and began sending long-range reconnaissance patrols from Uta, a staging town east of Elista.[236]

The Kalmyks are mobilised

It was not long before the Russians began partisan operations inside the Kalmyk ASSR, which included the entire expanse of the Kalmyk Steppe. The Ic, *Major* Poltermann, requested permission from the divisional commander to raise a local volunteer militia from the nomadic Kalmyk tribes that would help them to guard the flanks. *Oberstleutnant* Bernd Freytag von Loringhoven, who at the time was in Poltava, quickly made some phone calls and located an interpreter for him who had knowledge of the Kalmyk people and, best of all, could speak their language fluently.[237] This officer turned out to be *Sonderführer* Dr Otto Doll, whose real name was Dr Otmar Werva, although another source states that his real name was Rudolf Vrba.[238] Whichever was the case, what is known is that Dr Doll had been born in Russia before the First World War and had served as a White Russian officer during the Russian Civil War.[239]

After the war he had immigrated to the Sudetenland and had joined the German Armed Forces Secret Service (the *Abwehr*), in 1938. When summoned to the headquarters of *16. Infanterie-Division* he had been working in the *Abwehr* office in Feodosia, in the Crimea. His present rank was that of Lance Corporal, but because he was the only individual the Germans could find who spoke Tibetan (the language of the Kalmyks), he was initially promoted to *Sonderführer* and eventually reached the rank of *Major* in the *Heer*.[240] Because of his genuine concern for them, Dr Doll came to be much admired and loved by the people with whom he would share the next two years. He immediately set about organising the Kalmyks, raising the first unit titled *Abwehrtrupp 103* in the middle of August 1942.[241] This force included an initial strength of two cavalry squadrons with about 150 horsemen in each squadron (company).

The title *Abwehrtrupp 103* was soon changed to *Kalmyken Abteilung Dr Doll,* when the formation reached battalion size in September 1942. By the autumn, the formation had reached regimental strength and was now referred to as *Kalmuken-Verbände Dr Doll.* It was eventually renamed as the *Kalmückisches Kavalleriekorps* (abbreviated to KKK) within the German Army in the spring of 1943. By then the unit contained about 5,000 men. In September 1942 twenty-five squadrons of 100 horsemen each were organised throughout the Kalmyk region.[242] The mission of these units was to protect the Kalmyk settlements and help fight the communist guerrillas. This they did, as well as to cover the extended flanks of *16. Infanterie-Division.* The Kalmyks employed guerrilla tactics as well and operated with swiftness and stealth. The partisan bands often did not know that they were being attacked until the Kalmyks were in their midst. Having an intimate knowledge of the countryside, and being accustomed to the harsh weather, the Kalmyk cavalry would seek their revenge on their tormentors. One author attested to their prowess as horsemen and guerrilla fighters:

> These masters of small-scale cavalry warfare soon proved themselves to be of inestimable value with their cavalry raids and reconnaissance expeditions into the Soviet interior.[243]

Moreover, the Kalmyk squadrons protected the exposed flanks of the German troops concentrated at Utta, Chalkuta, and Justa, on both sides of the Elista–Astrakhan road. They were also excellent fighters not only against Soviet partisans, but regular Russian forces, and excelled as scouts. In fact, this reconnaissance and scout work was so invaluable that the commander of *16. Infanterie-Division,* General Graf von Schwerin said in late November 1942 that the duties taken on by his division would have proved impossible to accomplish had it not been for the reliable assistance and cooperation given to his unit by the Kalmyks. That help was often passionate. The Kalmyks, long oppressed by the communists, set about eliminating their enemy with a willingness and vengeance that even appalled some of the German officers. Although the Germans considered them as undisciplined fighters, they nevertheless respected their fighting prowess. There was never any doubt about their effectives and zeal as attested to by this remark:

> Though the Kalmyks were totally without discipline in the western sense, they launched themselves passionately into their work. Indeed, they set

> about wiping out groups of Russians in the Steppes with such ardour that the German Army at times had to intervene to prevent atrocities.[244]

This enthusiasm was, as stated earlier, brought about by the benevolent administration, which the German command wisely chose to follow. In fact, the initial speech made to the Kalmyk leaders was short and simple:

> The land is yours. You are free from the oppression of the Tsars and Bolsheviks... In order to keep power you must fight against the Soviet authority and its supporters.[245]

Fight they did. In fact, soon after the last Soviet NKVD units had left Elista, five units of thirty to forty men each had been independently raised by the Kalmyks at their own initiative. By December 1942 the Germans had recruited no less than 3,000 men,[246] with a German cadre staff of seventy-five officers and NCOs.[247] Most of the Germans were located in the principal headquarters staff. There were forty German officers and NCOs there, but an equal number of Kalmyks.[248] Unfortunately, this German benevolence did not extend to all the people living in the Kalmyk ASSR. One source reported that *Einsatzkommando 11a* sent an *SD-Teilkommando* to Elista and before the end of 1942, ninety-three Jewish families had been rounded up and killed. The body count was around 300.[249] What would have been the reaction of the Kalmyks, one wonders, if they had known that these men who belonged to *Einsatzgruppe D* had proudly recorded that in the first twelve months of the Russian campaign, the unit had 'liquidated at least 90,000 Asiatics, commissars, and Jews'. [250]

Meanwhile Dr Doll had begun to lead the unit, while his Chief of Staff was a Kalmyk leader named Baldan Metabon.[251] At least one of the soon to be organised battalions was led by *Major* Abushinov.[252] In Elista, *Ortskommandantur I. / 649* provided support and weapons (mostly captured arms) to the Kalmyk squadrons. In December 1942 a squadron of Kalmyks attacked a battalion (the 59th Destruction Battalion) of Russian partisans and achieved their single greatest victory to date: the destruction of half of the guerrilla battalion near Ulan Tug, south of Utta.[253] The arrival of the Soviet winter offensive in and around Stalingrad, however, begun on 19 November 1942, would eventually bring a halt to the German occupation of the Kalmyk region. By January 1943 the German *16. Infanterie-Division (motorisiert)* was in retreat, as well as the rest of Army Group's 'A' and 'B'. With them left countless tens of thousands of Caucasian peoples who had collaborated with the Axis forces, as well as their dependents. Dr Doll, together with his assistants, tried to explain the situation to the Kalmyk leadership after assembling all of the tribes. It was a low point in morale:

> [The Kalmyks] at first refused to believe that their trust in the Germans had plunged them into an adventure that might mean the end of their existence as a people. In long columns, including women, children, herds, they made their way towards the Ukraine.[254]

The Kalmyks numbered 10,000-15,000 people altogether. This left about 75-80,000 Kalmyk people who chose to stay behind for one reason or another. The decision was made to leave several cavalry squadrons in order to harass the advancing Russians. Those who did not wish to leave with the Germans and wanted to try their luck by staying, volunteered. One 'division', which was equivalent to a reinforced battalion in strength, contained five cavalry squadrons (the 9th, 10th, 11th, 15th, and 16th) and remained behind to continue the fight using guerrilla warfare. Soon after the Red Army arrived, the region was flooded with NKVD forces looking for these Kalmyk cavalrymen.[255] It is quite certain that by the end of 1943, the NKVD had eliminated these Kalmyk squadrons. There is very little that a courageous horseman can do against the power of machine guns, tanks and artillery. As for other peoples recruited from the Caucasus region, Hitler had stated flatly that he trusted the various Muslim populations of the Caucasus, declaring at a military conference in December 1942:

> For the time being I consider the formation of these battalions of purely Caucasian peoples as very risky, while I don't see any danger in the establishment of purely Muslim units... In spite of all the declarations from Rosenberg and the military, I don't trust the Armenians either. ... I don't know about these Georgians. They do not belong to the Turkic peoples... I consider only the Muslims to be reliable.... All the others I deem unreliable.[256]

If Hitler considered the Muslims to be reliable, Stalin found them to be fittingly untrustworthy enough to eliminate their national republics and exile entire races of them. Based on their support for the Germans, Moscow made sure that the Kalmyk people were included in this group:[257] On 27 December 1943, the Presidium of the Supreme Soviet issued a decree which liquidated the Kalmyck ASSR and listed a series of crimes against the state the Kalmyk people had committed, guaranteeing them a forced relocation to Siberia:

> Taking into consideration that in the period of occupation by German-Fascist invaders of the Kalmyk ASSR, many Kalmyks betrayed the motherland, joined organized German military detachments to fight against the Red Army, handed over to the Germans honest Soviet citizens, seized and handed over to the Germans kolhoz livestock evacuated from Rostov Oblast and Ukraine, and after the expulsion of the occupation by the Red Army organised bands and actively opposed organs of Soviet power so as to restore their destroyed German masters, commit bandit raids on kolkhozes and terrorise the surrounding population...[258]

1943

In the beginning of 1943, and in the midst of the withdrawal, Dr Doll was able to create a Kalmyk Cavalry Regiment based on a three-battalion unit. As stated earlier, each battalion was named a 'division' and contained around 750 men and a HQ's Staff of six officers and NCOs. This was equivalent to a reinforced battalion. In January Dr Doll organised three such 'divisions' but one month later he had four. In each 'division' there were five cavalry squadrons of 150 mean each plus a Squadron HQ's Staff of five officers and NCOs. Each squadron contained three *Vzvod,* which were the equivalent of a cavalry platoon, and had a complement of forty-eight men each plus a platoon staff of three officers and NCOs.[259] On 18 January 1943, ten cavalry squadrons of the Kalmyk Legion were located just east of Salsk.[260] The unit was withdrawing right alongside *Kosaken Regiment von Jungschultz* (Cossack Cavalry Regiment 'von Jungschultz'). This had been done for protection against attacks by superior enemy forces. The withdrawal followed the route of the Manych River all the way to Rostov. Since the unit had been officially formed on 17 October 1942, it had been referred to by the Germans as the *'Kalmücken-Legion'*,[261] although the Kalmyks themselves referred to their formation as the *'Kalmyckij Kavalerijskij Korpus'* (Kalmyk Cavalry Corps).[262]

On 22 January 1943 the three-battalion strong Kalmyk regiment was transferred to *3. Panzer-Division*. It was immediately relocated west-northwest of Bela Glina as the lynchpin between *3. Panzer-Division* and *444. Sicherungs-Division.*[263] By then the Soviet winter offensive had been going on for two months and the German *6. Armee,* which had been surrounded at Stalingrad, was close to being destroyed. The Germans had attempted to relieve the trapped *6. Armee* but had failed to break the siege. There followed a general withdrawal from the Caucasus Mountains that often times resembled a race to see who would reach Rostov first: the Germans or the Russians. During this general withdrawal a large portion of the Kalmyk population followed the German retreat westwards, as their husbands and sons were serving the *Kalmuken-Verbände Dr Doll.*

The author Paul Carell,[264] states that at the end of January 1943, the Germans, whose principal units in the area of Tikhoretsk were the *3. Panzer-Division* and *111. Infanterie-Division,* were racing from there to try to reach Rostov before the Russians captured the city and trapped all German forces still in the Caucasus.[265]

In February 1943 the Germans changed the title of the unit to *Kalmücken-Verbände Dr.Doll* (Kalmyk Formation Dr Doll).[266]That same month, the regiment and the *Kosaken-Regiment von Jungschultz* withdrew alongside the *3. Panzer-Division* until they reached Taganrog, where they were then attached to *Feldkommandantur 200.* Both units were now assigned to coastal guard duty by the Sea of Azov.[267] In early March 1943, while the Kalmyk formation was under the control of the *444. Sicherungs-Division,* Field Marshal von Kleist ordered that all Cossack units be sent to Kherson in the Ukraine with the objective of merging them all together into a larger armed and therefore more effective fighting force. The ignorance of higher authorities, who believed that if you were opposed to Stalin and rode a horse then you must be a Cossack, caused the Kalmyk cavalry formation to be sent there as well.[268]

However, it soon became evident to the German commanders at Kherson that 'there had been a mistake'. How could one supervise a volunteer from Smolensk and a Kalmyk horseman who had spent all his life on the Steppe using the same rules? This question was too problematic for the Germans and so the Kalmyk formation was separated from the Cossacks and withdrawn.[269] It was in March 1943 that the Kalmyks received their first arms since withdrawing from the Kalmyk Steppe. It included 1,000 Dutch rifles and 35,000 rounds for these weapons.[270] Before this, the units had been armed with sabres and mostly Russian rifles. They were the first of what would be a plethora of various weapons from half a dozen different nations. By 18 April the strength of the unit was some 2,200 men and as of the 28th, there were seventy-nine Kalmyk officers, 353 NCOs, and 2,029 men, plus 2,030 horses and camels.[271] By the end of April 1943 the Kalmyks were still under the newly formed German *6. Armee,* established after the original *6. Armee* was destroyed at Stalingrad. At the time it was performing coastal guard duty by Mariupol, some 150 kilometres (100 miles) west of Taganrog. The Kalmyks next moved to Zaporizhia on the lower Dnieper River and were placed under the control of *Oberfeldkommandantur 397*. On 23 May there were sixty-seven Kalmyk officers, 374 NCOs, and 2,917 men. The formation had also acquired an amazing 4,600 horses and camels. By August 1943 the title of the *Kalmücken-Verbände Dr Doll* was changed to the *Kalmückisches Kavalleriekorps* (Kalmyk Cavalry Corps). It was at this time that the order of battle for the unit was organized as follows:

CO: *Major* Ottmar Rudolf Werba (AKA Dr Doll)
Adjutant: *Major* Eduard Bataev [272]
Ia: *Major* Baldan Metabon
Liaison: *Major* Kallmeyer [273]
1st Division - CO: *Major* Lukyanov Cilgirov
1st, 4th, 7th, 8th, 18th squadrons
2nd Division - CO: *Major* Boldyrev Mukubenov
5th, 6th, 12th, 20th, 23rd squadrons
3rd Division - CO: *Major* Abushinov Cilgirov
3rd, 14th, 17th, 21st, 25th squadrons
4th Division - CO: *Major* Konokov Savkaev
2nd, 13th, 19th, 22nd, 24th squadrons

It should be noted that the Chief of Staff, Baldan Metabon, who held the post from June 1943 until March 1944, was a non-Kalmyk Mongol who had previously been a member of the Soviet 110th Cavalry Division. From May until July 1944, Kalmyk Major Mukeben Chachlysev assumed this post. When Chachlysev and Dr Doll were killed in battle in July 1944, Captain Dordzi Arbakov assumed the post of Chief of Staff. Another valuable officer, Lieutenant Kuskin, the Chief of the Kalmyk Field Police Troop, died in September 1944. Colonel Eduard Bataev would assume command of the Kalmyk formation upon the death of Doll.[274] The strength of the unit on 21 July 1943 was as follows:

Table 12. Strength of the Kalmyken Kavallerie Korps on 21 July 1943.

German Staff	Kalmyks	Grand Total
71 + 68[275]	3,000	3,139
Horses/Camels	Rifles	Pistols
4,600	2,000	85
Machine Pistols	Light Machineguns	Heavy Machineguns
61	5	1
Light Mortars (62 mm)		
14		

The KKK continued to serve behind the lines throughout 1943. In July 1943 it was listed under *Kommandeur der Osttruppen z.b.V. 721* (Commander of Eastern Troops 721) by Krivoi-Rog.[276] By the end of 1943 the unit was under *4. Panzerarmee* and tasked with guarding the rear of the German divisions in the Nikopol bridgehead. It was here that once again the Kalmyks proved their worth. The defensive positions of the Germans at the Nikopol bridgehead were in the shape of an arc approximately 112.5 kilometres (75 miles) long. The depth of the combat area was no more than 10-14 kilometres (6-8.5 miles) from the eastern bank of the Dnieper River. The *Plavna,* an extensive, swampy area also lay in this region. The area was ideal for Soviet guerrillas and indeed was swarming with partisans. However, the Germans had one ace in the hole: the Kalmyk Cavalry Formation. One author described very succinctly just how much the German *Landser* appreciated them:

> These clandestine forces in the inaccessible hiding places of the swamps would have been a serious danger to the German lines but for Senior Sergeant Willi Lilienthal. This man from Hamburg turned up at the end of November 1943 with the Kalmyk Major Abushinov. With him came five cavalry squadrons – 1,200 Klamyk volunteers from the yurt villages of the Kalmyk Steppe. These mortal enemies of the Russians had been fighting on the German side since the summer of 1942. With their wives and families, they had followed 16. Panzer Grenadier Division from the wide-open spaces around Elista all the way to the west. There were no better scouts and no better hunters of partisans. They kept the franc-tireurs of the Plavna in check. [277]

In fact, this was one the of the Kalmyk 'divisions' (the 3rd).[278] The rest were performing security duty up and down the length of the Nikopol bridgehead on both sides of the Dnieper.[279] The unit was executing rear area security and anti-partisan duty for the *XL. Panzerkorps*. This duty was not without losses however, for by 2 December the 3rd 'Division' under *Major* Abushinov had lost 200 men killed or wounded. The 1st 'Division' of the *Kalmückisches Kavalleriekorps* was under the command of *Major* L. Cilgirov. Together with *Major* A. Cilgirov's 3rd 'Division' and *Hauptmann* Munster and his *Geheim Feldpolizei Trupp 721,* these three units would take part in an anti-guerrilla sweep in late December 1943. *Abwehrtrupp 201* would also participate in an ancillary role.

The aim of the operation was the destruction of Russian Major Kirpa's partisan band in the *Plavna* swamps. The operation netted fifty guerrillas killed and thirty-two captured. More importantly, it kept the partisans from the backs of the German defenders at the Nikopol bridgehead. As well as they performed their missions in fighting their hated enemy, the Kalmyk nation experienced a lack of understanding from many German commands that they were forced to come under. Having Asiatic features, they were not treated like the Cossacks, who, it was thought, were transplanted Aryans. As a result, and despite their extreme value to the German command, they even experienced some bigotry:

> They carried out their task to the best of their ability. But the consequences of their transplantation into an alien world soon began to show up. Doll had never tried to convert Kalmyks into soldiers in the Western sense. He knew that it couldn't be done. The result was that they now became an endless nuisance to the German military authorities. Soon one headquarters or another was demanding that they be disarmed. It was mandatory that they be separated from their wives and children. The Kalmyks, for their part, reacted as they could not help reacting – like uprooted, homeless, misunderstood, and unjustly attacked individuals. And what the Germans refused to give them they took for themselves.[280]

1944

The next area of operations for the *Kalmückisches Kavalleriekorps*was in the Dnepropetrovsk– Dievka region in January 1944, before it moved on and crossed the Hungarian frontier in February. It was in February that Gottlob Berger, the head of the SS Recruiting Office, had requested the *Gestapo*'s consent to do away with the national insignias of peoples of the Caucasus that had been recruited to work in Germany. This request only covered the Tartars, Cossacks and Kalmyks, while the other Slavic peoples were still deemed too unreliable and needed to be easily recognised.[281] In that same month the *Kalmückisches Kavalleriekorps* came under the control of *Oberfeldkommandantur 372* in Lublin, Poland.[282] By February, the KKK was attached to the *213. Sicherungs-Division* for operational purposes.[283]

The Kalmyk volunteers were now relegated to performing anti-guerrilla operations against the Polish underground army. In this new environment the Kalmyks encountered a different climate and fauna. The dry, wide-open steppes were long gone and instead were replaced by woods, marshes, and hills that were unfamiliar to the Kalmyks. Their employment in these new surroundings would lower the effectiveness of the Kalmyk units, although alongside their beloved commander, Dr Doll, they continued to do their best. In June 1944 the unit was still in the Lublin area, where a large anti-partisan operation was launched against guerrillas entrenched in the Bilgoraj Forest. The Germans had amassed a sizable force for the drive and included the following formations:

Ground Units:
Sonderdienst-Bataillon[284]
CO: *SS-Sturmbannführer* Helmut Pfaffenroth.
Sonderdienst Bataillon
CO: *Rechtsrat* Dr Jaensch.
154. Reserve-Division
CO: *Generalleutnant* Altrichter
174. Reserve-Division
CO: *Generalleutnant* Eberhardt
213. Sicherungs-Division
CO: *Generalleutnant* Lendle
Kalmückisches Kavalleriekorps (attached to *213. Sicherungs-Division*)
CO: *Oberst* Dr. Doll
Landesschützen Bataillon 115 (Regional Defence Battalion 115)
1.(mot.) Gendarmerie Bataillon (motorisiert) (1st Motorised Gendarmerie Battalion)
5th Hungarian Infantry Division (only parts, the bulk of the unit was at Kobrin).[285]
Air Support: *1. Staffel der Luftwaffe Fliegergruppe 7* [286]

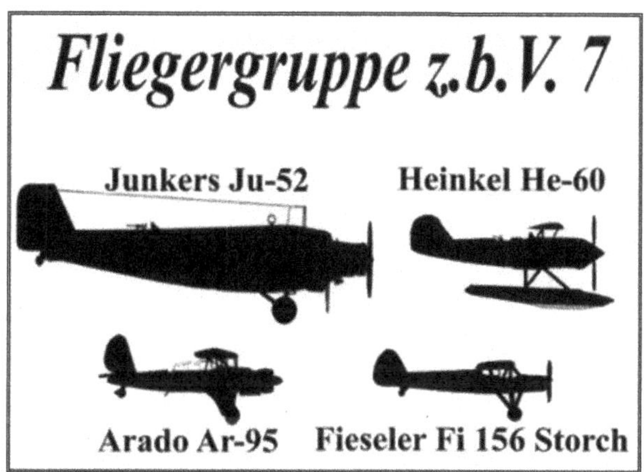

Figure 35. The various planes employed by Fliegergruppe z.b.V. 7. *(Author's line drawing)*

The Germans listed Polish Home Army losses as 898 killed, while '193 bandits and 531 bandit helpers' were apprehended. Axis losses were placed at 102 killed and 202 wounded. Captured equipment included 2 radio sets, 8 light machine guns, 3 anti-tank weapons (bazookas), 24 machine pistols, 2 mortars, 40 rifles, 230 hand grenades, 22,000 rounds of rifle ammunition, 2,500 rounds of machine pistol ammunition, 400 kg of explosives and 370 fuses.[287] There the KKK performed all too well, eliminating any guerrillas they found, but their behaviour did not change and they continued to be misunderstood.

The Germans always failed to comprehend how the Kalmyks felt. These people had been uprooted from their ancestral home, had basically given everything up for the Germans and felt that the Third Reich was indebted to them. Therefore, it was felt that the responsibility of the Germans was to supply the Kalmyks with their every need. If those needs were not met, then they felt justified in removing the property and livestock of the local peasants, as they needed it. Pretty soon the local German authorities were complaining about the formation once again.

In a way, it is hard to blame the Kalmyks for taking this attitude, but it made them seem more and more like free-booters of the Thirty Years' War. It was in July 1944 that the KKK was committed to fighting on the front lines against regular Russian units. Tragedy befell the unit when its beloved and much-admired commander, *Major* Doll and some other Kalmyk leaders were killed. The loss of their German commander was so great that the unit became demoralised for a time and had to be withdrawn for several weeks. The interim commander was now to be *Oberstleutnant* Bergen,[288] a Reich German whose *nom-de-guerre* was 'Pipgorra'.[289] Slowly, the unit's morale was once again raised, but not to the level at which it had been before the death of their beloved commander. On 6 July 1944, the KKK could count on the following forces and arms at its disposal:

Table 13. Strength of the Kalmückisches Kavalleriekorps on 6 July 1944.

Officers	NCOs	Enlisted Men	Total
147	374	2,917	3,438
horses/camels	rifles	pistols	machine pistols
3,800/800	2,166[290]	246	163[291]
light machine guns	60 mm mortars	*Panjewagen*	PKW and LKW light trucks
21	9	500	8

In the autumn, the unit was stationed in the Radom district and was still there when, in January 1945, the Soviet winter offensive began. The German front line cracked all along the Eastern Front. It was during this chaotic period in the war that the Red Army forces finally trapped and conclusively defeated the KKK near Kielce.[292] It was eventually decided that Colonel Eduard Bataev would assume command. What remnants remained of the KKK after the Soviet offensive in January 1945 withdrew into Austria in February. It is interesting to note that shortly before the Soviet offensive, the strength of the KKK had been increased to around 5,000 men.

This had been done by the ruthless conscription of all available manpower. Kalmyk men older than 45 years of age and younger than 18 had not been drafted into the corps before 1944.[293] Interestingly, it appears that plans had been in the works to include the KKK into the forming *Kaukasicher-Waffen-Verbände der-SS*. One unconfirmed report states that the *SS Hauptamt* (SS Main Office) had, on 8 January 1945, authorised the transfer of the KKK into the newly organised Caucasian SS Cavalry formation.[294] It would appear that the idea was dropped either because of the Soviet winter offensive, which began a few days later, or because the KKK had already been earmarked for the Vlasov Army. Perhaps it was on account of both, but in any case, we shall never really know.

The remnants of the corps withdrew through Silesia and eventually reached Austria in March 1945 when it was finally dissolved and its survivors were absorbed into the 600th and 650th (Russian Army of Liberation) Infantry Divisions.[295] This occurred at the Neuhammer Training Camp.[296] The Kalmyk people experienced the same fate that awaited tens of thousands of other Soviet citizens who had chosen to cast their lot with the Germans. It was their sad fate in life to have put their trust in one dictatorial regime in order to get rid of an equally despotic government. In the end, historian Olaf Caroe put it quite succinctly, when he said of them:

> It was their tragedy that, like the Kalmyks in the seventeenth century, they were used as pawns in the struggle of two contending empires on the chessboard of power-politics. In such a contest their own aims, however noble, could not be realised.[297]

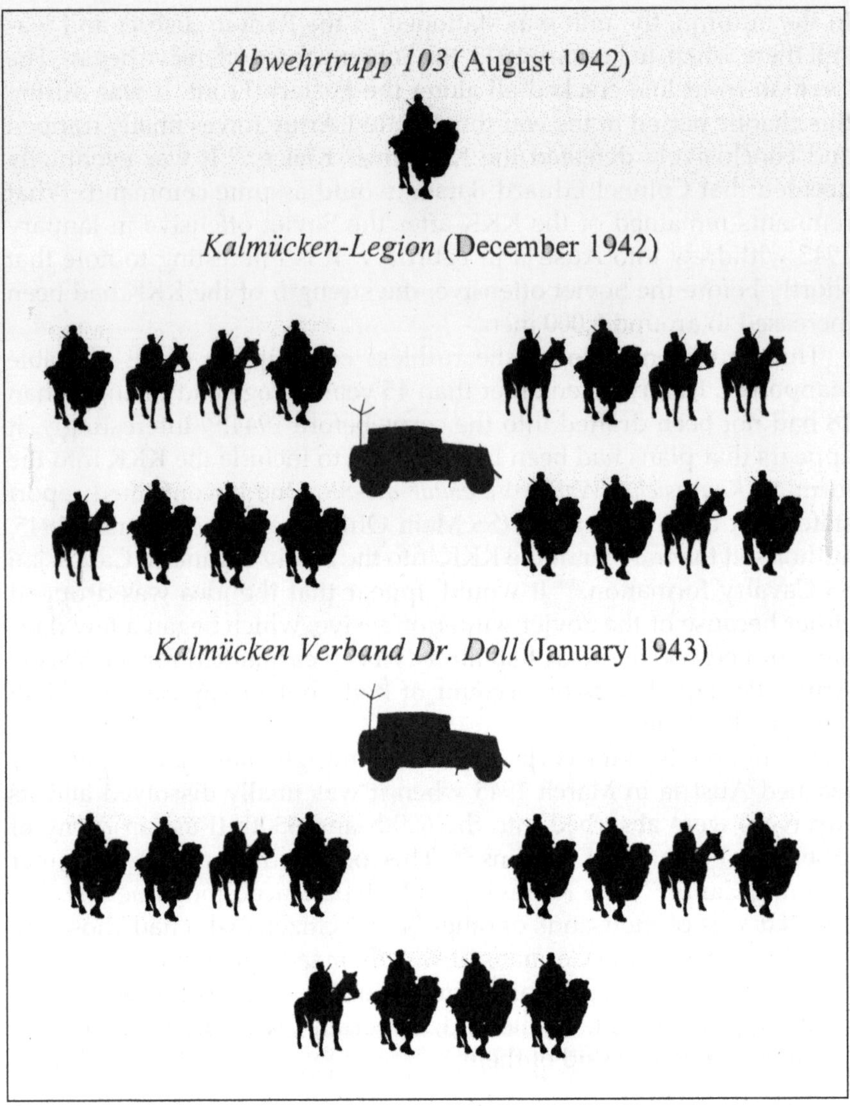

Figure 36. The Kalmyk cavalry formation, 1942-1943. *(Author's line drawing)*

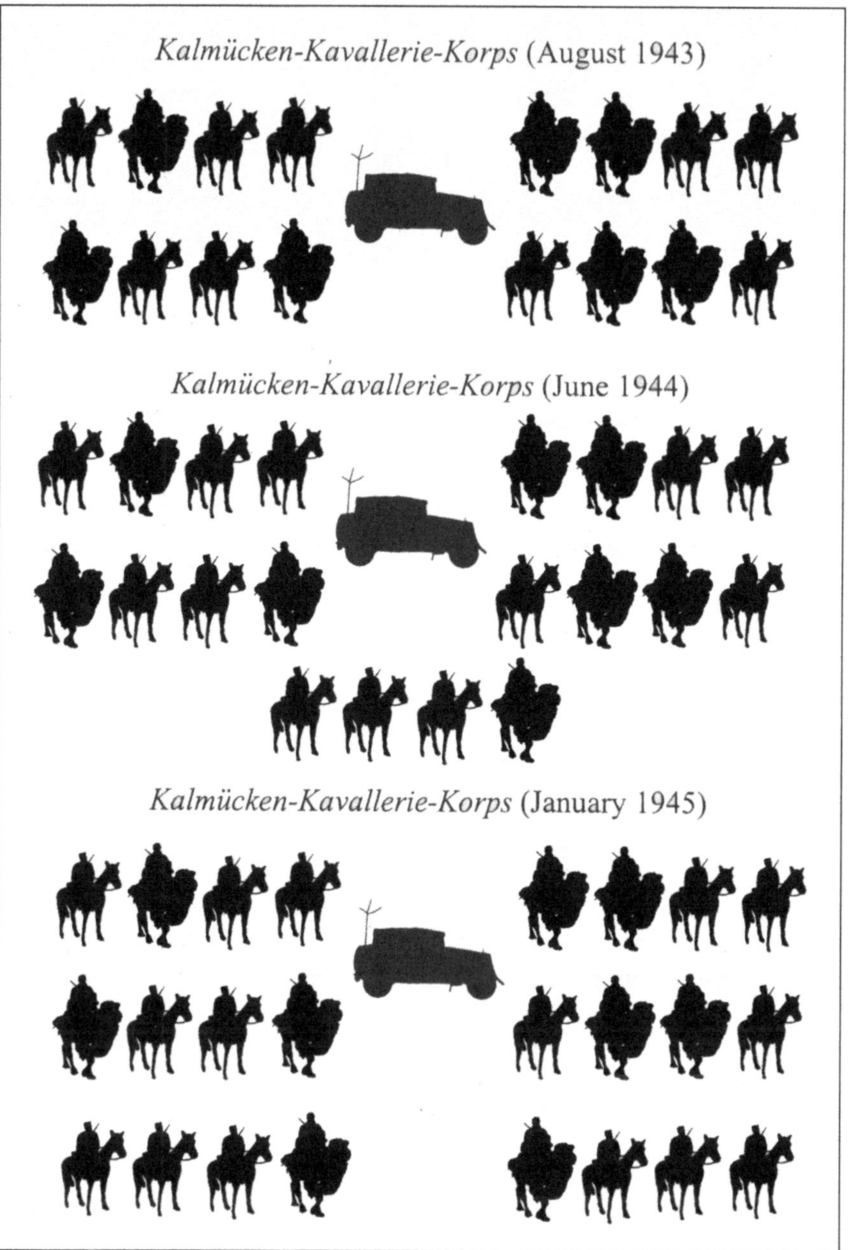

Figure 37. The Kalmyk cavalry formation, 1943-1944. *(Author's line drawing)*

Chapter Nine

CONCLUSIONS

From a military point of view, we can safely argue that the contribution to the Nazi war effort of the forces covered in this book can be described as minimal and relatively insignificant to the outcome of the war. However, during the war, these tens of thousands of volunteers provided thousands of photographs and hundreds of reels of film for the German propaganda office. In that sense, these units were a Godsend to the Third Reich, because it gave the impression that many people in the world were supporting Nazi Germany. If one is to believe the propaganda that came with these photographs and films, one would think that the majority of the world was behind the Germans. This, of course, was the point of the German effort. It is not that these formations were created strictly for propaganda purposes. We know that some, like the Arab formations, were established in the hope that once Germany had conquered the Middle East, they would serve as the basis for a satellite army that would help the Third Reich to control that region. Another reason why these exotic units were established was more practical and basic: pure military necessity. This was especially true as the war turned against the Germans, and a nation of 80 million people found itself fighting the world.

The recruitment of Arab volunteers is quite an interesting story. When the opportunity presented itself in the spring of 1941 on account of the Iraqi Army uprising against British interests in Iraq, the Third Reich was caught unaware. The German command reacted late and haphazardly, being simply caught flatfooted. Their assistance to the Iraqis was only ready after the British had crushed the uprising. This missed opportunity that developed in the Middle East in the spring and summer of 1941, pretty much sums up early German efforts to support Arab independence. In other words, Nazi Germany had not given any thought on the subject.

Fascist Italy was also a problem that was never addressed properly or decisively. Benito Mussolini was adamantly opposed to granting even semi-autonomy to the people of the region. The Libyans had staged a twenty-year revolt against Italian rule in Libya, which the Italians supressed rather ruthlessly. This uprising against Italian rule could only be put down with great difficulty. It was therefore a non-starter for Mussolini that the Arab people be granted even the status of a satellite Axis nation. Consequently, as the war progressed, no concrete promises were ever made by the Germans to the people of the region regarding what a victorious Third Reich could mean to them. Only vague promises were ever made to the volunteers from the regions of North Africa and the Middle East. The same can be said of German promises made to Muslim volunteers from the Balkans and the USSR. This was because Hitler's plan for the East did not envision any sort of semi-autonomy or nation-state for the *Ostvölker* (Eastern Peoples).

What would have happened had the Third Reich won the war, is up to speculation. Certainly, we can surmise that if any of these people were to have been allowed to have a state, that nation would have to have been an Axis satellite state, completely dependent and wholly benefitting Nazi Germany. If this is the case, why did these men volunteer in the first place? Based on all available evidence, we can conclude that the various Muslim peoples who lived in North Africa, the Middle East, the Balkans and the USSR joined the German Armed Forces for potentially the following principal reasons. And while each volunteer may have had one, two, or more reasons for joining the German Armed Forces, it must also be remembered that some Muslims were forcibly conscripted into the German Army. This, too, needs to be factored into the equation as to why they served:

1. To fight British and French imperialism in North Africa and the Middle East.
2. To resist Jewish attempts to establish a state in Palestine.
3. Hatred of the Jews.
4. Continued racial and religious hatred in the Balkans between the Serbians, Croatians and Bosnian Muslims.
5. Fear and hatred of communism and its Soviet system.
6. Hatred of Stalin and the Stalinist regime.
7. A desire for self-determination.
8. A desire for adventure.
9. A desire for some sort of personal gain.
10. A desire to be 'on the winning side'.[298]

For the most part, 99.99 per cent of the Muslim volunteers who served in the German *Heer* (army) and / or *Waffen-SS*, did so for one or more of the above-mentioned reasons. We cannot consider the overwhelming majority of these men as Nazi racists, for they did not meet the strict Aryan racial requirements for the Germans to consider them their equals. Instead, we can think of this Muslim–Nazi partnership not as a bonafide military union, but as a form of military expediency, rather than an actual coalition or partnership of various peoples, all working together equally for a common cause. The old Arab proverb, 'the enemy of my enemy, is my friend' is the guidepost that one should use in trying to understand Nazi–Muslim relations during the Second World War. For these volunteers, it was not so much *what* the Nazis had to offer them, but rather what would be destroyed as a result of that Nazi victory.

BIBLIOGRAPHY

Doctoral Dissertations-

Pronin, Alexander. *Guerrilla Warfare in the German Occupied Soviet Territories 1941-1945*. Georgetown: Georgetown University Graduate School, 1965.

Primary Sources

NARA T-78, Roll 410

NARA T-78, Roll 645

NARA T-175, Roll 77

NARA T-175, Roll 140

NARA T-175, Roll 162

NARA T-175, Roll 168

NARA T-354. Roll 161

NARA T-314, Roll 661

NARA T-311, Roll 286

NARA T-313, Roll 194

NARA T-315, Roll 2214

NARA T-501, Roll 249

NARA T-501, Roll 256

NARA T-263, Tscherim Soobzokov name file, and NARA T-85, INS file

Case 2:15-cv-6831-SDW-LDW; 02-16-2016, Aslan T. Soobzokov (Tscherim Soobzokov), Plaintiff, v. Eric Lichtblau; Houghton, Mifflin and Harcourt, Defendants.

BStU - Bundesbeauftragter für die Unterlagen des Staatssicherheitsdienstes der ehemaligen Deutschen Demokratischen Republik, Berlin (Stasi Records Archive, East Germany), MfS HA IX/11, FV 6/74, Bd 25, pp BStU 000124-000125.

Personnel File for *SS-Sturmbannführer* Egon Zill, Berlin Document Centre – now referred to as the *Bundesarchiv*, Berlin-Lichterfelde.

Personnel file for *SS-Standartenführer der Reserve* Arved Theuermann, Berlin Document Centre – now referred to as the *Bundesarchiv*, Berlin-Lichterfelde.

Personnel File for *Waffen-Standartenführer der-SS* Kutschuk Ulagaj, Berlin Document Centre – now referred to as the *Bundesarchiv*, Berlin-Lichterfelde.

Post-war SHAEF interview found in file of Tscherim Soobzokov, and subsequent interview by the FBI Office for Special Investigations. Berlin Document Centre – now referred to as the *Bundesarchiv*, Berlin-Lichterfelde.

Völkischer Beobachter ('People's Observer') newspaper, dated 12 January 1944.

SS-Hauptamt. *Dienstalterliste der Schutzstaffel NSDAP. Stand von 9. November 1944*. Berlin: Gedruckt in Reichsdruckerei, 1944.

Trial of the Major War Criminals before the International Military Tribunal. Nuremberg: U.S. Army, 1946, 22 volumes.

Felmy, Helmut. *German Exploitation of Arab Nationalist Movements in World War II.* MS No.P-207: United States Army in Europe: U.S. Army Historical Division, 1946.

Secondary Sources

Achcar, Gilbert. *Le Arabe et la Shoah. La guerre israélo-arabe des récits*. Paradou: Actes Sud, 2009.

Alexiev, Alex. *Soviet Nationalities in German Wartime Strategy, 1941-1945.* Santa Monica: Rand Corporation, 1982.

Anders, Wladyslaw. *Hitler's Defeat in Russia.* Chicago: Henry Regnery Company, 1953.

Bensoussa,n Georges, editor. *Antisemitisme et Negationnisme dans le Monde Arabo-Musulman: La Derive. Revue Histoire de la Shoah. le Monde Juif.* Paris: Somogy éditions dart, 2004.

Bostom, Andrew G. *The Muftis Islamic Jew-Hatred: What the Nazis Learned from the Muslim Pope.* Jacksonville: Create Space Independent Publishing Platform, 2013.

Busch, Erich. *Die Fallschirmjäger Chronik 1935-1945*. Friedberg: Podzun Palla Verlag, 1983.

Caballero-Jurado, Dr Carlos. *La Espada del Islam: Voluntarios Arabes en el Ejercito Aleman 1941-1945.* Alicante: Garcia Hispan, Editor, 1990.

Carell, Paul. *Hitler Moves East: The Russo-German War, 1941-1943*. Boston: Little, Brown and Company. 1964.

Carell, Paul. *Scorched Earth: The Russo-German War, 1943-1944*. Boston: Little, Brown and Company. 1970.

Carnier, Dr. Pier Arrigo. *L'armata Cosacca in Italia 1944-1945*. Grupo Ugo Mursia Editore, 1990.

Caroe, Olaf. *Soviet Empire: The Turks of Central Asia and Stalinism*. London: MacMillan & Co. Ltd., 1954.

Curtiss, John Shelton. *The Russian Revolutions of 1917*. New York: D. Van Nostrand Company, Inc., 1957.

Dalin, David G. and John F. Rothman. *Icon of Evil: Hitlers Mufti and the Rise of Radical Islam: Hitlers Mufti and the Rise of Radical Islam.* London: Routledge, 2009.

Dallin, Alexander. *German Rule in Russia 1941-1945. A Study of Occupation Policies*. London: Macmillan & Co. Ltd., 1957.

Ganter, Theresa M. *Searching for a New German Identity: Heiner Müller and the Geschichtsdrama*. Lausanne: Peter Lang 2008.

Gelvin, James L. *The Modern Middle East*. New York: Oxford University Press, 2005.

Gershoni, Israel, editor. *Arab Responses to Fascism and Nazism: Attraction and Repulsion*. Austin: University of Texas Press, 2014.

Grenkevich, Leonid. *The Soviet Partisan Movement 1941-1944*. London: Frank Cass, 1999.

Gruenthal, Heide-Marie. *Nacht Über Europa: Die Faschistische Okkupationspolitik in Polen (1939- 1945)*. Köln: Pahl- Rugenstein Verlag, 1989.

Heilbrunn, Otto and Aubrey Dixon. *Communist Guerrilla Warfare*. London: George Allen & Unwin Ltd., 1954.

Herf, Jeffrey. *Nazi Propaganda for the Arab World*. New Haven: Yale University Press, 2009.

Hillgruber, Andreas. *Die Räumung der Krim 1944*. Berlin: Verlag E. S. Mittler & Sohn, 1959.

Hinze, Rolf. *Rückzugkämpf in der Ukraine 1943/44*. Neustadt: Verlag Dr. Rolf Hinze, 1991.

Hnilicka, Karl. *Das Ende auf dem Balkan 1944/45*. Zürich: Musterschmidt-Göttingen Verlag, 1970.

Hnilicka, Karl. *Das Ende auf dem Balkan 1944/45*. Musterschmidt - Göttingen Verlag: Zürich, 1970.

Hoffman, Joachim. *Die Ostlegionen 1941-1943*. Verlag Rombach Freiburg, 1986.

Khalidi, Rashid. *Resurrecting Empire: Western Footprints and America's Perilous Path in the Middle East*. Boston: Beacon Press, 2004.

Kleitmann, Dr K.G. *Die Waffen-SS: eine Dokumentation*. Osnabrück: Verlag 'Der Freiwillige' GmbH, 1965.

Küntzel, Matthias. *Jihad and Jew-Hatred: Islamism, Nazism and the Roots of 9/11*. Candor: Telos Press Publishing, 2007.

Lambert, Pierre Philippe and Gerard Le Marec. *Les Francais Sous Le Casque Allemand: Europe 1941-1945*. Paris: Jacques Grancher, 1994.

Lepre, George. *Himmlers Bosnian Division: The Waffen-SS Handschar Division, 1943-1945*. Atglen: Schiffer Publishing, 1997.

Lichtblau, Eric. *The Nazis Next Door: How America Became a Safe Home for Hitler's Men*. Houghton, Mifflin and Harcourt: New York, 2014.

Littlejohn, David. *The Patriotic Traitors. The History of Collaboration in German-Occupied Europe, 1940-45*. Doubleday & Company, Inc.: Garden City, New York, 1972.

Lucas, James. *War on the Eastern Front 1941-1945*. London: Janes Publishing Company, 1979.

Mallmann, Klaus-Michael and Martin Cüppers. *Halbmond und Hakenkreuz. Das Dritte Reich, die Araber und Palästina*. Darmstadt: Wissenschaftliche Buchgesellschaft, 2006.

Mehner, Kurt. *Die Waffen-SS und Polizei 1939-1945*. Norderstedt: Militär-Verlag Klaus D. Patzwall, 1995.

Mendelsohn, John, Editor. *Covert Warfare: Intelligence, Counter-Intelligence, and Military Deception During the World War II Era*. New York: Garland Publishing, 1979.

Motadel, David. *Islam and Nazi Germanys War.* Harvard Belknap Press, 2017.

Mulligan, Timothy Patrick. *The Politics of Illusion and Empire: German Occupation Policy in the Soviet Union, 1942-1943.* New York: Praeger Publishers, 1988.

Muñoz, Antonio J. *Modernism, Colonialism and Arab Nationalism: Essays on the Modern Middle East.* New York: Europa Books, 2010.

Muñoz, Antonio J. *Hitler's Eastern Legions, Volume II – The Osttruppen.* New York: Europa Books, 1997.

Muñoz, Antonio J. *For Czar and Country: A History of the Russian Guard Corps, 1941-1945.* New York: Europa Books, 1999.

Muñoz, Antonio J. *The Last Levy: Waffen-SS Officer Roster, 1 March 1945.* New York: Europa Books, 2001.

Muñoz, Antonio J. *Forgotten Legions: Obscure Formations of the Waffen-SS, 1943-1945.* Boulder: Paladin Press, 1991.

Muñoz Antonio J. *Lions of the Desert: Arab Volunteers in the German Army 1941-1945.* New York: Europa Books, Inc., 1995.

Muñoz, Antonio J. *Hitler's Green Army: The German Order Police and Its Auxiliaries, 1939-1945, Volume 2 - Eastern Europe and the Balkans.* Europa Books: New York, 2006.

Neufeldt, Hans-Joachim, Jürgen Huck and Georg Tessin. *Zur Geschichte der Ordnungspolizei 1936-1945.* Schriften des Bundesarchivs: Boppard-am-Rhein, 1957.

Nicosia, Francis R. *Germany and the Arab World.* Cambridge: Cambridge University Press, 2015.

Nicosia, Francis R. and Boğac A. Ergene. *Nazism, The Holocaust, and the Middle East: Arab and Turkish Responses.* New York: Berghahn Books, 2018.

Piekalkiewicz, Janusz. *The Cavalry of World War II.* New York: Stein and Day, 1980.

Redzic, Enver. *Bosnia and Herzegovina in the Second World War.* New York: Frank Cass, 2005.

Rubin, Barry and Wolfgang G. Schwanitz. *Nazis, Islamists, and the Making of the Modern Middle East.* New Haven: Yale University Press, 2014.

Seidler, Franz W. *Die Kollaboration 1939-1945.* Berlin: F. A. Herbig Verlargsbuchhandlung, 1995.

Tessin, Georg. *Verbände und Truppen der Deutschen Wehrmacht und Waffen-SS 1939-1945.* Osnabrück: Biblio Verlag, 1975-1999. 18 Volumes.

Tessin, Georg and Norbert Kannapin. *Waffen-SS und Ordnungspolizei im Kriegeinsatz 1939-1945.* Biblio Verlag: Osnabrück, 2000.

Thorwald, Jürgen. *The Illusion: Soviet Soldiers in Hitler's Armies.* New York: Harcourt Brace Jovanovich, 1975.

Trigg, Jonathan. *Hitlers Jihadis: Muslim Volunteer of the Waffen-SS.* Kent: Spellmount Publishers, Ltd., 2012.

Werhas, Mario and Božidar Mikulčić. *13. SS Division Handschar.* Zagreb: Despot Infinitus, 2018.

Wieviorka, Olivier. Translated by Jane Marie Todd. *The French Resistance.* Harvard: Belknap Press, an Imprint of Harvard University Press, 2016.

Wistrich, Robert S. *Hitler's Apocalypse: Jews and the Nazi Legacy.* London: Weidenfeld & Nicolson, 1985.

Yerger, Mark C. *Allgemeine-SS.* Schiffer Publishing: Atglen, 1997.

ENDNOTES

1 *General der Flieger* Helmut Felmy. *German Exploitation of Arab Nationalist Movements in World War II.* MS No.P-207: United States Army in Europe: U.S. Army Historical Division, 1946.

2 Currently, many people (even within Israel) consider the current right-wing government of Benjamin Netanyahu to be leaning in an authoritarian direction. Some have called his present government as apartheid. For example, under Netanyahu, the illegal seizure of Palestinian land has continued in the West Bank. In addition, under current Israeli law, Palestinians living in Israel are, in all things, second class citizens. The fear within the left and moderate elements in Israel, is that the hardliners in the government will force Netanyahu's policies further to the right, thus diminishing what was a thriving democracy.

3 One of the principal reasons for the rise in popularity in Europe, and elsewhere, of fascism and communism was the fact that millions of people felt democracy had failed them. Rampant unemployment and poverty increased the suffering of the working classes. The depression that hit the world beginning in 1929 was the final straw. Millions now supported these radical political parties, who were promising to end the suffering of the people. The result was the Second World War. Understanding this, most politicians in Europe resolved to never again fail their people, lest they be tempted by extreme political parties again. This is why most democracies in Europe today have a mixed economy, where the working class receive free health care and education, even though capitalism is practised. Franklin Delano Roosevelt wanted to do the same in the United States, by offering what would have been a second 'New Deal'. However, his death from the long-term effects of polio, and an intransigent Republican-controlled Congress, prevented FDR from achieving this dream.

4 Although £10 million pounds today sounds like very little, back then it was a lot of money. In 2024 terms, the £10 million that the United Kingdom was spending yearly on the Palestine mandate, would be worth £540,891,706.

5 In the 1930s Menachem Begin was a wanted man. He had been labelled a terrorist by the British authorities for his involvement in numerous

bombings in Palestine that had caused dozens of British and Palestinian lives. This is a perfect paradigm of the often quoted saying, 'one man's terrorist is another man's freedom fighter'.

6 Dr Carlos Caballero-Jurado. *La Espada del Islam: Voluntarios Arabes en el Ejercito Aleman 1941-1945.* Alicante: Garcia Hispan, Editor, 1990.

7 Pierre Philippe Lambert and Gerard Le Marec. *Les Francais Sous Le Casque Allemand: Europe 1941-1945.* Paris: Jacques Grancher, 1994.

8 Antonio Muñoz. *Lions of the Desert: Arab Volunteers in the German Army 1941-1945.* New York: Europa Books, Inc., 1995.

9 The term 'Middle East' is a phrase to denote a region that was known as the Near East. It is therefore a western creation. In 1943, while the Second World War was raging, American military planners began to refer to the Near East as the 'Middle East'. The term stuck in western lore and is used today.

10 The Canaanites were an ancient Semitic-speaking people who inhabited the land of Canaan, an area roughly corresponding to present-day Israel, Palestine, Lebanon, and parts of Jordan and Syria, during the Bronze Age and Iron Age. They are mentioned in various ancient texts, including Egyptian and Mesopotamian records, as well as in the Hebrew Bible. The Canaanites were known for their advanced civilization, which included urban centres, agriculture, trade networks, and artistic achievements. They were skilled merchants and seafarers, engaging in commerce with neighbouring civilizations such as the Egyptians, Phoenicians, and Hittites. Canaanite society was organised into city-states, each ruled by a king or local leader. Their religion was polytheistic, with a pantheon of gods and goddesses, including Baal, El, and Asherah. They practised various rituals and sacrifices, often involving fertility rites and ceremonies to ensure agricultural abundance. The Canaanites' cultural and linguistic influence was significant in the ancient Near East, and their legacy persisted through subsequent civilizations, such as the Phoenicians, who emerged as a maritime power in the Mediterranean, spreading Canaanite culture and trade throughout the region. The Hebrew Bible portrays the Canaanites in a negative light, often depicting them as idolatrous and immoral, and describes the Israelites' conquest of Canaan under Joshua. However, archaeological evidence suggests a more complex and nuanced picture of Canaanite society, and their history is an important part of the broader cultural landscape of the ancient Near East. To understand why the Canaanites were depicted so negatively by the Jews in the Old Testament, one must remember that history is written by the victor, and not by the loser. The same can be said of the Etruscans. Most of what we know about the Etruscans comes from the Romans, who defeated them. Like the Israelites, the Romans had only bad things to say about the Etruscans.

11 The Kingdom of Israel had twelve tribes, while the Kingdom of Judah had two main tribes: Judah and Benjamin. After the death of King

Solomon, the united monarchy split into two separate kingdoms: the northern Kingdom of Israel and the southern Kingdom of Judah. The northern Kingdom of Israel comprised ten tribes: Reuben, Simeon, Dan, Naphtali, Gad, Asher, Issachar, Zebulun, Ephraim, and Manasseh. This kingdom was centred around the capital city of Samaria. The southern Kingdom of Judah included the tribes of Judah and Benjamin, and its capital was Jerusalem. Over time, the term 'Jews' came to refer primarily to the people of the Kingdom of Judah, while the term 'Israelites' encompassed the broader group of people from both the Kingdom of Israel and the Kingdom of Judah.

12 One account was written by a Jewish scholar, Flavius Josephus, who was born in 37CE in Jerusalem and died 100AD in Rome in 100CE.

13 James L. Gelvin. *The Modern Middle East.* New York: Oxford University Press, 2005, p. 206.

14 The Alfred Dreyfus affair was a significant political scandal that rocked France in the late nineteenth and early twentieth centuries. Alfred Dreyfus, the only French army officer of Jewish descent, was falsely accused of treason in 1894 for allegedly passing military secrets to the German Empire. The case against Dreyfus was built on flimsy evidence and fuelled by anti-Semitic sentiments prevalent in French society at the time. Despite lacking concrete proof, Dreyfus was convicted in a military court-martial and sentenced to life imprisonment on Devil's Island, a penal colony off the coast of French Guiana. A few years later, evidence emerged suggesting that another officer, Major Ferdinand Walsin Esterhazy, was the real traitor. Despite this revelation, the French military, government, and many members of the public refused to accept Dreyfus's innocence due to deep-seated anti-Semitic beliefs. The case dragged on for years, with numerous twists and turns, including a second trial for Dreyfus in 1899, where he was again found guilty, but this time with extenuating circumstances, and subsequently pardoned by the French president. It was not until 1906 that Dreyfus was officially exonerated and reinstated in the French army with the rank of major. The Dreyfus affair exposed deep flaws in the French justice system, highlighted the persistence of anti-Semitism in Europe, and had far-reaching consequences for French society and politics. It also contributed to the development of modern concepts of justice, including the importance of due process and the presumption of innocence.

15 Gelvin, op. cit., p. 205.

16 John Shelton Curtiss. *The Russian Revolutions of 1917.* New York: D. Van Nostrand Company, Inc., 1957, p. 30.

17 Representative bias occurs when we make judgments based on how people or situations match particular stereotypes.

18 The term 'Pale of Settlement' refers to a territory within the Russian Empire where Jews were required to reside by law. The Pale was established in 1791 by Catherine the Great, and its borders changed

over time. Initially, the Pale of Settlement included parts of modern-day Ukraine, Belarus, Lithuania, Moldova, and western Russia. Jews were restricted from living outside the Pale without special permission, although there were some exceptions for professionals, merchants, and military personnel. The purpose of establishing the Pale was to confine the Jewish population to specific areas and limit their interaction with the broader Russian population. This policy was part of a broader pattern of discrimination and persecution against Jews in the Russian Empire. The Pale of Settlement existed until the early twentieth century, when it was gradually abolished following the Russian Revolution and the subsequent establishment of the Soviet Union. However, discrimination against Jews persisted in various forms throughout the region's history.

19 In 1917, Palestine was an Ottoman region with a small minority Jewish population.

20 The way that Isma'il Pasha got Egypt greatly into debt has partly to do with the American Civil War. When the war between the North and South in the United States broke out in 1861, the Union immediately placed a blockade on southern goods earmarked for Europe. This included cotton. At the time, the southern United States supplied the bulk of the cotton that was feeding the textile mills in England and other nations. Once southern cotton was no longer available on the European market, the price of cotton skyrocketed. Isma'il Pasha saw a way to raise collateral to help finance his grandiose infrastructure plans to modernize Egypt, by growing cotton in Egypt and selling it on the European market. He took disadvantagous loans from British and French bankers to help pay for the infrastructure projects. While the price of cotton remained high, he was able to pay the exorbitant interest rates. However, when the American Civil War ended, and the south could once again sell its cotton to Europe, cotton prices on the world market collapsed, and Egypt very quickly got into debt.

21 The Dual Control system was implemented in Egypt in 1801. Under this system, both Britain and France were supposed to supervise Egypt's finances, aiming to prevent the accumulation of debts and maintain stability in the region. However, in practice, it was largely dominated by the British, leading to increased British influence in Egyptian affairs. It ended in 1882 when the British occupied the country.

22 Egypt was nominally part of the Ottoman Empire until 1914. However, by the late nineteenth century, Egypt had effectively become a semi-autonomous province under the rule of the Muhammad Ali dynasty, which had gained significant control over the region. The British occupation of Egypt in 1882 further diminished Ottoman influence, and Egypt effectively became a British protectorate, although it remained technically part of the Ottoman Empire until 1914, when it was formally declared a British protectorate.

23 Sharif Hussein bin Ali (1853-1931). Sharif Hussein had four sons, Abdullah, Faisal, Ali, and Zeid. Abdullah would become the first ruler of Jordan (originally called 'Transjordan'), while his brother Faisal would be the first ruler of Iraq. Ali became King of Hejaz and Grand Sharif of Mecca from October 1924 until he was deposed by Ibn Saud (Abdulaziz bin Abdul Rahman Al Saud) in December 1925. Zaid led the Arab northern army alongside T. E. Lawrence during the First World War. After the war, he would become the head of the royal houses of Iraq and Syria.

24 Rashid Khalidi. *Resurrecting Empire: Western Footprints and America's Perilous Path in the Middle East.* Boston: Beacon Press, 2004, p. 104.

25 The United Kingdom kept a tight leash on both King Abdullah and King Faisal. In many ways, their rule was mere illusion, as the government in London wielded power from behind the scenes. This was particularly true because from the very beginning, Transjordan was not an economically viable state. It has always depended (and still does so today) on foreign financial support. Today it is the Saudi Arabians and Americans who provide that financial help, while back in the 1920s-1950s it was the United Kingdom. In the case of Iraq, its oil was the target of BP (British Petroleum), who exploited this Iraqi natural resource for the benefit of the United Kingdom under favourable terms given by King Faisal. When Iraqis asserted their independence in the early 1950s and expelled their colonial master, the London government performed one last act of mischief, when they separated the southern province of Kuwait (which has vast deposits of oil) from the rest of the nation of Iraq and recognised it as a separate kingdom.

26 In ancient times, the land originally belonged to the Canaanites. The Philistines and Israelites invaded the Kingdom of Caanan and eventually wiped out the Canaanites, taking their land. Thereupon the Philistines and Israelites fought each other, with the Israelites eventually winning.

27 The term *'Yishuv'* refers to the Jewish community in the pre-state period of Israel, particularly during the late nineteenth and early to mid-twentieth centuries. The *Yishuv* emerged as Jewish immigration to Palestine increased, driven by various factors such as religious, political, and social motivations, including the desire to establish a Jewish homeland in the land of Israel (then part of the Ottoman Empire, later under British control). The *Yishuv* encompassed various aspects of Jewish life in Palestine, including agricultural settlements (kibbutzim and moshavim), urban communities, cultural institutions, educational initiatives, and self-defence organisations. Despite facing challenges such as Arab-Jewish tensions, British restrictions on Jewish immigration, and economic difficulties, the *Yishuv* grew and developed over time. The *Yishuv* played a significant role in laying the groundwork for the establishment of the modern State of Israel in 1948. Many of its institutions, ideologies, and leaders became foundational elements of Israeli society and government following independence.

28 The JNF Agency really did have an unwritten policy of evicting people after purchasing Palestinian land. It was a long-game strategy of supplanting Arabs with Jews. The Jews had conquered the land in ancient times from the Canaanites but lost the land over hundreds of years to the Assyrians, the Babylonians, the Persians, the Macedonians the Romans, and finally, the Arabs under the green banner of Islam. During all that time, Arab numbers in the region increased. The *Yishuv's* plan meant to reverse that trend so that once again Jews could become a majority there and therefore, by force of numbers, claim the land for themselves.

29 The blueprint of the Zionists was simple: create a sufficiently large enough population of Jews living in Palestine, with the long-term goal of establishing a *de facto* Jewish state. The strategy was as simple as it was effective. The problem was that not enough Jews wanted to emigrate to Palestine in the 1920s and 1930s. Of course, with the persecution of Europe's Jews beginning in the mid-to-late 1930s, and the start of the Second World War, this all changed.

30 Franz W. Seidler. *Die Kollaboration 1939-1945.* Berlin: F. A. Herbig Verlargsbuchhandlung, 1995, p. 263.

31 Seidler, op. cit., p. 264.

32 *Wehrmacht:* German Armed Forces.

33 *Phalange Africaine:* African Phalanx.

34 One of the tasks of a properly functioning national military force, is to prepare for any and all eventualities. Peacetime is not merely the time for the armed forces to practise and to train its troops. It also involves writing up and preparing for contingency plans for any possible eventualities. For example, I am sure that somewhere in the Pentagon, there is a plan filed away in a drawer, concerning a possible US invasion of neutral Switzerland, should the need ever arise.

35 The Germans gave him the title 'Grand' Mufti, to elevate his importance in both the Arab and western world.

36 Seidler, op. cit., pp. 212, 263.

37 Felmy, op. cit., p. 13.

38 There are two cases of photographic evidence that show African volunteers, who were most likely Muslim. Both wear the *Feldheer* uniform, while one is clearly sporting a *Freis Arabien* arm patch.

39 Georg Tessin. *Verbände und Truppen der Deutschen Wehrmacht und Waffen SS 1939-1945.* Osnabrück: Biblio Verlag, 1974-2010, 18 Volumes., Vol. 9, p. 13.

40 Major Theodor von Hippel was a junior officer during the First World War, who served with *General* Paul von Lettow-Vorbeck and his Askari troops in East Africa.

41 This formation was the size of a reinforced regiment.

42 These companies were directly under the control of the regimental headquarters.

43 This battalion was established on 22 October 1942.

44 This was the German-Arab Training Battalion.

45 Of the original thirty Arab volunteers, fifteen had recently been promoted to the rank of second lieutenant.

46 Tessin, op. cit., vol. 5, p. 278.

47 'Arko' stood for *Artillerie-Kommandeur*, or Artillery Commander. This staff controlled all the artillery units directly attached to the corps headquarters.

48 *Truppenübungsplatz Doberitz* was located near Dallgow-Döberitz (Brandenburg District), just west of the German capital of Berlin.

49 The Kalmyk Autonomous Soviet Socialist Republic (ASSR) was a political entity within the Soviet Union, established in 1935. In that year, the Soviet government granted the Kalmyks an autonomous republic within the RSFSR, recognising their distinct identity. However, the republic's existence was short lived. In 1943 the Soviet government, under Joseph Stalin, accused the Kalmyk people of collaborating with Nazi Germany and engaged in large-scale repression. The Kalmyk people were forcibly deported to Siberia and Central Asia, and the Kalmyk ASSR was abolished.

50 Telex from *General der Flieger*, Helmuth Felmy, dated 28 October 1942 to *Oberkommandos der Wehrmacht.*

51 In the last week of May 1942, *3. Panzer-Division* was attached to *XL. Panzerkorps,* which itself was a part of *6. Armee.* The other major unit of *XL. Panzerkorps* at this time was *16. Infanterie-Division (motorisiert).* The *3. Panzer-Division* was positioned on the right flank of *SonderVerbände 287,* in and around the town of Mozdok.

52 Felmy, op. cit., pp. 22-4.

53 Meyer-Ricks was the Chief of Staff of the *Generalkommando z.b.V.*

54 NARA Microfilm T-315, Roll 2214, Frame 387.

55 Ibid., Frame 401.

56 The Askari were African native troops employed by the Kaiser's Army in German East Africa. Before the beginning of the First World War, the elementary *Schutztruppe* unit was the *Feld Kompanie* (field company) which on paper was supposed to contain seven to eight German officers and NCOs and around 160 Askaris, although each field company could contain anywhere from 150-200 men. Each company also contained two machine gun squads.

57 Carlos Caballero-Jurado. *La Espada del Islam: Voluntarios Arabes en el Ejercito Aleman 1941-1945.* Alicante: Garcia Hispan, Editor, 1990, p. 175.

58 In 1960, as President Charles de Gaulle was planning to give up French-controlled Algeria, the overwhelming majority of the *Pieds-Noirs* rejected Algerian independence and resisted de Gaulle's plan. A segment of the *Légion étrangère Français* (French Foreign Legion) participated on the side of the *Organisation armée secrète* (OAS, 'Secret Army Organisation'), which was resisting Algerian independence. The French Foreign Legion took part in a coup that temporarily stopped Algerian independence, but after a few days, the coup failed. After Algeria was granted its freedom, about 800,000 *Pieds-Noirs* immigrated to Metropolitan France, where they encountered discrimination. The *Pieds-Noirs* in France found it difficult to obtain jobs and even housing. Many people thought them to be less than French. About 200,000 *Pieds-Noirs* remained in Algeria, but they too experienced resentment and discrimination at the hands of the Algerian population, who saw them as colonisers. Five years after Algeria gained its independence (1965) only 100,000 *Pieds-Noirs* remained in the former French colony. By 1969 only 50,000 were living in Algeria, and by 1993 only 30,000 *Pieds-Noirs* could be found, most of them elderly retirees.

59 David Littlejohn, *The Patriotic Traitors: The History of Collaboration in German Occupied Europe, 1940-45*. London: Heinemann, 1972, p. 255.

60 Felmy, op. cit., p. 28.

61 Felmy, op. cit., p. 29.

62 These sub-units included *Artillerie-Kommandeur (Arko) 168, Korps-Nachrichten-Bataillon 468, Korps-Nachschubtruppen 468, and Panzer-Spähkompanie 468.*

63 MIA: missing in action.

64 Felmy, op. cit., p. 31.

65 Ibid., pp. 31-2.

66 Published in the *Daily Mail* newspaper, 1 April 1944.

67 John Mendelsohn, Editor. *Covert Warfare: Intelligence, Counter-Intelligence, and Military Deception During the World War II Era.* New York: Garland Publishing, 1979, p. 18.

68 Antonio Munoz. *Lions of the Desert: Arab Volunteers in the German Army 1941-1945.* New York: Europa Books, 1995, p. 18.

69 This parachute engineer battalion was later expanded to become *21. Fallschirmpionier Regiment* in June 1944. Witzig was promoted to the rank of Major shortly after assuming command of the regiment. The regiment, however, was disbanded a month later, in July.

70 Erich Busch. *Die Fallschirmjäger Chronik 1935-1945.* Friedberg: Podzun Palla Verlag, 1983, p. 165.

71 This area had a series of heavily fortified concrete fortifications that had been built before the war by the colonial French Army. The *Afrika Korps* and Italian 1st Army called it the Mareth Line. The Axis forces were hoping that these defences could help halt the advance of the British 8th

Army coming from Egypt through Libya. In December 1942, a Tunisian battalion composed of Arab volunteers was made a part of *21. Panzer-Division*. It was stationed in Toudjane and employed as a rear area guard in December 1942 but was not really physically attached to *21. Panzer-Division* until mid-January 1943, when Rommel's *Afrika Korps* reached the Mareth Line defences.

72 Felmy, op. cit., p. 33.

73 After the Second World War, the camp was temporarily shut down. After the withdrawal of the Red Army from Austria and the re-establishment of the Austrian state, discussions abounded as to what to do with the land. Many wanted the area to be turned into farmland and for five or six villages to be created there. Eventually, the ground was once again made a military training area. It was renamed *Truppenübungsplatz Allentsteig* in 1964 and employed by the Federal Austrian Army. The training area is still in use today by the Austrian Army.

74 Felmy, op. cit., pp. 33-4.

75 Heeresgruppe, hereafter referred to as *HG* in this table.

76 OB Südost: Oberbefehlshaber Südost.

77 Felmy, op. cit., p. 37

78 The Arab 845th Infantry Battalion had arrived in Salonika on 13 August 1943 and was immediately assigned to *Kampfgruppe Eberlein,* a temporary battlegroup which was also composed of *Sicherungs Regiment 639.* This security regiment was temporarily subordinate to *104. Jäger-Division*. The commander of the battlegroup was *Oberst* Dr August Ritter von Eberlein, while *Sicherungs Regiment 639* was led by his son, Major von Eberlein. On 25 February 1945 *Oberst* von Eberlein's son, Major von Eberlein, would be captured by the 4th Battalion of the 6th Krajina Brigade (4th Krajina Division) after the partisans attacked the train carrying the headquarters of *Sicherungs Regiment 639.*

79 Felmy, op. cit., p. 38.

80 Here Major General Serafis used the term 'Moroccans' to refer to the Muslim volunteers of *845. Infanterie Bataillon.*

81 Major General Sarafis used the term 'Battalionists' to denote Greek collaborator units.

82 Major General Stefanos Sarafis. *ELAS: Greek Resistance Army*. London: Merlin Press, 1980, p. 441.

83 Felmy, op. cit., pp. 36-7.

84 Tessin, op. cit., Vol. 6, p. 122.

85 This division was led by *Generalmajor* Fritz Becker.

86 This *Grenadier Alarm Regiment 92* was created from two training and replacement battalions that supplied *Panzergrenadier Brigade 92*

with replacements: *Ersatz und Ausbildungs Bataillon 92*, and *Infanterie Ausbildungs Bataillon 92 (motorisiert)*.

87 Felmy, op. cit., p. 39.

88 The way that many of these Europeans came to serve in front of Berlin was through the particular German unit fighting there. For example, in March 1945 the *11. SS-Freiwilligen-Panzergrenadier-Division Nordland*, which normally contained Germans, Danes, and Norwegians, also received about two dozen English and South African members of the 'Legion of St. George': British and South African citizens who were serving in the *Waffen- SS*. These men wore the *Waffen-SS* uniform with a particular SS cuff band. What made this cuff band so different was that it was the only *Waffen-SS* cuff band written in a language other than German. The cuff band was black with silver thread and the writing read: 'British Free Corps' in English. The *SS-Nordland-Division* took part in the Battle for Berlin in April 1945. The Spaniards were *Waffen-SS* members serving with *101. SS-Spanische-Kompanie*, which was known informally in Spanish as *'unidad Ezquerra'* (after its commander). This Spanish company was initially attached to *I. Bataillon, SS-Freiwilligen-Panzergrenadier-Regiment 70* of the *28. SS-Freiwilligen-Panzergrenadier-Division 'Wallonien'* that also fought in the battle for Berlin. Shortly before the battle began, the Spaniards were transferred to the *SS-Nordland-Division*. The Arabs were serving under *9. Fallschirmjäger-Division*, which also fought along the Oder River in April 1945. A battalion of Latvians from *15. Waffen-Grenadier-Division der-SS (lettische Nr. 1)* also defended the German capital. The French who fought alongside the Germans in Berlin were members of the *33. Waffen-Grenadier-Division der-SS 'Charlemagne'* - a 7,840-man *Waffen-SS* division that had been created in the fall of 1944 from French volunteers. For the battle of Berlin, only one battalion of French SS volunteers took part in the fighting. The Russian and Belarusian volunteers who took part in the defence of Berlin (less than 150) were auxiliary police members of the *SS-Sicherheitsdienst* who happened to be in the capital at the time. A few Swedes also took part in the defence of the German capital while serving in the *SS-Nordland-Division*.

89 From the staff of *Festungs Infanterie Regiments 733, Festungs Infanterie Regiment 746* and *III. Bataillon* of *Festungs Infanterie Regiment 733*.

90 From the staff of *Festungs Infanterie Regiments 938* with *III. Bataillon* of *Festungs Infanterie Regiment 999* and *Festungs Infanterie Bataillon 1009*.

91 From the staff of *Festungs Infanterie Regiment 965* with *II. Bataillon* and *VIII. Bataillon* of *Festungs Infanterie Regiment 999*.

92 From *Füsilier Bataillon Rhodos*.

93 From the staff of *Artillerie Regiment 141* with *Heeres Küsten Artillerie Abteilungen 819, 820, 821* and *III. Bataillon* of *Artillerie Regiment 619*.

94 From *Alarm Regiment Athen*.

95 From *Pionier Bataillon 264* and *Pionier Sicherungs Kompanie 705.*

96 Ibid.

97 Littlejohn, op. cit., p. 183.

98 Olivier Wieviorka, *The French Resistance*, published in 2016 by Harvard University Press. Book review by Prof. Jeremy Black in the *Journal of World History*, June 2019, Vol. 30 Issue 1/2, pp. 255-6.

99 The *Carlingue* were Frenchmen who worked as police auxiliaries for either the *Gestapo, SS Sicherheitsdienst* or the German Army's *Geheim Feldpolizei* (Secret Field Police).

100 Lambert, 210.

101 Remember that British forces stationed on the air and naval base on the island of Malta were destroying most of the men, weapons, equipment and munitions that both Italy and Germany were sending to North Africa. The situation became so bad, that the Italians proposed an airborne and naval invasion of Malta in 1942, but the German parachute corps had been so badly wrecked during the battle for Crete in 1941, that Adolf Hitler absolutely refused to employ his paratroopers in another such mission.

102 Yugoslavia was established at the end of the First World War from mostly Austro-Hungarian territory. Until 1928, the nation was known as the Kingdom of the Serbs, Croats and Slovenes, before it was changed to Yugoslavia. The ethnic and religious rivalries that existed in 1941, had been established hundreds of years earlier, during the period of the Byzantine Empire and the rise of the Ottoman Turks. There is a saying that applies to the Balkans: 'The mountains have long memories and the people there never forgive'.

103 The New Testament was put together in 325CE at the Council of Nicaea. The Old Testament is the Jewish Bible. Christians, however, believe not only in the Old Testament, but the New Testament as well. The New Testament comprises the writings of the early church patricians, including the original apostles.

104 *The Holy Bible*. King James Version, Mathew Chapter 13, verses 13-20.

105 The Serbian General Staff, which was always anti-German and anti-Austrian, had done this because the Prince Regent, Paul Karadjordjević, had signed a non-aggression treaty with Nazi Germany a few days earlier. In his place, the still-young 17-year-old Serbian heir to the throne, Peter II, was installed.

106 The term 'republic' is deceiving, given that each of these regions did not have a separate currency, like a nation-state has, nor actual power to alter the central government in Belgrade. They were in fact provinces of the country, rather than actual separate states, supposedly all bound together by their 'love' of a socialist-communist system.

107 Of course, after tasting a few years of Bulgarian occupation, the attitude altered, but initially the Macedonians welcomed the change from the Serbian dominated political scene. For a time, the most pro-Bulgarian elements, including IMRO, or the Inner Macedonian Revolutionary Organisation even hoped for a declaration of Macedonian independence and a rebirth of the Macedonian glory that was built by Alexander the Great, but the Bulgarians were never interested in Macedonian independence and only played this political card in order to help keep control of the region.

108 The Germans often did not differentiate between Judaism and Communism and called them by the collective title of 'Bolshevism'.

109 *Trial of the Major War Criminals before the International Military Tribunal.* Nuremberg: U.S. Army, 1946, 22 vols., testimony of Robert Brill.

110 The *Ustaše* were Croatian political troops, much like the SS, of Croatian Fascist dictator, Ante Pavelić. While the Germans had initially wanted Croatia to be ruled by a moderate Croatian leader of the Croat Peasant Party, the Italians, who had backed the Croat extremists, insisted on Pavelić being made leader.

111 *Poglavnik* was the Croatian equivalent to *Führer.*

112 Muslims adhere to dietary laws and guidelines outlined in Islamic teachings, which are primarily derived from the *Quran* (the holy book of Islam) and the *Hadith* (sayings and actions of the Prophet Muhammad, blessings be upon him). These dietary laws are known as *'halal'* (permissible) and *'haram'* (forbidden). There are some key dietary requirements and principles for Muslims. They are permitted to consume foods that are considered *halal,* such as meat from animals that have been slaughtered according to Islamic guidelines, known as *'zabihah.'* This involves invoking the name of Allah at the time of slaughter and ensuring that the animal is slaughtered by cutting the throat and draining the blood. Poultry, fish, and seafood are generally considered *halal,* as long as they are prepared in accordance with Islamic principles. Fruits, vegetables, grains, and dairy products are also considered *halal,* as long as they are not contaminated with *haram* ingredients or substances.

113 One source states that the projected number was actually 20,000 Muslim recruits, out of which several hundreds were to be Albanian Muslims.

114 The scimitar was a short sword with a curved blade that broadens toward the point. It was employed mainly by Muslim forces.

115 *Waffen-Gebirgsjäger-Regiment der-SS No. 27.*

116 Personnel File – Egon Zill, Berlin Document Centre – now referred to as the *Bundesarchiv,* Berlin-Lichterfelde.

117 The *Ostheer* recruited many peoples living in the Soviet Union. A good number of them were Muslim, like the Turkestani people, the

Azerbaijanis, Kyrgyzstanis, people from Uzbekistan, Tajikistan, the Chechens and Kazakhstan.

118 Theresa M. Ganter. *Searching for a New German Identity: Heiner Müller and the Geschichtsdrama*. Lausanne: Peter Lang 2008, p. 278.

119 Sauberzweig had served as an ordnance officer in the German Army during the interwar period. He first served in a cavalry regiment and then in an artillery regiment. Although he was born in Prussia, he later went on to serve in Austria, where he became a member of the General Staff of *XVII. Armeekorps,* whose headquarters was stationed in Linz, before it was moved to Vienna. Earlier, Sauberzweig's military career had also included a stint with the Prussian *8. Infanterie Regiment* before becoming a general staff officer of the *Reichswehr* on 1 October 1930.

120 The word *'Muselgermanen'* is considered a pejorative term. It is a German word that combines *'Musel'* (a derogatory term for Muslims) with *'Germanen'* (Germans). It is derogatory because it carries negative connotations of otherness, implying that Muslims are somehow of less value or worth than Germans.

121 Sauberzweig had recently been promoted to this rank.

122 Dizdarević worked to convince Džanić to lead the rebellion. Džanić was the puppet, and Dizdarević was the puppet master.

123 From a document, dated 17 September 1943, posted online. https://www.scribd.com/document/324299253/Semso-Alihodzic-o-pobuni-u-Villefranche-u-17-09-1943. Accessed 11 April 2017.

124 Translation: '13th SS Volunteer Bosnia Herzegovina Mountain Division [Croatia No. 1]'.

125 Front page article (two far-right columns) in the *Völkischer Beobachter* ('People's Observer') newspaper, dated 12 January 1944.

126 Siegfried Kasche was an SS general who was an envoy of the German Ministry of Foreign Affairs and was second in command in this Foreign Ministry delegation to the Independent State of Croatia.

127 Enver Redzic. *Bosnia and Herzegovina in the Second World War*. New York: Frank Cass, 2005, p. 179.

128 The *SS-Kama-Division* had been assigned the ancillary number '23'. In the *Waffen-SS* Battle Order, it was the 23rd Division, and following custom, its battalion-sized units were all numbered '23'. The two SS mountain infantry regiments of this second Muslim SS division were numbered '55' and '56'.

129 Dr K. G. Kleitmann, *Die Waffen SS: eine Dokumentation*. Osnabrück: Verlag 'Der Freiwillige' GmbH, 1965, p. 423.

130 The men of the division wore a special red Fez with SS insignia.

131 The battle group was composed of the reconnaissance battalion of the division.

132 Redzic. op. cit., p. 91.

133 Antonio J. Muñoz, *Hitler's Eastern Legions, Volume II - The Osttruppen*. New York: Europa Books, 1997, p. 24.

134 The division's 2nd Cadre Regiment went through reorganisation several times. First it was purged of all Volga Tartars, Azerbaijanis, and Armenians in April 1944. The unit was now filled with Russian and Ukrainian volunteers. Two months later, in June the regiment was once again purged, this time of Ukrainians who were transferred out and the unit became a purely Russian formation.

135 After June 1944, the regiment was supplied purely Ukrainian volunteers.

136 Ibid.

137 Jürgen Thorwald. *The Illusion: Soviet Soldiers in Hitler's Armies*. New York: Harcourt Brace Jovanovich, 1975, p. 233.

138 In mid-November 1933, Theuermann took command of the 10th SA Brigade 'Pommern-West'. In that capacity, he held the rank of *SA-Brigadeführer*. On 30 June 1934, during the so-called Night of the Long Knives, in which Hitler eliminated most of the SA top brass, he was arrested, ostensibly because of his close association with Hans-Adam Otto von Heydebreck, a top SA leader who was executed that very day. During his trial, he was accused of being an indolent officer who shirked his responsibilities, including keeping discipline within the ranks. If that was the case, it was a trumped-up charge, as his military career displayed the opposite of a lazy shirker. In August of 1934 he was expelled from the SA. In December 1934, he served on the staff of the NSDAP's training structures (AW) as *AW-Oberführer*. In 1935 he joined the SS and quickly rose through the ranks.

139 Bundesarchiv Dienststelle Berlin, Lichterfelde – *SS-Standartenführer der Reserve* Arved Theuermann.

140 The Higher SS District (*SS Oberabschnitt*) was a territorial administrative division within the structure of the Schutzstaffel (SS), the paramilitary organisation of Nazi Germany. The *SS-Oberabschnitt* units were part of the broader SS administrative structure, which included higher-level commands such as *SS-Obergruppenführer* (Senior Group Leader) and *SS-Gruppenführer* (Group Leader), as well as lower-level units such as *SS-Standarten* (Regiments) and *SS-Sturmbann* (Battalions).

141 Mark C. Yerger, *Allgemeine-SS*. Atglen: Schiffer Publishing, 1997, p. 69.

142 Personnel file for *SS-Standartenführer der Reserve* Arved Theuermann, Berlin Document Centre – now referred to as the *Bundesarchiv*, Berlin-Lichterfelde.

143 NARA T-175, Roll 168, Frame 2700372.

144 Ibid., Frame 2700380.

145 Ibid., Frame 2700386.

146 That is, the battalions containing the Turkestani, Georgians, and North Caucasian volunteers.

147 NARA T-175, Roll 168, Frame 2700388-92.

148 Ibid., Frame 2700459.

149 Pier Arrigo Carnier. *L'armata Cosacca in Italia 1944-1945.* Milan: Grupo Ugo Mursia Editore, 1990, p. 27.

150 *Amtsgruppe D* of the *SS-Hauptamt* was the liaison office between the SS and men from other countries. The sections in *Amtsgruppe D* were: *I – Planung, II - Germanische Leitstelle, III - Freiwilligen Leitstelle Ost, IV – Verwaltung, V - Germansiche-SS Erziehung Germansiche Leithefte.*

151 NARA Microfilm Series T-175, Roll 168, Frame 2700388.

152 Joachim Hoffmann. *Die Ostlegionen 1941-1943.* Freiburg: Verlag Rombach, 1986, p. 164.

153 NARA T-78, Roll 645, Frame 000778.

154 Littlejohn, op. cit., p. 365

155 Tessin, op. cit. Vols. 12 & 13.

156 A '?' mark indicates that this unit was 'possibly' used, but there is no definitive proof.

157 The Volga Finnish battalion was made up of men from the Mordvins, Udmurt and the Mari tribes. They were all Eastern Orthodox Christians, so they would have ended up in either the Armenian or Georgian regiment in the brigade.

158 The 804th and 806th Azerbaijani Battalions were later sent to reinforce the German 162nd (Turkic) Infantry Division.

159 In May 1944 the men from this unit were withdrawn from the 2nd Volunteer Cadre Regiment and became the IV Battalion of the 917th Grenadier Regiment of 242nd Static Infantry Division.

160 According to German sources, Paul Theurer was in reality the liaison officer to Cossack General Domanov and his Special Armed Cossack Corps stationed in northeastern Italy.

161 NARA Microfilm Series T-175, Roll 168, Frame 2700321.

162 NARA T-175, Roll 140, Frame 2668442.

163 Personnel file for *SS-Standartenführer der Reserve* Arved Theuermann, Berlin Document Centre – now referred to as the *Bundesarchiv,* Berlin-Lichterfelde.

164 Personnel File for *Waffen-Standartenführer der-SS* Kutschuk Ulagaj, Berlin Document Centre – now referred to as the *Bundesarchiv,* Berlin-Lichterfelde.

165 Antonio J. Munoz. *For Czar and Country: A History of the Russian Guard Corps, 1941-1945.* New York: Europa Books, 1999, p. 13.

166 Personnel File for *Waffen-Standartenführer der-SS* Kutschuk Ulagaj, Berlin Document Centre – now referred to as the *Bundesarchiv*, Berlin-Lichterfelde.

167 The Circassian Genocide refers to the mass expulsion, forced resettlement, and killings of Circassian people, primarily by the Russian Empire, during the Caucasian War in the mid-nineteenth century. The Circassians are an ethnic group indigenous to the North Caucasus region, primarily inhabiting the area of Circassia, which is now part of modern-day Russia. The Circassian Genocide occurred between 1860 and 1869, although some aspects of the violence and displacement continued beyond this period. The Russian Empire sought to expand its territory into the Caucasus region and gain control over strategic areas and trade routes. The Circassians fiercely resisted Russian expansion, leading to a prolonged and brutal conflict known as the Caucasian War. During the war, Russian forces employed tactics such as mass deportations, forced marches, and the destruction of villages to subdue the Circassian resistance. The Circassian population faced widespread violence, displacement, and starvation as Russian forces sought to quell their opposition. Estimates of the death toll vary, but it is believed that about 900,000-1 million Circassians perished as a result of the genocide, either through direct violence or the death due to the harsh conditions of displacement. Many Circassians were forcibly expelled from their homeland and deported to the Ottoman Empire and other regions, resulting in a significant diaspora. Part of the reason for the genocide was religious. The Circassians were overwhelmingly Muslim, and the Russians were attempting to spread Eastern Orthodox Christianity to Circassian lands. The Circassian Genocide remains a deeply contentious and sensitive issue, with Circassian communities around the world advocating for recognition and remembrance of the atrocities committed against their ancestors. However, the Russian government has been reluctant to acknowledge the events as genocide, leading to ongoing debate and controversy surrounding the historical narrative of the Caucasian War and its aftermath.

168 Here Soobzokov is referring to the 800th North Caucasian Infantry Battalion.

169 NARA T-263, Tscherim Soobzokov name file, and NARA T-85, INS file.

170 Ibid, Tscherim Soobzokov by this meant that Axis held territory was shrinking.

171 NARA T-263, Tscherim Soobzokov name file, and Breitman, Richard. *Tscherim Soobzokov*, https://sgp.fas.org/eprint/breitman.pdf; and Case 2:15-cv-6831-SDW-LDW; 02-16-2016, Aslan T. Soobzokov (Tscherim Soobzokov), Plaintiff, v. Eric Lichtblau; Houghton, Mifflin and Harcourt, Defendants.

172 Personnel File for *Waffen-Standartenführer der-SS* Kutschuk Ulagaj, Berlin Document Centre – now referred to as the *Bundesarchiv*, Berlin-Lichterfelde.

173 Ibid.

174 LVF: *Légion des volontaires français* (Legion of French Volunteers).

175 Personnel File for *Waffen-Standartenführer der-SS* Kutschuk Ulagaj, Berlin Document Centre – now referred to as the *Bundesarchiv,* Berlin-Lichterfelde.

176 Antonio J. Munoz. *The Last Levy: Waffen-SS Officer Roster, 1 March 1945.* New York: Europa Books, 2001, pp. 96-7.

177 NARA, T-175, Roll 168, Frame 2700458.

178 Carnier, op cit., pp. 159-60.

179 Berlin Document Centre. Post-war SHAEF interview found in file of Tscherim Soobzokov, and subsequent interview by the FBI Office for Special Investigations.

180 *BStU - Bundesbeauftragter für die Unterlagen des Staatssicherheitsdienstes der ehemaligen Deutschen Demokratischen Republik,* Berlin - Stasi Records Archive, East Germany, MfS HA IX/11, FV 6/74, Bd 25, pp BStU 000124-000125. Since 2021, now a part of the *Bundesarchiv.*

181 Dr Olzscha was promoted to *SS-Hauptsturmführer* on 1 September 1944. He left his job that same month in the SS- FHA and was posted as the commander of the *I. Bataillon* of *SS-Waffengruppe Turkestan* in the *Osttürkischer-Waffen-Verbände der-SS.*

182 The *General Generalgouvernement* was the part of Poland run by the German army and not annexed by Germany.

183 This SS brigade had been created in July 1944 by renaming the SS penal formation, *SS-Sonderverband Dirlewanger.* The unit was composed of criminals, poachers, communists, as well as all kinds of degenerates from German society.

184 Antonio J. Muñoz. *Forgotten Legions: Obscure Formations of the Waffen-SS, 1943-1945.* Boulder: Paladin Press, 1991, p. 352.

185 Ibid., pp. 169-70.

186 Ibid., p. 172.

187 Ibid., p. 258.

188 NARA Microfilm T -175, Roll 162, Frame 2695084.

189 NARA T-501, Roll 249, Frame 000338.

190 Ibid.

191 NARA T-314, Roll 661, Frame 000439.

192 Ibid.

193 Karl von Krempler was born on 26 May 1896, in Pirot, which was part of the Kingdom of Serbia. He was the offspring of an Austrian engineer and Tereza Krempler. He served in the Austro-Hungarian Army during the First World War and became a *Waffen-SS* officer during the Second

World War. Krempler spoke three languages: German, Serbian, and Ottoman Turkish.

194 NARA Microfilm T-314, roll 661, Frame 001119 and NARA Microfilm T-501, roll 256, Frame 000374 and 000777, and NARA T-311, Roll 286, Frame 000125 and Otto Kumm. *7. SS-Gebirgs-Division Prinz Eugen im Bild.* Osnabrück: Munin Verlag, 1983, p. 159.

195 Tomasevich, op. cit., pp. 321, 328, and 331.

196 NARA T-313, Roll 194, Frame 7454441.

197 NARA T-501, Roll 256, Frames 000006, 000089, 000142, 000314, 000318, 000352, 000550-59, 000777-78, and NARA T-311, Roll 286, Frame 000125.

198 NARA T-501, Roll 256, Frames 000352 and 000374, and Tomasevich, op cit. p. 229.

199 Ibid., Roll 256, Frame 000414, and Tomasevich, op. cit., pp. 407-408.

200 This unit was made up of Italians who had decided to join the Yugoslav guerrillas.

201 Tomasevich, op. cit., p. 225.

202 Headquarters of the German Order police.

203 NARA Microfilm T-311, Roll 286, Frame 000125, and NARA T-78, Roll 410, Frames 6378310-72. And Hans-Joachim Neufeldt, Jürgen Huck and Georg Tessin. *Zur Geschichte der Ordnungspolizei 1936-1945*. Schriften des Bundesarchivs: Boppard-am-Rhein, 1957. Part 2, p. 71, and Karl Hnilicka. *Das Ende auf dem Balkan 1944/45*. Musterschmidt - Göttingen Verlag: Zürich, 1970.

204 Tomasevich, op. cit., pp. 409-11.

205 Tomasevich, ibid., p. 410.

206 Olaf Caroe. *Soviet Empire: The Turks of Central Asia and Stalinism*. London: MacMillan & Co. Ltd., 1954, p. 243.

207 Alexander Dallin. *German Rule in Russia 1941-1945. A Study of Occupation Policies.* London: MacMillan & Co. Ltd., 1957, p. 635.

208 Ibid., pp. 254, 256.

209 Ibid., p. 257.

210 Otto Heilbrunn and Aubrey Dixon. *Communist Guerrilla Warfare*. London: George Allen & Unwin Ltd., 1954, p. 129.

211 Dallin, op. cit., pp. 258-9.

212 Georg Tessin and Norbert Kannapin. *Waffen-SS und Ordnungspolizei im Kriegeinsatz 1939-1945*. Biblio Verlag: Osnabrück, 2000, p. 595.

213 Rolf Hinze. *Rückzugkämpf in der Ukraine 1943/44*. Neustadt: Verlag Dr. Rolf Hinze, 1991, p. 545.

214 Andreas Hillgruber. *Die Räumung der Krim 1944*. Berlin: Verlag E. S. Mittler & Sohn, 1959, p. 234.

215 Ibid., p. 40 and Hinze, op. cit., p. 565.

216 Kleitmann, op. cit., p. 513.

217 Kurt Mehner. *Die Waffen-SS und Polizei 1939-1945.* Norderstedt: Militär-Verlag Klaus D. Patzwall, 1995, p. 325.

218 SS-Hauptamt. *Dienstalterliste der Schutzstaffel NSDAP. Stand von 9. November 1944.* Berlin: Gedruckt in Reichsdruckerei, 1944.

219 NARA T-175, Roll 77, Frame 2593584.

220 Kleitmann, op. cit., p. 379.

221 One unverified source says that at peak strength the brigade contained 3,520 officers, NCOs and enlisted men.

222 Dallin, op. cit., pp. 260-5.

223 Littlejohn, op. cit., p. 253.

224 Ibid., p. 325.

225 Muñoz, *Forgotten Legions*, op. cit., pp. 174, 368.

226 Dr Frank H. Vizetelly, Editor. Funk & Wagnalls *New Standard Encyclopaedia.* New York: Funk & Wagnalls Company, 1931. Vol. 17, pp. 20-1.

227 Caroe, op. cit., p. 71.

228 Wladyslaw Anders. *Hitler's Defeat in Russia.* Chicago: Henry Regnery Company, 1953, p. 177.

229 Otto J. Pohl. *Ethnic Cleansing in the USSR, 1937-1949.* Westport: Greenwood Press, 1999, p. 62.

230 Timothy Patrick Mulligan. *The Politics of Illusion and Empire: German Occupation Policy in the Soviet Union, 1942-1943.* New York: Praeger Publishers, 1988, p. 128.

231 Alexiev, Alex. *Soviet Nationalities in German Wartime Strategy, 1941-1945.* Santa Monica: Rand Corporation, 1982, p. 21.

232 Ibid., p. 23.

233 Leonid Grenkevich. *The Soviet Partisan Movement 1941-1944.* London: Frank Cass, 1999, p. 132.

234 James Lucas. *War on the Eastern Front 1941-1945.* London: Janes Publishing Company, 1979, pp. 114-15.

235 On 13 November 1942 *Generalmajor* Gerhard Graf von Schwerin assumed command of the division and led the unit until 20. May 1943.

236 Paul Carell. *Hitler Moves East 1941-1943.* Little, Brown and Company: Boston, 1964. p. 507.

237 Thorwald, op. cit., pp. 70-1.

238 Janusz Piekalkiewicz. *The Cavalry of World War II.* New York: Stein and Day, 1980, p. 218.

239 George F. Nafziger. *The German Order of Battle: Waffen-SS and Other Units in World War II*. Combined Publishing: Pennsylvania, 2001, p. 217.

240 Littlejohn, op. cit., p. 363.

241 Hoffmann, op cit. p. 20.

242 Alexander Pronin. *Guerrilla Warfare in the German Occupied Soviet Territories 1941-1945*. Georgetown: Georgetown University Graduate School, 1965, p. 219.

243 Piekalkiewicz, op. cit., p. 218.

244 Ibid.

245 Pronin, op. cit., p. 227.

246 Mulligan, op. cit., p. 128.

247 Mulligan, op. cit., p. 128.

248 Pronin, op. cit., p. 230.

249 Hoffmann, op. cit., p. 104n.

250 Thorwald, op. cit., p. 230.

251 Richard Landwehr. 'The Kalmucken-Verbände Dr. Doll, 1942-1945' in *Siegrunen Magazine*. Brookings, 1994. Number 56, Spring 1994, p. 17.

252 Paul Carell. *Scorched Earth: The Russo-German War, 1943-1944*. Boston: Little, Brown and Company. 1970, p. 385.

253 Piekalkiewicz, op. cit., p. 218.

254 Thorwald, op. cit., p. 78.

255 Antonio J. Muñoz. *Hitler's Green Army: The German Order Police and Its Auxiliaries, 1939-1945, Volume 2 - Eastern Europe and the Balkans*. Europa Books: New York, 2006, p. 126.

256 FHQ, '*Lagesbesprechung*,', 12 December 1942.

257 Dallin, op. cit., p. 251.

258 Pohl, op. cit., p. 64.

259 Pronin, op. cit., p. 230.

260 Hoffmann, op. cit., p. 193.

261 Nafziger, op. cit., p. 217.

262 Hoffmann, op. cit., p.115.

263 NARS Microfilm T-315, Roll 2214, Frame 365.

264 Paul Carell's detailed history of the Russo-German War spanned two volumes; however, he ended his history of that conflict in July 1944, failing to write a description of the campaign for the last year of the war. In spite of this, his two-volume history is considered a classic and a 'must read' for any serious student of the war in the East. Not many people know that Paul Carell's real name was Paul Schmidt, and that during the war he was Adolf Hitler's Press Secretary.

265 Carell, *Scorched Earth,* op. cit., p. 140.

266 Nafziger, op. cit., p. 217.

267 Hoffmann, op. cit., p. 115.

268 Littlejohn, op. cit., p. 319.

269 Newland, Samuel J. *Cossacks in the German Army 1941-1945.* Portland: Frank Cass, 1991, p. 38.

270 Hoffmann, op. cit., p. 116.

271 Ibid., p. 136.

272 Eduard Bataev was a pseudonym. His real name was Erdne Dordziev.

273 By August 1944 *Hauptmann* Baron von Kutzschenbach had assumed this post.

274 Hoffmann, op. cit., pp. 132-3.

275 Sixty-eight Germans were attached from *Landesschützen Bataillon 917,* while an additional seventy-one were on staff on a regular basis.

276 Hoffmann, op. cit., p. 138.

277 Carell, *Scorched Earth,* op. cit., p. 385.

278 Hoffmann, op. cit., p. 120.

279 Hoffmann, op. cit., p. 118.

280 Thorwald, op. cit., p. 78.

281 Dallin, op cit. Pages 447-8.

282 Muñoz, 'German SS, Police, and Auxiliary Forces in Poland', op. cit., p. 33.

283 Hoffmann, op. cit., p. 143.

284 The *Sonderdienst* were battalions of ethnic-German Poles who served in this paramilitary organiszation. They served as guards, auxiliary police, operated in anti-partisan sweeps and towards the end of the war, were thrown into the front lines. They were usually led by a German SS officer. For example, *Sonderdienst Ersatz Bataillon Lublin* was commanded by *SS-Sturmbannführer* Anton Binner.

285 Dr. Leo W.G. Niehorster. *The Royal Hungarian Army, 1920-1945.* New York: Europa Books, 1998, p. 167.

286 Muñoz, German SS, Police, and Auxiliary Forces in Poland, op. cit., p. 33.

287 Heide-Marie Gruenthal. *Nacht Über Europa: Die Faschistische Okkupationspolitik in Polen (1939-1945).* Köln: Pahl-Rugenstein Verlag, 1989, p. 300.

288 Hoffmann, op. cit., p. 144.

289 Martin Bergen was born on 6 May 1908, in Frödau, East Prussia. He was almost 69 years old when he died on 16 April 1977, in Rössing, Hildesheim, Lower Saxony, West Germany.

290 Of this number, 1,092 were German manufactured, 1,025 were Russian Negat rifles, and forty-three were Dutch. The forty-three Dutch rifles were all that remained of the approximately 1,000 that were given to the men in the corps in early 1943. Perhaps they had been withdrawn because only 35,000 rounds of ammunition had been distributed for them.

291 Of this figure, thirty-three were German MP-40 and 135 were the popular Russian made PPS.

292 Hoffmann, op. cit., p. 153.

293 Ibid., p. 136.

294 Ibid., p. 152.

295 Pronin, op. cit., p. 229.

296 Thorwald, op. cit., p. 78.

297 Caroe, op. cit., p. 246.

298 In the case of the war, a good number of the volunteers joined the *Wehrmacht* during the victorious war years 1939-1942.

NAME INDEX

UNIT INDEX

German Brigades

German Regiments

German Battalions

German Companies

Armoured Trains

German Battlegroups

Abwehr, Brandenburg, and Geheim Feldpolizei

Eastern Volunteer Formations

Murder Kommandos

SS Formations

Luftwaffe